UCEN

SPORT examined

Paul Beashel
Andy Sibson
John Taylor

CONTENTS

ACKNOWLEDGEMENTS

Photo credits

All photos supplied by Getty Images, apart from the following:

- p.1 (top), p.8, p.23 (bottom), p.70, p.90, p.92 (left), p.93, p.114, p.115, p.116, p.117, p.121, p154, p.158 (bottom), p.162, p.169, p.234, p.235, p.237, p.238, p.240, p.261 photographed by Simon Punter.

- p.9 photographed by Paul Beashel.

- p.16 and p.17 Stromotion photos by Dartfish.

- p.18, p.46 (top), p.113, p.167 Photodisc 10 (NT).

- p.32, p.138, p.142 (top), p.144, p.145 (left), p.149, p.191, p.193 Actionplus Sports Images.

- p.46 (top right) Photodisc 51 (NT).

- p.92 (middle), p.93, p.147 Photofusion Picture Library.

- p.108 Alamy Images.

- p.127 (bottom) Kobal Picture Library.

- p.142 (bottom) Supersport Photographs/Eileen Langsley.

- p.148 (right) TopGolf Game Centre, Watford, www.topgolf.co.uk.

- p.180 Science Photo Library/Maximilian Stock Ltd.

- p.263 Offside Sports Photography.

Picture research by Getty Images and Sue Sharp.

Dear Student,

Welcome to the world of sport. We are very pleased that you have decided to study physical education and sport. Over the next two years you will acquire a wealth of knowledge about your own body and how it stands up to the stresses and strains of modern sport. We are sure that you are already aware that sport makes many physical demands. However, our bodies are extremely adaptable. With a well-planned and sustained training programme you will certainly improve your sporting performance.

A thorough and wide-ranging knowledge of the workings of the body is essential for an understanding of sporting performance. Nevertheless your own performance will not improve merely by reading books about sport or by watching sport on television. It is on the games field, in the gym or in the swimming pool that your sporting knowledge is applied and becomes of real value.

We know that you will get a great deal of fun and enjoyment from your course as you improve your sporting skills. You will also have the opportunity to gain a valuable GCSE in Physical Education. For us and for thousands of people around the world, sport is a daily inspiration and a challenge. We hope that you too will continue to enjoy sport for the rest of your life, and we wish you every success on this course.

Paul Beashel
Andy Sibson
John Taylor

SPECIFICATION STRUCTURE

This book has been written to match precisely the requirements of the OCR GCSE Physical Education syllabus. At the start of each chapter we have set out the necessary key words, together with a summary of the specification requirements separately. At the end of each chapter there is a set of OCR examination-style questions. The specification is divided into three main sections as described below.

Factors affecting participation and performance

You will need a sound knowledge of how your body works in order to understand sporting performance and so the body systems important for physical activity and sport are described in detail. You will discover how physical activity benefits our physical, social and mental health and you will develop a fuller understanding of all the reasons why we should keep physically active.

Many sporting activities require us to learn new skills in order to be successful. You will gain important practical knowledge about how we learn and how our learning can be influenced by a wide range of factors, such as our motivation and mental preparation.

Here you will learn about the many factors which determine whether or not you choose to take part in sport and how you develop your ability. You will analyse the way in which your attitude in sport is influenced by the people around you, including your family, friends, teachers and also by the media. Local and national sports organisations and their facilities in your area will also affect your sporting choices.

The relationship between health, fitness and practical activity

This section clarifies the links between health and fitness and describes the various factors which can affect your ability to remain healthy and perform well in sporting activity. You will understand the various components necessary for good health and for skill-related fitness and be able to describe how all of these components can be improved by applying the principles and methods of training.

Most importantly, you will learn how to plan, implement and monitor a six-week personal exercise programme (PEP). This PEP will be designed using the training principles and will demonstrate your knowledge of how to use a variety of training methods to improve your own or someone else's sporting performance.

Risk assessment in physical activity

Sport is not only exciting it is also potentially dangerous. You will need to know how to assess the risks in a wide range of sporting activities in order to prevent accidents and injuries. You must also be able to recognise and treat simple physical activity and performance-type injuries.

The world of sport covers a wide variety of activities. Enjoyment is the main reason why we take part in sport and physical recreation. We do not know in which sports you will specialise. Therefore we have designed our book to give you the knowledge, principles and skills that are the basis of sporting performance. We know that we all learn in different ways, so we have included many different types of activities throughout the book. We hope that not only will you enjoy them but that they will stimulate you and lead you to success in your OCR Physical Education examination.

Analysis of performance

Analysis of performance

- Rules, regulations and terminology
- Observation and analysis
- Evaluation of performance compared with the Perfect Model
- Planning strategies, tactics, practices and training to improve performance
- Understanding the principles and roles of sports leadership
- Analysing performance task

1 Analysis of performance

All of us involved in sport want to improve our performance. We train hard and practise our skills so that in competition we can produce our very best. To improve our performance we must first be able to analyse it. Learning the skills of analysing sporting action will help us to improve our own performance. We can also learn to analyse the performance of others and so work towards becoming a coach. This takes time, effort and experience.

Analysing performance

Your teacher will assess your ability to analyse performance during an interview with you. You will be questioned after you have completed the analysing performance task (see page 31) and will focus on the sport or activity investigated for the task. Your teacher may ask questions such as those below. We have assumed you are analysing the performance of a student. The analysis could of course be of your own performance.

1 Can you describe in simple terms what the student is trying to achieve in this aspect of the game or activity?
2 Can you suggest any obvious weaknesses in his or her performance? Describe what these are.
3 Why do you think he or she has this weakness?
   - What is causing it?
   - What do you suggest he or she might do to remedy this weakness in either skill or technique?
   - In what ways might you be able to help the student to improve performance? Can you suggest any practice or training methods?
4 Can you identify any skills or techniques which he or she does really well in the chosen activity? Explain why you think he or she does them well. How do you think the student might refine these skills or techniques even further?

This chapter will help you to develop your analysis of performance skills.

activity

Analysing performance

Watch a group of your classmates playing a small sided game, for example, indoor hockey or netball. Try to decide who is the most effective player. Now explain why his or her performance is so effective. Is the player fitter? Faster-thinking? Harder-working? More skilful?

You can use the checklist on Worksheet 1 to help.

2

KEYWORDS

Analyse: to examine in detail and to explain

Arousal: level of motivation and alertness when taking part in sport

Data: facts or information

Drill: training by repeating a technique or skill

Evaluate: to decide what is good and what needs to improve

Feedback: information about the outcome of a performance

Motivation: determination to achieve

Observe: to watch carefully

Perfect Model: a mental image of the correct technique

Performance: how well a task is completed

Skill: the learned ability to choose and perform the right techniques at the right time

Strategy: long term plan for success in sport

Tactics: methods we use to put strategies into practice in a game

Technique: basic movements in sport.

Key to Exam Success

For your GCSE you will need to know:

- the rules and regulations of your chosen sport and how to apply them as a player, coach, referee or judge. You should be able to use technical terms when describing your sport
- how to observe and analyse a performance and how to give feedback to the performer
- how to evaluate a performance, how to compare it with the 'Perfect Model' and how to provide comprehensive and detailed feedback
- the importance of leadership in sport and the different roles of sports leadership.

66 KEY THOUGHT 99

'Preparation is the key to success in sport.'

Rules, regulations and terminology

activity

What would happen if...?
Imagine if these sports changed their laws:

- cricket – no lbw law
- football – no offside law
- hockey – the ball is allowed to touch the feet during play
- athletics – no lanes for the 200m
- tennis – no second service.

Discuss how each sport might change as a result of these new laws.

Think about your favourite sport. Have any rule changes been made in recent years? You may need to research the official rules.

Why do you need to know the rules and regulations?

You will often be asked to referee, umpire or score during PE lessons. GCSE assessment includes your ability to apply the rules and regulations, also called laws, as an official in charge of a match. When refereeing you must think about the rules of the activity and how to make sure that the players obey them. Every time you are asked to referee you should take the opportunity to practise, as you will then improve. As an official you need to show the players that you understand the rules thoroughly. They also want to see you make confident decisions and to control the game fairly but firmly.

Your teacher will assess your knowledge and understanding of the rules of your chosen sport.

You will need to demonstrate this knowledge by refereeing or umpiring a game or a match. You will also be asked questions about the rules and basic tactics. You should take a pride in knowing the rules and also playing and refereeing fairly at all times. Ultimate Frisbee has included this idea in the official rules of the game. There is no referee. Players simply referee the game as they play – even at the world championships!

Keeping up to date with the rules of your sport

You should also keep up to date with rule changes. Every governing body reviews the rules of its sport on a regular basis. It may change the rules to make the game safer; for example, in rugby union, players must now stay on their feet at rucks. Rule changes may also be introduced to speed up the game; for example, in volleyball, teams now score a point every time

they win a rally, not just when they win from their own serve.

Often changes affect the way that the game is played and coached. In 1992 FIFA changed the rules so that goalkeepers could not pick up a ball that was passed to them by their own team. This stopped teams wasting time or using the goalkeeper as a 'safety' player. Defenders had to change their tactics as a result. Attackers began to run down back passes instead of leaving the goalkeeper to pick up the ball. The pace of the game increased and now we see many goalkeepers being forced into mistakes.

activity

Sports quiz

Choose a sport. It would be good if this is your Analysis of Performance assessment sport. Research the rules and produce a ten-question quiz to test participants' knowledge of the rules. Look for some obscure rules or situations to baffle your friends. If you like, use ICT to make your quiz interactive.

Why do coaches modify rules?

Sometimes coaches and teachers modify the rules of the game in training to develop skills or to create a new challenge. In some football games, players may only be allowed to control the ball with one or two touches in order to encourage movement and passing. Some rules will complicate the game too much for beginners; for example, in PE lessons the three-second and other time rules are rarely used in basketball, and in hockey lessons young players do not have to worry about offside. Some sports have different rules for junior games: for example, high fives netball, which is a five-a-side game with players rotating positions and roles.

What is terminology?

When you talk about your sport you will often use technical terms such as 'lbw' or 'offside'. These technical terms are called terminology. You probably know a lot of sports terminology already, but if you are going to coach effectively you need to know which terms to use to describe your sport. It is very important that you know the names of the skills and techniques of your sport when analysing performance.

Look at this example of terminology from badminton:

> 'You may play a forehand or a backhand shot. It may be a clear, a drive, a drop shot, a hairpin drop shot or a smash.'

You should be able to describe each shot and suggest to a player when he or she could use it as a tactic. Once everybody knows the terminology it is much easier to talk about the sport. Terminology includes examples of techniques, skills, strategies, tactics and rules.

Observation and analysis

The first stage in coaching is observing and analysing a performance. We have to watch a sportsperson in action and try to break down the movement into parts. If we watched a long jump we would need to look at the run-up, the take-off, the action in the air and the landing. Only when we have completed this part can we go on to evaluate the performance and explain to the performer how improvement can be made. At this second stage we can compare the jump in our mind with what we would like to see and then suggest to the athlete how he or she could do better.

Many coaches today use technology to help them to analyse performance. However, most of the time you will have to carry out live observation. That is to say, you must watch a player performing and then make decisions about the quality of the performance. This requires

activity

Terminology test

Are there any special terms in your chosen sport? Think about equipment, rules, techniques and strategies. Produce a list of terms on small cards, then pass the cards amongst your class. Each person has to explain the term to the rest of the class. If they do not know the answer you will have to make sure that you can explain it.

a lot of planning and practice. You can use a four-step approach to learn how to observe and analyse.

The four-step approach

The four-step approach begins with observing a simple activity involving one person. It builds up to a complex situation with many players in action.

Step 1
Observe and analyse a single technique – for example, a forward roll. In this situation you can control the environment, decide when the roll takes place and where you should stand to watch.

Step 2
Observe and analyse a single technique in action – for example, a forehand drive in tennis. This is a technique that requires a feed, that is someone to throw the ball for the player to hit. You are still in control of most of the situation, but the feed will vary and the player has to move to play the shot. There is much more to look at and to analyse.

Step 3
Observe an individual competitive performance – for example, a player in a badminton match. You can decide where to stand to observe the player, but you cannot decide which shots will be played. You will have to concentrate on just a few parts of the performance or you will get very confused. You will now be observing skill and tactics.

Step 4
Observe a competitive team performance – for example, a basketball team playing a match. In this situation you must focus on one or two aspects of performance and observe them carefully. Both team skill and team tactics can be observed.

Step 1: How do you analyse a specific technique?

You must know what the very best technique looks like. We call this the Perfect Model. You can then compare what you are seeing with the **Perfect Model** in your head. To build up this image you might use books, photographs, video footage or an expert performer. Your PE teacher, or one of your group, may be able to demonstrate during a lesson.

Before observing the technique you must break it down into a number of simple parts. You can then concentrate on each part in turn as the performer repeats the technique. Making a list of the different parts of the technique will help you to analyse in detail.

For example, if we were looking at a forward roll, we would look at the starting position, especially the hands and the head, the shape of the body during the roll and the finishing position, particularly of the arms. We would compare each part of the movement with the same part from our image of the Perfect Model.

You must decide where to stand to get the best view before observing any performance. You could view from either side, from the front or from behind, and also in some cases from above or below. The position you choose will depend on the specific technique that you are observing, the nature of the sport and on your knowledge of the sport. An experienced javelin coach will first note whether the athlete is right- or left-

handed and will then view the run-up and throw from a number of different positions. Safety would also be an important consideration for the coach in this event.

Step 2: Analysing a technique in action

When observing a technique in action you should use a help sheet to list the points you will be looking for before you begin.

Here is an example of a technique to analyse the overhead clear in badminton.

You might want to look separately at:

- movement into position
- foot placement and body position under the shuttlecock
- arm and racket preparation
- hitting action and follow-through.

Before observing this technique you must decide who is going to feed the shuttle to the player. A feeder in this context means another player or coach who throws, kicks or places the ball or shuttle in the best position so that the technique can be practised. If the feed is not accurate, the player will not be able to play the shot that you wish to see. Top coaches in sports such as volleyball have to pass tests to make sure that they can feed a ball accurately to the right place for each technique to be practised. When practising, the feeder has a very important role and should be told exactly how and where to feed. He or she must take the job very seriously.

Using ICT

Observation and analysis are much easier if you can slow down the action and study it in detail. Using ICT can help you to do this. There are many CD-ROMS and DVDs available which show footage of different sports. The web has examples too. If you have the facilities, you can make your own video using editing software. The simplest way of slowing down the action is to use a digital video camera and to watch the technique on the camera LCD screen.

activity ☺☺☺

Where to stand

Choose a technique from a sport of your choice and consider where you should stand to observe it. Is it best to stay in one place? Do you need to observe from a number of different angles to get an overall picture – for example, from the side, the front and from behind? Are you better placed at ground level or should you observe from above?

activity ☺☺☺

Observing a technique in action

Select a technique from a sport that requires a feeder. Write down a list of the parts of the technique that you wish to observe. Decide who is to feed and give precise instructions to the feeder. Then observe the technique in action and analyse the performance.

Step 3: How do you analyse a competitive individual performance?

A performer will use a range of techniques and skills very rapidly during competition. Your analysis must focus on these and also consider a number of other factors, such as fitness, tactics and strategies. Better performers will know both their own and their rivals' strengths and weaknesses. As a result they will be able to develop a plan or strategy in order to win. To achieve their strategy they will decide which particular tactics they can use during the competition. For example, suppose that a 1,500-metre runner knows that she has a much faster finish than the other competitors in a race. Her strategy is to have the race run at as slow a pace as possible in order that she has enough energy left for her sprint finish. Her tactic will probably be to take the lead and then try to keep the pace as slow as possible. Her opponents may have other ideas and she may have to rethink her tactics as the race progresses.

In planning your observation you should think about your performer's plan, performance and evaluation:

The plan

What overall strategy does the performer have and what tactics are they attempting to use? When you know these you can look at how effective they are within the game. If they are not effective you must look for reasons.

The performance

This includes the techniques and skills in action. By looking at these you can see if poor performance or technique is preventing your player from being skilful and carrying out his or her tactics.

The fitness level of your player is also a vital factor. Tired people perform less well. You must look carefully at fitness levels. If in doubt, ask the performer how he or she feels.

The evaluation

Good decision-making within the game is essential. If your performer is

activity 😊😊

Analysing an individual competitive performance

Observe a group member playing a competitive game and assess his or her performance. Use the three factors, the plan, the performance and the evaluation, to focus your observation. Discuss your findings with the player and suggest ways to improve.

anticipating the opponent's moves and selecting successful moves then his or her performance will be good. You must analyse the decisions made by your player. This is especially important if your player is losing and needs your help as a coach to select better tactics.

Step 4: How do you analyse a competitive team performance?

In a team game you can observe either an individual player within the team or the performance of the team as a whole.

Individual performance

If you are focusing on an individual player you should not only look at his or her individual competitive performance, but at his or her contribution to the team effort. This will differ according to the sport, but might include running off the ball to support in attack, supporting in defence by covering others and getting back to mark opponents. The attitude of the player should also be assessed – for example, whether he or she encourages or criticises others – as this can play an important part in team games.

activity

Using data to analyse performance

Choose a sport and decide on the data to be gathered in order to analyse team performance. This may be the number of successful passes, tackles, attacks, etc. Have at least two observers for each team or player. Observe a team or player for a period of time and note everything that happens on a checklist. The checklist below can be used for football or hockey but you will need to adapt it to suit other sports. You may also wish to observe a particular player using a similar checklist.

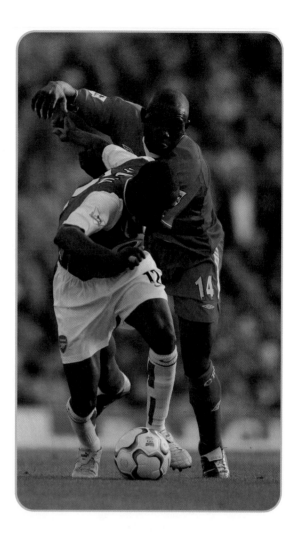

Team performance

You can also observe and analyse the team performance as a whole. A team will have an overall strategy and a chosen set of tactics. You will need to decide which aspect of the performance will be your focus; top teams have a number of assistant coaches who only look at attack or defence. If you try to look at everything you will find that there are too many things happening for you to analyse easily.

This example from football shows how data could be gathered on a number of aspects of a team performance:

Date:	Period of observation (minutes):	Tally total
Aspects observed	Record each incident with a tally mark	
Pass completed		
Possession lost		
Successful tackle		
Unsuccessful tackle		
Shot off target		
Shot on target		

How do you analyse a strategy?

A **strategy** is a plan for success in sport. A team of talented individuals will need to work together on their tactics and strategies to ensure success. Without a strategy team performance will suffer.

You can gather data to analyse the effectiveness of a strategy. Coaches and players have to select strategies in many sports. Sometimes the strategies are very different:

■ A tennis player might stay at the baseline throughout a match or serve and volley – that is, run to the net to cut off shots from their opponent.

■ Badminton pairs will often play 'front and back', with one player taking the short shots while the other takes those to the rear of the court. Others choose to play side-to-side, with each player covering one side of the court from the net to the baseline.

■ Basketball teams might use a 'man-to-man' defence or 'zone' defence.

■ Some athletes in middle distance events will run as fast as they can from the start and hope to 'hang on' to their lead. Others will pace themselves, then speed up and sprint to the finish.

■ Throwers and jumpers often complete their first attempt at less than 100% effort to make sure that they do not produce a foul. Others try their hardest each time, but sometimes 'no-jump' or 'no-throw' throughout the competition.

Wise coaches will ensure that players are able to switch strategies and or tactics to suit specific situations.

activity

Analysing a strategy

Consider this example from football and then decide how you could observe, gather data and advise the managers.

Mickey and **Johanne** are two experienced football managers in a local league.

Mickey believes that his team will be more successful in getting the ball into the opposition penalty area if his goalkeeper always plays the ball out to a full back to restart play. He thinks that his players will keep possession and create scoring opportunities for his strikers in the opposition penalty area.

Johanne has told his goalkeeper always to kick the ball as far up the pitch as possible. He thinks that this will lead to more scoring opportunities in the opposition penalty area.

Neither manager has any facts to back up his beliefs.

Can you find some facts to support one of the managers?

You could gather data by observing a number of live football matches on TV. You will need to decide what to look for, and create a rota of observers so that each match has at least two people watching the entire 90 minutes. Once you have collected enough information you will know which is the best strategy.

You might wish to send the results to your local club to help their manager!

Evaluation of performance compared with the Perfect Model

We have seen that the first stage in coaching is observing and analysing performance. The second stage is to evaluate the performance and to provide feedback to the performer.

- **Evaluating** a performance means deciding what is good and what needs improvement.

- Providing **feedback** means giving information about the performance to the performer.

Giving feedback is a very important stage as the performer needs to know how to improve. The coach must be careful to provide accurate feedback in a positive way. Providing incorrect advice or giving

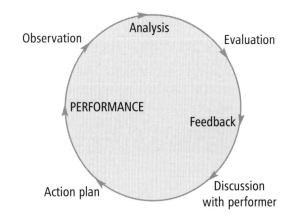
feedback in a thoughtless manner can damage the performer's confidence. A good coach will always allow the performer the opportunity to comment on his or her performance. You can use the coaching model on the right to guide your observation, analysis, evaluation and feedback.

Observation — Analysis — Evaluation — Feedback — Discussion with performer — Action plan — PERFORMANCE

activity

Back to basics

For this activity you need to put yourself in the position of a complete beginner. Attempt a simple technique in your chosen sport – for example, a set shot in basketball or netball, a serve in tennis or badminton, or a penalty kick in football – but use your non-preferred hand or foot. Do you have to think about the action? Are you able to perform it as quickly? How different was it? What expectations do you have of yourself when playing like this?

Coach the basics

Try coaching a group member to perform a simple technique with the non-preferred hand or foot. How easy is it to correct errors?

Evaluating a performance

When you evaluate a performance you should be clear about the standard of performance that you are expecting. Players can be at the beginner, intermediate or advanced level. It is important that coaches and players understand the level at which the players are performing. A lack of understanding can lead to unreasonable expectations of novice players. This in turn can create pressure and tension, which affects performance and slows the learning process.

The Perfect Model

You must know what the very best technique looks like – the Perfect Model (see page 8). You can then compare what you are seeing with your mental image.

Strengths and weaknesses

Whenever you observe a performance you should look for strengths and weaknesses. When giving feedback it is important to tell the performer about the good things you have seen before talking about the weaknesses.

Feedback

It is impossible to learn skills effectively without knowing whether or not our efforts are successful. We use the word **feedback** to cover all the ways in which we learn about our performance. Not all feedback is useful to us. It is the role of the teacher or coach to highlight the important parts of the feedback in order to assist our skill learning. Too much information at the early stages of learning is unhelpful.

How much feedback?

As beginners we can only cope with a small amount of verbal or visual feedback. With experience we begin to get the feel of movements which work for us and bring about success. Gradually we are able to handle more information and learn to evaluate the success or otherwise of our own performance. Our coach is able to fine-tune our movements and we are able to respond to comments more readily.

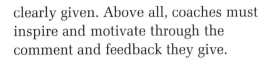

When is feedback given?

A running commentary on our attempts can get in the way of our learning. Rather than give feedback after each and every attempt, it is often more useful if the coach comments at key moments. As performers become more experienced, they will realise when they are making errors and will not need to be told.

Any feedback should be easy to understand and instructions should be

clearly given. Above all, coaches must inspire and motivate through the comment and feedback they give.

Using technology and data to improve performance

There are a number of different types of aids that coaches can use to help improve performance. These are:

- technical information
- video recordings of player performance
- statistical analysis
- fitness monitoring and analysis equipment
- interactive white boards.

You may have the opportunity to try some of these during your GCSE course. They can provide a lot of evidence to support your feedback to performers.

activity

Which is the Perfect Model?

Working in pairs, look at the two long jumpers in the photographs below. One is the Perfect Model. The other is also a very good performer. Discuss the strengths and weaknesses of each performer with your partner. What do they both have in common? Look at the take off, action in the air and landing.

Planning strategies, tactics, practices and training to improve performance

After observing, analysing and evaluating performance, you must plan to improve performance. You have looked at performances, compared them with the Perfect Model and decided what needs to be done to improve them. Now you have to consider how you can ensure that this improvement takes place. You must be able to plan practices and training sessions to improve fitness, techniques and skills. You will also need to show that you understand the strategies and tactics of your sport. Chapter 11, Training principles, shows you how to construct an exercise programme and how to organise a training session. Your PEP will include research into training methods. In this section you will learn about the practical side of coaching.

activity

Looking at arousal

Work in groups of about 12. Each player in turn attempts three free shots in netball or basketball under normal conditions. They then repeat it with a supportive audience, a totally silent audience and a hostile audience. The rest of the group provide the audience.

Discuss the results. Did the audience affect performance? How did the performer feel about each type of audience?

How do coaches plan to improve performance?

It is vital that coaches know their players so that they can plan programmes that match the player's level of ability and experience. Analysis of performance plays a large part in enabling a coach to prepare training sessions. It provides specific information which enables him or her to select activities and drills to suit the needs of the players. A good coach will also understand the personality of each player and will know how best to motivate each individual in the team.

Motivation and arousal

In sport the level of motivation and alertness is called **arousal**. If your arousal level is not high enough, you may feel bored and you will perform badly. If your arousal gets too high you may become anxious and worried. This creates tension, which causes your performance to become less effective. Coaches must look very carefully at the personality of different players and the nature of the sport before deciding on the level of motivation needed. For example, most snooker players need

support to remain calm and focused before a major competition. Increasing their level of arousal is likely to lead to poor performance.

How do coaches improve different types of skill?

We can put skills in sport into two different groups.

- **Closed** skills are skills not affected by the sporting environment.

- **Open** skills are skills that are affected by the whole sporting environment such as other players and the weather.

Inverted U theory

A graph showing Performance (low to high) on the vertical axis and Arousal (low, moderate, high) on the horizontal axis, with an inverted U-shaped curve.

Closed skills

Closed skills are relatively easy to train. In gymnastics and archery, for example, competition is very similar to training. Closed skills are also found within 'open' games, for example, bowling the ball in cricket, taking penalties in football or taking a free throw in basketball. In all these activities the coach has to try to create the pressure that a player may feel within a competitive situation if the player is to be fully match-prepared. This can be done by:

- setting 'closed' drills when the player is tired

- creating pressure by rewarding success or punishing failure (in the sporting sense, of doing an extra run)

- simulating the match with recorded crowd noise

- creating pressure by having team mates talking at, and trying to put off, the performer.

Open skills

Open skills are performed within open activities where it is difficult to predict what will happen next. Most sports are open in this sense, including invasion games and racket sports. Coaches need to provide their performers with as wide a variety of experiences as possible so that they can practise their skills in many different situations. To help them perform skilfully and develop tactical understanding, the coach needs to allow them to make their own decisions during game play. The best coaches know when to advise and when to let their players take control for themselves.

Putting skills into action

Tactical skill is the ability to choose the right plan of action when taking part in sport. Different types of sport require us to use different strategies and tactics. In order to develop our tactical skill we need to understand the needs of our sport.

What are strategies and tactics in sport?

- **Strategies** are plans that we think out in advance of the sporting competition. They are methods of putting us in the best position to defeat our opponents.

- **Tactics** are what we use to put our strategies into action. Tactics can also be worked out in advance, but they will often need to be adapted to the real situation during competition. Tactics involve planning and team work.

Strategies and tactics will be very different for different types of games. For example, an invasion game like rugby involves large numbers of players, a variety of set plays as well as an opportunity for individuals to respond to many different situations. It gives many choices to players, such as kicking, passing or running with the ball. By contrast, in a judo competition there is only one opponent to worry about and there are a limited number of attacking or defending moves to make.

Beginners are not able to cope with complex strategies. They will need simple tactics such as 'Pass the ball to a player who is free'. More skilful players are able to give time and attention to strategies and tactics.

What sort of strategies and tactics are used in sport?

Strategies and tactics become more important as the level of competition increases.

When developing a strategy the coach will focus on:

- teamwork
- the game plan
- team formation
- restarts and set plays.

Teamwork

A successful team will have good teamwork. This means that all members of the team understand the agreed strategy. They also put the tactics for each game into practice by working as a unit. Managers, coaches and captains have important roles to play in teamwork. The motivation to work hard for each other has to be developed through training and team-building activities. A coach will also try to make sure that all the players are in their best positions during the game. For example, a tall, powerful footballer is likely to be in the centre of defence or attack, not expected to play in the middle of the midfield area where a quicker, more mobile player is required.

Game plan

In some matches and competitions, players and teams talk of a game plan. This is the set of tactics for use in a particular game. The game plan will be based on their own strengths and the weaknesses of the opposition.

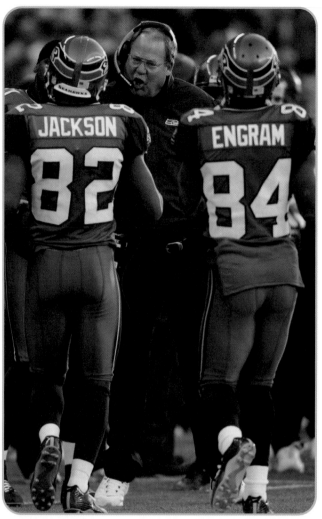

Formations

Teams can use different formations; that is, the players can take up different positions on the field of play. Some sports have rules limiting where the players can move during the game. In netball these restrictions present certain problems to be solved. In basketball there are few restrictions on the positions of players, so teams can be more flexible. Everyone discusses the formations in football. Some teams choose to have four defenders, four midfield players and two attackers (4:4:2). Others play with three central defenders, five midfielders and two attackers (3:5:2). Attack-minded teams or teams trying to score an equaliser in a cup-tie might play 4:3:3 or even 2:5:3.

Restarts and set plays

All games have restarts. In net games these are the serves. In invasion games they are free hits, throw-ins, corners, scrums, etc. These restarts give the team an opportunity to have free possession of the ball. At these times many teams use set plays which are practised during training.

How to develop strategies and tactics

To develop a strategy you will need to know:

- your own strengths and weaknesses

- the strengths and weaknesses of the opposition

- your level of fitness

- the importance of the competition

- any important environmental factors.

In a net game such as tennis, you might have considered all the factors above and decided your strategy. Let us say it is to move your opponent around the court in order to get her out of position and to tire her, allowing you to play a winning shot or to force an error. The tactic you use to achieve this might be to serve wide on both sides of the court and to come in to the net quickly.

In the game you might find that your tactics are not working because your opponent is returning your serve very well. In this case you will have to decide whether or not to continue with the same tactic or change it. If you change it you might stay at the baseline, but try to play disguised drop shots to draw the opponent forward and then lob or pass the ball beyond her. Alternatively, you might notice that her backhand is weak so you could decide to play most of your shots to her backhand side. Your tactics must be flexible to respond to the situations you meet during each game.

Training to improve performance

The objective of every training session must be to improve performance. Your analysis of performance will provide a focus for your training sessions. Each session must be well planned. The coach must guide the players through techniques and into skills. They must also develop strategies and tactics in preparation for competition. The players' fitness will have to be maintained or improved. Training must include three essential parts:

- Warm-up

- Main activity including skills training, fitness training, game and tactical development

- Warm-down.

Warm-up and warm-down
These are an essential part of any training session. They must be linked closely to the sporting activity. Full details are given in Chapter 11 (page 217).

Skills training
Skills practices in sport are often called **drills**. They are used to teach techniques and skills. A drill is a movement or number of movements that are repeated until they can be performed easily. Swimmers will spend many hours perfecting their strokes to improve efficiency. Dancers and gymnasts perform choreographed sequences of movement, but they must also develop their basic dance techniques during the main activity phase of training sessions.

Changing tactics
Working in groups, consider the following situations and make suggestions for strategies and tactics to help the individual player or improve team performance. You must explain to the whole group how you think your tactic or strategy will make a difference.

1 Your basketball team is losing heavily at half time. One player of average height but excellent all-round court movement has scored most of the opposition's points. Your zone defence has been unable to cope with him.

2 Your hockey team is winning 1–0 with 15 minutes remaining in the match. The opposition are playing almost entirely in your half. Your defenders are tired and keep hitting the ball away, but the opposition regain possession very quickly.

3 You are a middle distance runner. Both you and your rival have personal best times of 5 minutes for the mile (4 laps of the track). You plan to race at 75 seconds per lap and then out-sprint your rival to the finish. You begin the race and stay at the shoulder of the leader. However, after the first lap your rival speeds up to a pace of 65 seconds per lap.

You might practise techniques individually even if you are training for a team game. Small groups, or units, might also practise their skills separately from the rest of the team. An example might be the defenders working on defending crosses in hockey.

A series of techniques are often linked into a skilled movement that mirrors the game situation. This is a very important aspect of training because skill practices should always reflect the reality of the game situation.

How to design a drill

If a drill is to work it must be prepared carefully. Before the coach begins to lead the drill, every aspect of it must be planned and all equipment must be in place. This checklist can be used to ensure that no detail is missed when you plan your drills. By answering all the questions you will have prepared well.

- What is the drill trying to teach or improve?

- How many players are involved? What do they each do (feeder, performer, coach, ball collector)?

- What equipment is needed (bibs, balls, cones, goals, rackets, nets, posts, etc.)?

- What does the drill look like? Draw a diagram and write a key.

- What instructions will need to be given to explain the drill? Write them out.

- How many times do the players repeat the drill?

- What happens after the first player has completed the drill? Where does he or she go next?

- How do the players know if they have been successful?

Finally, you should evaluate your drill after it has been completed, as follows:

activity

Design a drill

Training sessions often involve identifying areas for improvement and then practising skills or techniques. With your teacher, decide on a technique that could be developed and design a drill to teach this technique to your group. You must plan the drill in enough detail for someone else to be able to teach it.

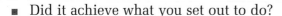

- Did it achieve what you set out to do?

- Were all the players able to follow your instructions?

- How would you change it if you did it again?

Types of skill training

Once a technique has been taught and learned, skill training can take one of four different forms, depending on the amount of opposition required.

Unopposed
We can learn techniques more easily if there is no opposition. In basketball, the shooter can practise the jump shot unopposed at first, and opposition can be introduced gradually as technique improves. In volleyball, team organisation often takes some time to learn. This is best practised with the coach feeding the ball rather than within the game itself, when the team will be under pressure from the opposition.

Passive opposition
Opposition is essential for some techniques to be learned. However, in the early stages of learning it is often best for opposition to be static or minimal. Learning how to tackle in rugby is far easier if the player with the ball stands still! This is known as passive opposition. It is much easier to learn how to keep control of a ball whilst dribbling in and out of a line of opponents when the opponents are not trying to steal it from you. Passive opposition drills are often used with beginners.

Active opposition
In order to make practices more realistic, the opposition must be real but limited in order for the techniques and skills to be learned. A common example of active opposition in football and hockey is the 3 v 1 possession drill in a grid square, where the player in the middle has to try to get the ball.

Pressure training
Pressure training is a method for putting a technique or skill under stress. It should only be used when a performer has developed the technique or skill to a high level. Pressure can be applied in a number of different ways:

- You might make the performer work very hard for a period of time. This combines skill and fitness work. As the performer tires, the skill level will drop. The practice will increase fitness levels and help the performer to play when tired. For example, in football, practice in heading the ball can be alternated with sprinting.

- Pressure can also be applied by forcing the performer to react very quickly. In basketball the jump shooter could receive the ball from a player who is between him and the basket. As the shooter receives it, the player runs at the shooter and attempts to block the shot. The pressure to receive the ball, prepare and execute the shot in a short period of time is similar to a competitive situation and will lead to improvement within the game itself.

activity

Designing practices

Choose a technique or skill from the sport of your choice. Describe how you would set up a number of drills to improve performance using the techniques outlined above. Then try them out with your group. You may find that some of your group cope well with all types of practice. Others will find that their performance drops off as the pressure increases.

How are games used to develop strategies and tactics?

Skills need to be transferred from the practice situation into the game situation. Practice games also let coaches try out strategies and practise tactics.

- **Modified** games give each player plenty of action and lots of time with the ball – for example, 5 v 5 hockey.

- **Conditioned** games have rule changes that focus on a particular skill or tactic. For example, two-touch football can develop good control and passing, but it also encourages support for the player with the ball. Conditioning the game can extend to providing areas of the pitch where the player with the ball cannot be tackled. If these are down both wings the teams are encouraged to play the ball wide because they can then keep possession until they wish to cross the ball. Once the habit of looking to create width in attack has been learned, the players will try to introduce it into normal games.

The use of games within training sessions also helps coaches to assess players' strengths, find out weaknesses and plan future sessions.

How do we plan and use fitness training?

Players must take responsibility for their own personal fitness.

This includes eating and drinking sensibly, avoiding smoking and recreational drugs and getting plenty of rest. Nevertheless fitness training should be part of all training sessions. Further details can be found on page 217. It can be part of the skills practices in the form of pressure drills, but should not exhaust players so much that they cannot concentrate on their skills. Regular fitness testing provides valuable feedback to coaches and players.

Understanding the principles and roles of sports leadership

When you analyse a team performance you look to see who influences the game. Players who influence those around them are leaders. Coaches, officials and others involved in sport can also be leaders. Your teacher will assess your own leadership ability, based upon your work during the GCSE course. It will include how well you demonstrate leadership through refereeing, organising and playing sport. You must always remember that good leadership has a direct impact on performance. If a game is refereed poorly, or a practice is disorganised, the players involved will not play to the best of their ability.

activity ☺☺☺

Organising a club tournament

Imagine that you have to organise a tournament for your club involving players or teams from the surrounding area. Make a list of all the things that need to be done before the day of the tournament. Then list all the jobs that will have to be done on the day. Do not forget the clearing up afterwards! You will not be able to do everything, so divide all the jobs between a number of people. You can give them job titles, such as secretary, referee coordinator, referee, scorer, equipment organiser, equipment helper, etc.

What makes a good leader in sport?

A good leader in sport is likely to have one or more of the following qualities:

- outstanding ability in the sport

- great enthusiasm

- sound judgement

- good motivational powers

- ability to read the game or sporting situation.

Captains of cricket teams have a lot of responsibility for making tactical decisions during games. When fielding they must decide who is to bowl and where the fielders are to be placed.

Captains in other sports do not usually make as many crucial decisions, but they must set an example to the players in their team and motivate them. This is very important when a team is losing.

Motivators on the pitch are players who perform reliably under pressure. The other players look to them for inspiration. Some players drift in and out of games. They may be highly skilful but are not good leaders. Sometimes the most skilful players, or the most popular players, are given the captaincy of a team. However, the real leaders in the team may be doing an excellent job without being recognised.

activity ☺☺☺

Follow the leader

Observe a competitive team performance. Look for leadership on the pitch. Give examples of when leadership is shown. Is it always the same players? Is it always the high-profile or popular ones, or can you find an unsung hero who leads well, but whose contribution is often overlooked?

What makes a good organiser in sport?

Sport needs organisers. Whether you are playing in a Sunday league netball team, or representing your country in the Commonwealth Games, you depend on many people to ensure that the event goes ahead smoothly. Sports organisers are needed at all levels in both professional and amateur sport and they carry out a wide range of roles. Some help to plan the event or take responsibility for the finance, while others will officiate. All these people are essential, although their work often goes unnoticed.

activity

Officials and sport

Do you know how many officials are required to control a game or event in your chosen sport? Research the answer and complete a checklist with details of each official and the roles they have.

Officials and sport

An official's central task, whether an umpire in tennis or a referee in rugby, is to enable sportspeople to take part in sport fairly and safely. Administrators organise events, but officials control the sporting action.

Officials must:

- have excellent knowledge of the sport and its rules

- apply rules firmly and fairly

- be patient, good with people and have a sense of humour!

- look after the safety of all those involved

- be in good physical condition.

Officials deserve respect and should not be taken for granted. Without them, organised sport would not exist.

Analysing performance task

As part of your GCSE course you are required to complete an analysing performance task. The investigation gives you an opportunity to show how much you know about your chosen sport. It can be an analysis of a partner or a self-analysis when performing a chosen activity. You may wish to analyse a team player, an official or an individual performer. In the checklist below we have assumed that you are analysing the performance of a male games player belonging to a local team.

Once you have selected your context and topic you must plan the investigation. The task is likely to take six weeks to complete and should amount to 5–6 sides of A4 paper when finished. By following the checklist below you can ensure that your investigation meets all of the examination requirements.

- Choose a member of a local team.
- Identify the person you are going to observe.
- State the game in which he is involved.
- State the position of your chosen person.
- Identify the important skills and techniques needed for him in his team.
- Observe him in a game situation.
- Analyse his performance with a view to identifying and describing his strengths in detail.
- Analyse his performance with a view to identifying and describing his weaknesses in detail.
- Suggest ways in which any of his strengths or weaknesses might be improved or corrected.
- Suggest what training methods or practice sessions might be used to improve his performance. Draw on knowledge of training methods and practices from the programme of study and used through the teaching of the practical activities.
- Identify some of the factors which affect performance in both positive and negative ways.
- After a period of six weeks' practice, assess how much improvement he has made and record it.
- Discuss your findings with the player and record his coments.
- In the case of a self-analysis, you must discuss your conclusions with a teacher and note his comments.

Factors affecting participation and performance

2 Skeleton and joints

- What does our skeleton do?
- What are the different types of joint?

6 Skill, motivation and mental preparation

- How do we learn skills?
- Types of skill
- Motivation and mental preparation
- Goal-setting

3 Muscles

- Our muscles in action
- Our major muscles
- Muscle training and development

4 The circulatory system

- The circulatory system in action
- Our heart and exercise
- What makes up our blood?

7 Social factors and participation

- Sport and leisure
- Why take part in sport?
- Sport in school
- Sport and society

8 Local and national facilities

- The structure of sport in England
- Who provides sports facilities?
- Sports facilities and participation

5 The respiratory system

- The respiratory system and sport
- How do we breathe?
- Factors affecting respiration

Skeleton and joints

Without our skeletal system we would look very different indeed. Our bodies would have no framework, our delicate organs would be unprotected, and we would be unable to move.

We are all limited in the choice of sport in which we might be successful because of the size of our skeletal system. At the highest sporting level, height is necessary for success at, for example, basketball, high jump and volleyball. However, even if we are of medium height we can still have some success in these sports if we are skilful and determined enough. Gymnasts usually have shorter limbs. This enables them to produce a burst of power very quickly and also to move their body with great control. Top-class rowers are usually very tall, with the necessary long levers to row a boat at speed.

Our skeleton has many joints. Our muscles are positioned around these joints. If we want to make a movement, our muscles contract and pull on the bones around the joints. In this way our whole body can move as quickly or as slowly as we want. The different arrangements of bones and joints, together with our muscles, allow us to perform intricate and powerful movement patterns in dance and gymnastics, as well as to make a full-blooded tackle in rugby.

activity

Joint observation

Roll up the sleeve of your right arm. Bend your elbow to bring your arm across your chest.

Look at the back of your hand and your forearm near the elbow as you wiggle your fingers. What's going on? Notice how your muscles create movement via some very long tendons. Now move your thumb around and note the muscles creating this movement.

KEYWORDS

Abduction: limb movement away from the middle line of the body

Adduction: limb movement towards the middle line of the body

Cartilage: a tough but flexible tissue which cushions and protects many bones in the skeleton

Extension: limb movement straightening a joint

Flexion: limb movement bending a joint

Joint: a place where two or more bones meet

Ligament: a band of tough fibrous tissue which bind bones together at the joint

Rotation: circular movement in which part of the body turns whilst the rest remains still

Skeleton: the bony framework of the body

Synovial joint: joint containing synovial fluid, allowing a wide range of movement

Tendon: strong cords of fibrous tissue which fix muscles to bone

Vertebrae: irregular bones which make up the vertebral column.

Key to Exam Success

For your GCSE you should be able to:

- describe and explain the functions of the skeleton and relate them to exercise
- know the names of the major bones and describe their roles in movement
- understand the structure of a synovial joint
- identify different types of joint and explain their function in movement
- describe the different terms used to explain movement
- explain the value of healthy and efficient joints in sport.

❝ KEY THOUGHT ❞

'Movement is a joint exercise with muscles.'

What does our skeleton do?

Our **skeleton** gives shape to our body, protects our organs, moves our body, supports our organs and produces blood.

Gives shape

Our body needs a framework and the skeleton gives shape to our bodies, enabling us to achieve a good posture.

When playing sport we need a firm basic shape from which to develop the many different body positions required, from a smash in tennis to a tuck in gymnastics. Sports such as golf, speed skating and riding also require a variety of sporting postures.

Protects

Our delicate organs need the protection of a strong structure of bone, particularly to prevent injury in contact sports such as rugby and judo. The cranium protects the brain, the vertebral column protects the spinal cord and the ribcage protects the heart and lungs.

Moves

Different sports require an extremely wide variety of muscle movements and different amounts of force, from the delicate touch required for a badminton drop shot to the power and control of the hammer throw.

Our muscles use our bones to cause movement. The muscles are attached to the skeleton, which is jointed to allow a wide range of movement. Different joints allow different types of movement.

Supports

We change our body position in most sports and in gymnastics and

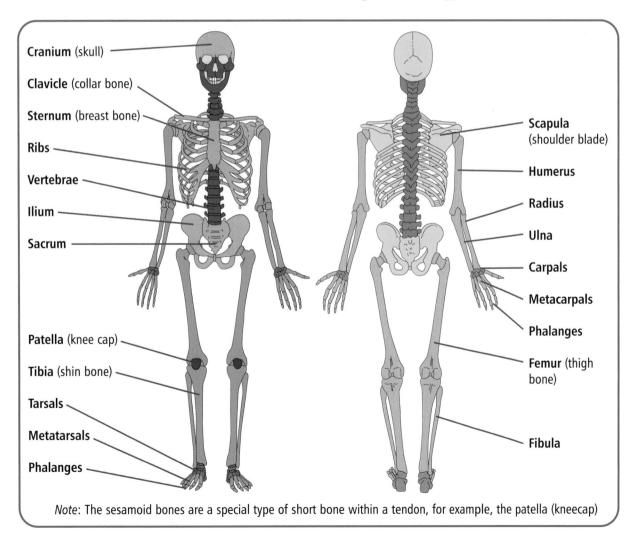

Cranium (skull)
Clavicle (collar bone)
Sternum (breast bone)
Ribs
Vertebrae
Ilium
Sacrum
Patella (knee cap)
Tibia (shin bone)
Tarsals
Metatarsals
Phalanges

Scapula (shoulder blade)
Humerus
Radius
Ulna
Carpals
Metacarpals
Phalanges
Femur (thigh bone)
Fibula

Note: The sesamoid bones are a special type of short bone within a tendon, for example, the patella (kneecap)

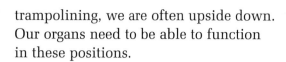

trampolining, we are often upside down. Our organs need to be able to function in these positions.

The skeleton holds our vital organs in place, the vertebral column playing a central part in supporting much of our body.

Produces blood

In sport, as in life in general, we need white blood cells for protection and red blood cells to provide the working muscles with oxygen. In endurance sports, the ability of the red blood cells to carry oxygen is vital for success. Red and white blood cells are produced in the bone marrow of the ribs, vertebrae and femur.

What are the main parts of our skeleton?

Bones in the upper body

The most important bones in the upper body are:

- the shoulder girdle

- the ribs and sternum

- the arms

- the wrist and hand.

The shoulder girdle

The shoulder girdle consists of two clavicles and two scapulas:

- **Clavicles** are thin, flat, slightly curved bones.

- **Scapulas** are large, flat bones with many muscles attached.

The shoulder girdle is only linked by muscles to our vertebral column. This

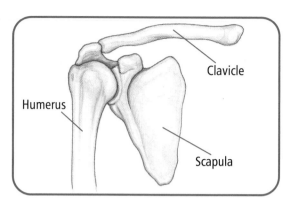

gives us great flexibility in our arms and shoulders, which is very helpful in sports such as gymnastics and swimming. However, it limits the force we can use.

The ribs and sternum

The sternum is a large, flat bone forming the front of the ribcage and giving it added strength.

- 12 pairs of ribs are joined to the vertebral column, but only 7 to the sternum.

- 3 pairs are joined to the seventh rib (false ribs) and 2 ribs are unattached (floating ribs).

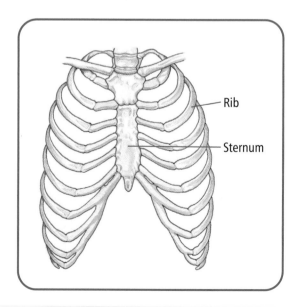

The ribcage protects our lungs and heart in combat and contact sports. It provides attachment for the intercostal muscles which are vital for deep breathing during strenuous exercise.

The arms

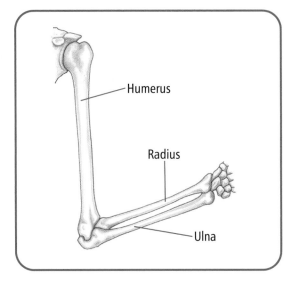

The arms consist of humerus, radius and ulna.

The long bones of the arm enable us to make major movements of the body, applying force over a large range of movement.

The wrist and hand

There are 8 carpal bones in the wrist, and 5 metacarpal bones and 14 phalanges in each hand.

The small bones of the hand enable us to make precise and delicate movements in sport.

Bones in the lower body

The most important bones in the lower body are:

- the pelvic girdle
- the legs, ankle and foot.

The pelvic girdle

The pelvic girdle is made up of two halves, each formed by three bones (including the ilium) which are fused together on each side. This forms a very stable joint with the vertebral column and passes the weight of the body to the legs. It supports the lower abdomen and provides a strong joint for the femur.

The female pelvis is wider and shallower than the male pelvis. This is to make childbearing easier, but it does make running less efficient.

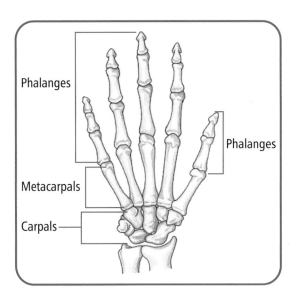

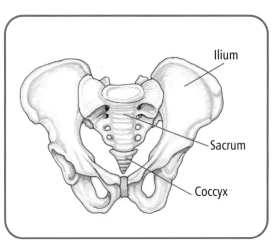

Legs

The legs consist of the femur, tibia and fibula. These long bones enable us to make major movements of the body, applying force over a large range of movement.

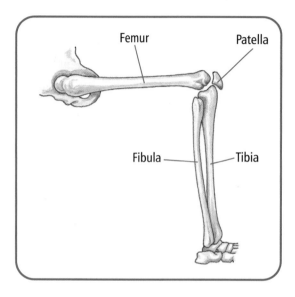

Ankle and foot

There are 7 tarsals in the ankle, and 5 metatarsals and 14 phalanges in each foot.

In order to perform most skilful actions, we need our feet to provide a solid base for our body. This is true of a drive in

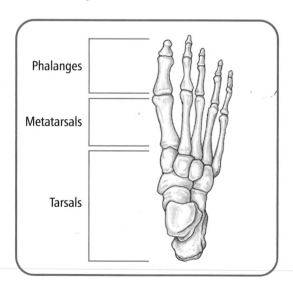

tennis, a shot in hockey or a take-off in the long jump. Even simple running requires a solid base for the thousands of steps which take place. All sportspeople should check the soles of their footwear for signs of abnormal wear.

How do we move?

Our body is flexible, and this is due to the combination of many of our joints. For example, our vertebral column has 33 small vertebrae, all of which can move a little. The result is that we can bend our back in many different ways in gymnastics, from performing a forward somersault to a backward walkover. The joints of our upper body allow us to serve in tennis and those of the lower body enable us to high-jump. In contrast to these powerful movements, the joints in our hands and wrist enable us to spin a ball in cricket, throw a dart and aim an arrow. We are able to adjust our body position constantly in sport and everyday life by using our muscles and joints together.

What are the different types of joint?

A **joint** is a place where two or more bones meet. The function of joints is to hold our bones together and to allow us to move our limbs and body.

Joints can be divided into three main groups, depending on the amount of movement they allow:

- immovable (fibrous) joints
- slightly movable (cartilaginous) joints
- freely movable (synovial) joints.

Immovable (fibrous) joints

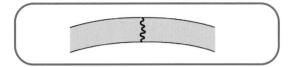

These are fixed joints with no movement possible between the bones. They have no significance in sport.

Slightly movable (cartilaginous) joints

- The bones have a pad of cartilage between them.

- Movement is possible between the bones.

- Examples are found in the joints between the ribs and sternum and between the vertebrae.

Note: the knee joint is a synovial joint although there are pads of cartilage within the joint capsule.

Freely movable (synovial) joints

Synovial joints are complex joints. The amount of movement they allow depends first of all on the shape of the bones within the joint. Movement will also depend on the arrangement of the muscles and their tendons around the joint, together with any ligaments which bind the bones together.

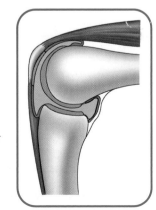

Synovial joints are found throughout the body including at the knee, hip and shoulder. They usually permit a wide variety of movement.

How are synovial joints constructed?

- **Hyaline cartilage** covers the head of the bones and the joint socket. It forms a hard, tough, slippery layer which protects bones and reduces friction in the joints.

- **Synovial membrane** forms a layer on the inside of the joint capsule and produces synovial fluid.

- **Synovial fluid** lubricates the joints and allows friction-free movement.

- A **joint capsule** made of fibrous tissue holds the bones together and protects the joint.

- **Ligaments** (not shown) hold the bones together. Made up of bands of tough fibrous tissue, the ligaments stretch to a limited amount and prevent dislocation.

What is cartilage?

Cartilage is a tough but flexible tissue.

Hyaline cartilage is found on the ends of our bones and around the joint socket in all our synovial joints. It is different from other forms of cartilage found in the body. For example, we have pads of tough cartilage in the vertebral column and knee which act as shock absorbers.

Many sportspeople suffer damage to the cartilage in the knee, especially in games like football. Since the cartilage does not have a blood supply, it does not repair itself easily. If the cartilage is torn it may be removed as this does not badly affect joint flexibility. However, the muscles around the knee will need strengthening to keep the joint stable.

What are ligaments?

Ligaments are bands of tough fibrous tissue which bind our bones together at joints. Some ligaments form a capsule which surrounds the joint and contains synovial fluid. Other ligaments remain outside the capsule, but also hold the joint stable. The ligaments make joints more stable by preventing excessive movement. They also limit the direction of movement. In general, the more ligaments around a joint, the stronger the joint will be.

If a lot of force is put on a ligament, it will stretch, although it can be damaged quite easily. In games like tennis, football and hockey, excessive twisting movements can cause damage to ligaments at the knee and ankle. The hip is a more stable joint because of the strength of the ligaments around it and therefore it is damaged less often. When ligaments are stretched or torn, this is known as a sprain (see page 268). The blood supply to ligaments is poor and so sprains heal slowly.

What are tendons?

Tendons are very strong cords of fibrous tissue which attach muscle to bone. They allow us to apply the power of the contracting muscles to the bones at the joint. They are made of tough fibres and are quite small so they can pass over joints and rough bone where the muscle itself would be damaged.

What are the different types of synovial joint?

Synovial joints have different structures, depending on how they work. This means the shape of the bones varies, as does the arrangement of the ligaments.

There are four basic types of synovial joint:

- ball and socket
- hinge
- gliding (plane)
- pivot.

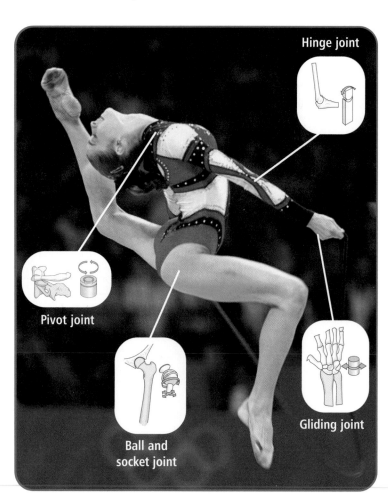

Hinge joint

Pivot joint

Gliding joint

Ball and socket joint

Ball and socket joint

- Moves freely in all directions
- Ligaments are often used to keep the joint stable
- Examples: hip and shoulder.

Hinge joint

- Movement is in one plane only
- Will open until it is straight
- Movement is limited because of the shape of the bones and the position of the ligaments
- Examples: elbow and knee.

Gliding (plane) joint

- One bone slides on top of another
- A little movement is possible in all directions
- Ligaments limit the movement
- Example: vertebrae, carpal bones in the hand.

Pivot joint

- Only rotation is possible because it has a 'ring-on-peg' structure
- Example: between the atlas and axis vertebrae in the neck.

Our joints and sport

Our different joints work smoothly together when we make skilled sporting movements. They must be capable of a full range of movement in order to help us perform well. The muscles, tendons and ligaments surrounding each joint must be strong enough to give stability to the joint.

The demands of sport put severe stress on our joints. We must ensure that our joints are in good condition to reduce the chance of injury and to give us the

opportunity to improve our sporting performance. We can do this by:

- eating a healthy diet to ensure strong bones, ligaments, tendons and cartilage
- strengthening the muscles around the joints to provide stability
- exercising regularly to prepare our joints for additional strain
- using flexibility exercises to increase the range of movement at the joints
- warming up thoroughly before each activity and warming down afterwards
- training to meet the needs of our particular sport.

How does our body move?

When we play sport we move our limbs in many different directions.
We use special words to describe these movements: **extension**, **flexion**, **abduction**, **adduction** and **rotation**.

Type of joint	Movement allowed
Ball and socket	Flexion and extension Abduction and adduction Rotation
Hinge	Flexion and extension
Gliding	Some gliding in all directions (no bending or circular movements)
Pivot	Rotation only

Our vertebral column and sport

This gymnast has bent her back into a hyperextension position. This should only be tried after much specialised training. Sportspeople can develop back injuries as a result of hyperextension.

The vertebral column of this tennis player is able to extend to allow him to serve with strength.

This diver is able to change her body position with great precision whilst moving at speed through the air. Our vertebrae and discs are arranged to form a flexible but strong unit.

It is very important for this rugby player that the weight pushing against his shoulders is passed to his legs through a straight vertebral column. A bent back with his vertebrae out of line could lead to injury.

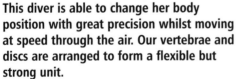

activity 😊😊

Movements at joints

Look at the pictures of movement on page 46. List the joints used and the type of movement shown, then try to think of examples of other sporting situations where the same, or a similar, action might be performed. Show your results in a table like the one below.

Photo	Joint(s) used	Movement	Further example(s)
A			
B			
C			
D			
E			

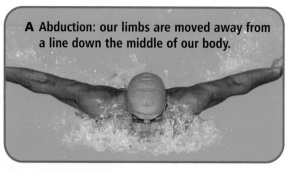

A Abduction: our limbs are moved away from a line down the middle of our body.

B Flexion: our limbs bend at a joint.

PARIS**2003**ST-DENIS

C Rotation: a circular movement in which part of the body turns whilst the rest remains still.

D Extension: our limbs straighten at a joint.

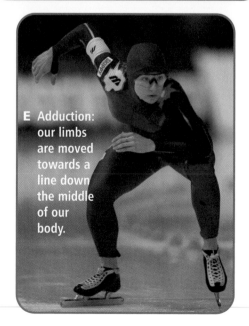

E Adduction: our limbs are moved towards a line down the middle of our body.

QUESTIONS

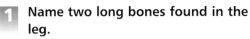

2 Skeleton and joints

1 **Name two long bones found in the leg.**

(2 marks)

2 **Where is the humerus bone found?**

(1 mark)

3 **Protection is one function of the skeleton. Give two others.**

(2 marks)

4 **Give two examples of bones protecting organs of the body.**

(4 marks)

5 **Name two flat bones.**

(2 marks)

6 **Explain the importance of each of the following in a synovial joint.**

a Synovial membrane *(1 mark)*
b Synovial fluid *(1 mark)*
c Hyaline cartilage. *(1 mark)*

7 **Name the type of synovial joint found between the:**

a carpal bones *(1 mark)*
b atlas and axis vertebrae. *(1 mark)*

8 **Stuart is a good hurdler. When clearing the hurdle his leading leg is straight.**

a Name the type of synovial joint found at his:

i knee *(1 mark)*
ii hip. *(1 mark)*

b Name the movement at his hip which:

i straightens his leg
ii will return his leg to the ground.

(2 marks)

c When his leg lands, what in his knee will absorb the shock?

(1 mark)

9 **Serena has been attending karate lessons for a year.**

a Describe the movement at her hip joint when:

i she performs a sideways kick

(1 mark)

ii her leg returns to a standing position.

(1 mark)

b What type of synovial joint is found at her:

i shoulder *(1 mark)*
ii elbow? *(1 mark)*

c Explain why her hip joint is more stable than her shoulder joint.

(2 marks)

d Name two of the three movements which are possible at the hip joint, but not at the knee joint.

(2 marks)
(Total 29 marks)

3 Muscles

Nearly all the movements of our body are caused by the contraction of our muscles. The speed and power which enables us to jump out of the way of danger also enables us to do well in contact sport. The muscles which control our vision in everyday life also allow us to follow the ball in racket sports. Our heart muscle beats constantly throughout our life to pump blood around our body and enable us to work, rest and play. Silent muscles within us meet the needs of our body for both energy and nutrients. Above all, our muscles have the special ability to change chemical energy into mechanical energy. This means that if we supply our muscles with food and oxygen they will produce movement. Without movement in sport, we can achieve nothing.

activity

Muscle analysis

Working with a partner, carry out the activities below while your partner identifies which major muscle groups are being used.

Examples of muscle groups include:

- upper back
- lower back
- upper arm
- lower arm
- chest
- shoulder
- stomach.

Begin by lying flat on your back. Then complete each action when instructed to do so by your partner.

Activity	Major muscle groups being used
Move to sit-up position	
Stand up	
Raise hands above head	
Raise one knee and hold for five seconds	
Complete one press-up	
From standing position, jump as high as possible	

Abduction: limb movement away from the middle line of the body

Adduction: limb movement towards the middle line of the body

Antagonist: muscle that works in combination with the prime mover to control movement at a joint

Atrophy: loss of muscle mass due to physical inactivity

Extension: limb movement straightening a joint

Fast-twitch muscle fibres: used for anaerobic activity, providing fast, powerful contractions for a short period

Flexion: limb movement bending a joint

Hypertrophy: growth of muscles as a result of regular physical activity

Insertion: the end of the muscle which is attached to the bone which moves

Isometric contraction: muscular contraction that results in no movement at a joint

Isotonic concentric contraction: muscular contraction where the muscle shortens, resulting in movement at a joint

Isotonic eccentric contraction: muscular contraction where the muscle lengthens, resulting in movement at a joint

Muscle tone: voluntary muscles in a state of very slight tension, ready and waiting to be used

Origin: the end of the muscle which is attached to the fixed bone

Posture: the way in which body parts are positioned in relation to one another

Prime mover: muscle that is responsible for movement at a joint

Rotation: a circular movement in which part of the body turns whilst the rest remains still

Slow-twitch muscle fibres: used for aerobic activity, providing contractions over a long period of time

Synergist: muscle that reduces unnecessary movement at a joint when prime mover contracts

Tendon: strong fibrous tissue that joins muscle to bone.

Key to Exam Success

For your GCSE you should be able to:

- know the importance of muscles and muscle action for sport, fitness and training
- understand the importance for sport, of fast- and slow-twitch muscle fibres
- know the name, position and functions of the main skeletal muscles of the body
- understand how muscles change when exercised
- describe and explain how muscles work in antagonistic pairs
- describe the role and function of tendons.

" KEY THOUGHT "

'Muscles are the machines of the body.'

Our muscles in action

All the movements we make happen as a result of the shortening (contracting) and lengthening (extending) of the voluntary muscles which are found around our joints. Our muscles can only pull; they cannot push.

Our muscles:

- enable us to move our body parts

- give us our own individual shape

- protect and keep in place our abdominal organs

- stabilise our joints during movement

- enable us to maintain a good posture

- help in the circulation of our blood

- generate body heat when they contract.

There are over 600 voluntary muscles in the body – 150 in the head and neck. Skeletal muscle accounts for over 40% of our body mass.

What are muscle fibres?

Our muscles are made up of many tiny thread-like fibres packed together in bundles. These fibres contract and make the muscle shorter. In voluntary muscle, the fibres come together at the ends of the muscles into a tough cord-like tendon. Each tendon is attached firmly to the bone. Voluntary muscles are usually long and thin. When they contract they become shorter and thicker.

We have two different types of fibres in our voluntary muscles: **fast-twitch** and **slow-twitch**.

Slow-twitch muscle fibres:

- have a very good oxygen supply

- work for a long time without tiring

- are not as strong as fast-twitch fibres

- take longer to contract

- are used in all types of exercise

- are used especially in aerobic activities which need cardiovascular fitness, such as long-distance running and cycling.

Fast-twitch muscle fibres:

- do not have a good oxygen supply

- tire very quickly

- are stronger than slow-twitch fibres

- contract very quickly

- are used when we need fast, powerful movements

- are used only in high-intensity exercise

- are used in anaerobic activities which need bursts of strength and power such as sprinting and jumping.

Our muscle fibres and sport

If we jog slowly, only a few of our slow-twitch muscle fibres contract to move our legs. When we increase our speed, we use more slow-twitch fibres. As we run faster, our fast-twitch fibres also start to contract to help out. More and more will start to work as we run even faster. At top speed, all of our fast- and slow-twitch muscle fibres will be working.

In many sports we need to use the different fibres at different times. In hockey, for example, we need to use our fast twitch fibres for quick sprints and our slow twitch fibres for jogging when not involved in the action.

Our muscles are usually an equal mixture of both fast- and slow-twitch fibres. The exact amount of each

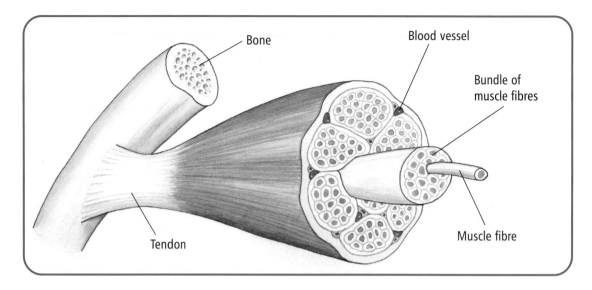

Bone

Blood vessel

Bundle of muscle fibres

Tendon

Muscle fibre

depends on what we inherit from our parents, and the mixture can vary widely. A person with more slow-twitch fibres is likely to be better at sports needing cardiovascular endurance such as cycling, running and swimming. Someone with more fast-twitch fibres is likely to be better at sprinting, throwing and jumping. For many team games we need both short bursts of activity and constant, less demanding activity. Our training programmes for games will therefore contain activities to develop both slow- and fast-twitch muscle fibres. We can train our muscle fibres to contract either more often (slow-twitch) or more powerfully (fast-twitch).

Our major muscles

Muscles of the upper body

Note: Movement terms are explained on page 46.

Biceps
- Location: front of the upper arm
- Function: flexes the forearm at the elbow

- Examples: drawing a bow in archery, rowing
- Strengthened by: curls of various sorts.

Triceps
- Location: back of the upper arm
- Function: extends the forearm at the elbow; extends the arm at the shoulder
- Examples: smash in badminton, throwing the javelin, press-ups
- Strengthened by: press-ups, triceps curls above the head.

Deltoids
- Location: front and rear of the shoulder
- Function: moves the arm in all directions at the shoulder; adducts (raises) the arm
- Examples: bowling in cricket
- Strengthened by: bent-over rowing, bench presses.

Trapezius
- Location: rear of the shoulders and neck
- Function: helps to raise and control the shoulder girdle; holds back the shoulders; moves head back and sideways

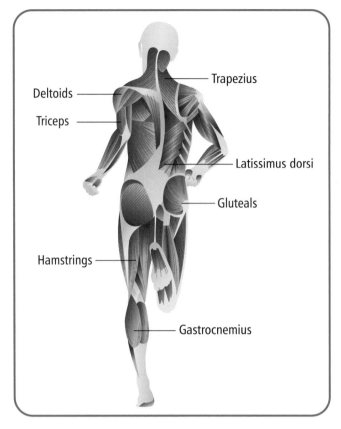

Deltoids —
Triceps —
Trapezius
Latissimus dorsi
Gluteals
Hamstrings —
Gastrocnemius —

- Examples: performing upward circles on the bar in gymnastics, pulling the body down in hurdling

- Strengthened by: sit-ups of various sorts.

Pectorals
Consist of pectoralis major and pectoralis minor.

- Location: front of the chest

- Function: adduct (raise) the arm and shoulder; used for deep breathing

- Examples: playing a forehand drive in tennis, putting the shot, front crawl

- Strengthened by: bench presses.

Muscles of the lower body

Hamstrings
Four separate muscles.

- Location: back of upper leg

- Function: extend the hip joint; flex the knee joint

- Examples: drawing the leg back before kicking a ball, jumping activities with knees bent before take-off

- Strengthened by: leg curls.

Quadriceps
Four separate muscles.

- Location: front of upper leg

- Function: flex the hip joint; extend the knee joint

- Examples: taking off in high jump, raising knee in running, kicking a ball

- Strengthened by: squats, leg extensions and leg presses.

- Examples: holding the head up in a rugby scrum, head back to follow high ball, head back in 'Fosbury Flop'

- Strengthened by: upright rowing.

Latissimus dorsi
- Location: lower back

- Functions: adducts (raises) and extends the arm at the shoulder

- Examples: butterfly stroke, rowing, pulling on the javelin

- Strengthened by: pull-downs.

Abdominals
Four separate muscles.

- Location: front of the abdomen

- Function: rotate, raise and allow the trunk to bend side to side; strengthen the abdominal wall; help with breathing

Gluteals

Consist of gluteus maximus and two other muscles.

- Location: form the buttocks

- Function: abduct (move away from body) and extend the hip joint

- Examples: stepping up during rock climbing, sidestepping, pulling back leg before kicking a ball

- Strengthened by: squats and leg presses.

Gastrocnemius

- Location: back of the lower leg

- Function: flexes the knee joint and points the toes

- Examples: running, take-off in jumps

- Strengthened by: heel raises.

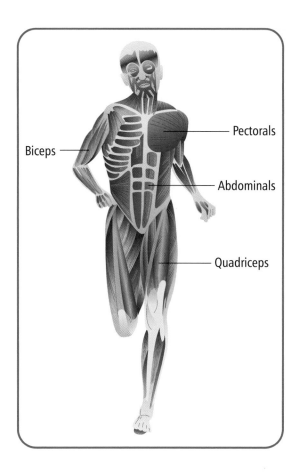

Biceps — Pectorals — Abdominals — Quadriceps

How do our muscles work together?

Our voluntary muscles can pull by contracting, but they cannot push. If one muscle contracts across a joint to bring two bones together, another muscle is needed to pull the bones apart again. Therefore muscles always work in pairs.

Even for simple body movements we need a large number of pairs of muscles to work together in different ways. Our muscles take on different roles depending on the movement we are performing.

activity

Muscle analysis using ICT

Using a digital camcorder, record a sporting movement – for example, a sprint start – and play it back in slow motion. Using the freeze-frame facility, try to identify exactly how the muscles work. Determine which muscles are the prime movers and the antagonists in the leg action, and which muscles are acting as extensors and which as flexors.

By moving the video on frame by frame, it should be possible to see how the roles of the muscles change. If a printer is available, print out each of the still frames and label the muscles and their actions.

They can work as:

- **flexors**, contracting to bend our joints

- **extensors**, contracting to straighten our joints

- **prime movers** (or **agonists**), contracting in order to start a movement

- **antagonists**, relaxing to allow a movement to take place

- **synergists**, contracting to reduce unnecessary movement at a joint when prime mover contracts.

How are our muscles attached to our bones?

Our voluntary muscles are usually attached to two or more different bones. The muscle fibres end in a strong flexible cord called a **tendon**. The tendon is fixed deeply into the bone and is very strongly attached. Tendons vary in shape and size. Some of our muscles are divided into more than one part. They may end in two or more different tendons, which may be fixed to different bones.

The extensor muscle contracts to straighten the joint

The main muscles used to produce a movement are called the prime movers

The flexor muscle contracts and bends the joint

Prime movers

Antagonistic muscles work against the prime mover to control the movement

As the prime movers contract the antagonist must relax to allow movement to take place

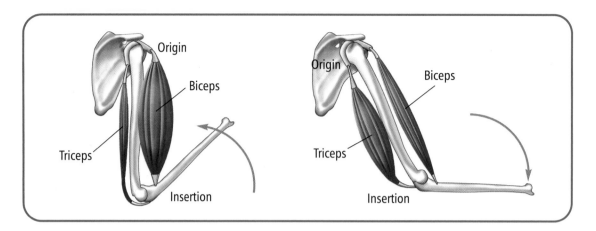

What are tendons?

Tendons are very strong cords of fibrous tissue which attach muscle to bone. They allow us to apply the power of the contracting muscles to the bones at the joint. They are made of tough fibres and are quite small so they can pass over joints and rough bone where the muscle itself would be damaged.

Tendons only stretch a little – much less than ligaments. Although they can be torn or bruised in contact sports, tendons are strong and the muscle itself is more likely to be damaged than the tendon.

Tendons can, however, be damaged by fierce muscle contraction. In squash, for example, players sometimes damage the Achilles tendon in the lower leg. Adolescents who overtrain through excessive running on hard surfaces may suffer from Osgood-Schlatter's disease, a condition caused by damage to the tendon below the kneecap.

Both tendons and ligaments respond to the stresses placed upon them. Regular exercise will improve the strength and flexibility of tendons and ligaments and make them less liable to injury during sporting action.

When our muscles make the bones around a joint move, usually one bone stays fixed and the other moves. The end of the muscle that is attached to the

activity

What am I doing?

From the following description, try to work out what action is being performed.

> The body begins in a standing position with the arms by the side. The deltoids contract to raise the arm so that it is parallel to the ground. The joints of the fingers are flexed to grip an object. The biceps contract slowly and then the triceps contract powerfully and the fingers extend as the object is released.

Write your own movement description, then see if your partner can work out what action is being performed. Be prepared to demonstrate some or all of the action if necessary. You may need to refine your description following discussion.

fixed bone is called the **origin**. The other end of the muscle is called the **insertion**. It is attached to the bone which moves. As the muscle contracts the insertion moves towards the origin.

How do our muscles work in pairs?

Our voluntary muscles are arranged in pairs around our joints to enable us to move. When a prime mover muscle contracts, the antagonist muscle must relax to allow a movement to take place. However, the antagonist muscle will keep some fibres contracting. This is to stop our prime mover moving the joint so hard that the antagonists are damaged.

Sometimes this system fails, for example, when sprinters are running flat out. In the upper legs when the knee is raised, the quadriceps are the prime movers and the hamstrings are the antagonists. Sprinters may tear their hamstrings and quickly come to a painful stop.

In isometric muscle action, both of the muscles of the pair at a joint contract at the same time and no movement is seen.

Muscle tone

Muscle tone is produced when voluntary muscles are in a state of very slight tension, ready and waiting to be used.

The way our prime movers and antagonists work against each other also gives us muscle tone. At any given time, some muscle fibres will be contracted whilst others are relaxed. This is true even when we are not moving. These contractions tighten the muscles a little, but are not strong enough to cause movement. Different fibres contract at different times in order to prevent tiredness setting in. This continuous slight contraction of our voluntary muscles is very important for good posture and keeps the body ready for instant action. Exercise improves muscle tone.

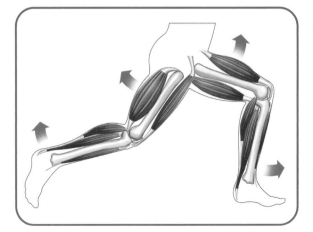

Muscle training and development

Our voluntary muscles have the ability to adapt in order to cope with the activities for which they are used. If we walk to school everyday, our leg muscles will adapt to this exercise and we will not find it difficult. If we move house and have an extra two kilometres to walk to and from school, at first we may find it tiring. However, after a few weeks our leg muscles will have learned to cope with the additional distance and we will find the walk easy again. This is exactly what happens when we train for sport. We put our muscles under an increased stress and they adapt to the new workload.

We all need a basic amount of muscular strength and cardiovascular fitness to cope with the demands of everyday life. Lifting and carrying involves strength, while walking and moving around requires stamina. As we get older it is important to maintain our fitness for life. Regular weight-bearing exercise can help prevent the weakening of bones and gentle, regular endurance exercise can help maintain cardiovascular fitness.

Muscle hypertrophy and atrophy

Our voluntary muscles become stronger the more they are exercised. If we train and exercise regularly over a long period, we will change our muscles. However, we must always remember that these changes are not permanent. The principle of **reversibility** applies (see page 212). This means that if we stop exercising, our muscles will return to their original state. 'If we don't use it, we lose it'!

Our muscles increase in size, strength and endurance when we follow a regular strength-training programme. This is called muscle **hypertrophy**. When we do not use our muscles regularly, they get smaller and weaker. We call this muscle **atrophy**. This loss of size and strength often happens when we are recovering from an injury. While waiting for a particular injury to heal, we should try to exercise the rest of the body as much as possible. Many joint injuries and weaknesses can be overcome by strengthening the muscles around the joints.

Our muscles adapt very well to an increased workload. If heavy weights are lifted, new muscle fibres develop and

the muscle grows in size and also becomes stronger. This hypertrophy is known as muscle bulk. A sprinter needs large, strong muscles to provide the power required. Sprinters will also have more fast-twitch muscle fibres than the average person. With training, these fibres will become able to use the stored energy in short bursts more efficiently.

Long-distance runners do not need muscle bulk. They use distance training to adapt their muscles to use energy more efficiently, in order to delay fatigue. In fact, carrying the extra weight of large muscles over a distance will be a disadvantage. Distance runners will have more slow-twitch fibres than the average person. Through training, these fibres will be able to use the stored energy in the muscle more efficiently and for longer.

The effects of exercise on bones, joints and muscles

What are the immediate effects of exercise on bones, joints and muscles?

- little effect on bones and joints
- increased flow of blood to working muscles
- muscles take up more oxygen from the blood
- muscles contract more often and more quickly
- more of the muscle fibres contract
- rise in temperature in the muscles.

What are the effects of regular training and exercise on bones, joints and muscles?

- bone width and bone density increases
- strengthens muscles, tendons and ligaments surrounding joints
- joint cartilage thickens, improving shock absorption at joints
- increased range of movement at joints (flexibility)
- muscles adjust to greater workload

- muscles increase in size (hypertrophy)

- depending on the type of training, the number of fast- or slow-twitch fibres will increase

- muscles can work harder and for longer.

What are the long-term benefits of exercise on bones, joints and muscles?

- increases bone strength and thickness

- increases stability of joints

- develops a full range of movement at joints

- increases muscular strength, muscular endurance and muscular power

- improves the muscles' capacity to tolerate fatigue by coping with lactic acid and oxygen debt.

activity

Feel the difference

This activity will help you to understand the three different ways in which muscles work.

1 Hold a textbook in your preferred hand with your arm extended by your side.

2 Bend your arm to raise the book to your shoulder. Place the fingers of your other hand on your biceps and feel the contraction. This is an isotonic, concentric contraction.

3 Slowly lower the book to the starting position and feel your biceps contracting as it lengthens. This is an isotonic, eccentric contraction.

4 Raise the book again but pause before your forearm is parallel to the floor. Hold the book steady and feel your biceps contracting. This is an isometric contraction as there is no movement taking place.

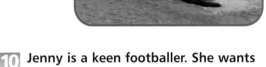

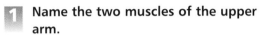 QUESTIONS

3 Muscles

1 Name the two muscles of the upper arm.

(2 marks)

2 Where are the pectoral muscles found?

(1 mark)

3 Name the main muscle strengthened by doing sit-ups.

(1 mark)

4 What do prime mover muscles do?

(1 mark)

5 How are muscles attached to bones?

(1 mark)

6 When the extensor muscle contracts at a joint, how does the joint move?

(1 mark)

7 What type of muscle is the heart muscle?

(1 mark)

8 What do we call the increase in muscle size due to training?

(1 mark)

9 Copy and complete the table below by matching muscles, type of movement and examples from sport.

(10 marks)

10 Jenny is a keen footballer. She wants to develop a more powerful shot.

a Name three muscles involved in kicking the ball.

(3 marks)

b Suggest a weight training exercise to develop strength in each of these muscles.

(3 marks)

c Name two muscles that work as an antagonistic pair when kicking a ball.

(2 marks)

d **i** Name the type of muscle fibre used when kicking a ball.

(1 mark)

   ii Explain why this type of fibre is used when playing football.

(2 marks)

e Name the type of muscle contraction taking place when kicking a ball:

   i in the kicking leg   *(1 mark)*
   ii in the standing leg.   *(1 mark)*

f Explain the difference between muscle hypertrophy and muscle atrophy.

(2 marks)

(Total 34 marks)

Muscle	Type of movement	Example from sport
	Control shoulder girdle	
Biceps		
		Bowling in cricket
	Abduct and extend hip joint	
Gastrocnemius		

4 The circulatory system

Our life depends upon a constant source of oxygen and nutrients in all the cells of the body. Our circulatory system works non-stop, 24 hours a day to deliver these vital supplies. The circulatory system also carries away carbon dioxide and other waste products.

activity
😊😊
😊

Recording heart rate

The simplest way to see how well our circulatory system is working is to measure our heart rate by taking our pulse. Our pulse is the surge of blood through our arteries which happens every time our heart beats. We must learn how to find and record our pulse accurately and quickly. This will enable us to assess how hard our circulatory system is working at any time.

We can easily measure our pulse rate at two specific places – in the neck at the carotid artery and in our wrist on the radial artery.

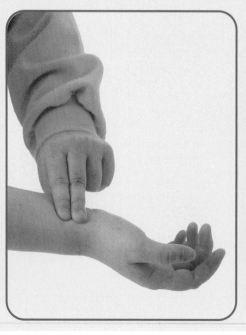

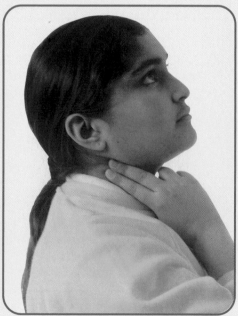

activity

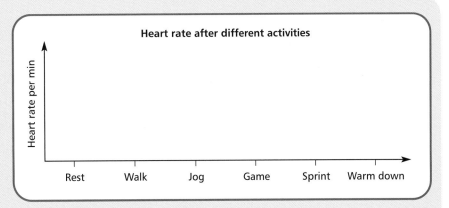

Heart rate after different activities

Heart rate per min

Rest Walk Jog Game Sprint Warm down

1 Practise counting the number of pulses felt over a time of 15 seconds. You must use your fingers and not your thumb. Try it at both the neck and wrist. Multiply your 15-second count by 4 to get your heart rate in beats per minute. (It should of course be the same at both your neck and wrist!)

2 Practise finding your carotid and radial pulses quickly. This is important when trying to count your pulse after exercise.

3 In pairs, practise counting the pulse of your partner using both the neck and wrist locations, while sitting down at rest.

4 One of you now walks at a brisk pace for one minute. Immediately after walking, the non-active partner measures the other's pulse over the first 15 seconds and records it in beats per minute.

5 Repeat the exercise with the roles reversed.

6 The first partner now jogs for three minutes at a slow pace. Repeat the pulse-taking and swap over.

7 You both now play a game, for instance, basketball, for 10–15 minutes. Repeat the pulse-taking.

8 Your partner sprints for a total of 20 seconds. Repeat the pulse-taking and swap over.

9 You both warm down for three minutes. Repeat the pulse-taking and swap over.

10 Record your results and those of your partner on a graph. Remember, you should not join the points plotted as the data you have collected is not continuous. Explain your results and set them out as shown in the table below.

Time period	Activity	Heart rate (beats per minute)	Explanation
	Rest		
1 minute	Walk		
3 minutes	Jog		
10–15 minutes	Play game (e.g. basketball)		
20 seconds	Sprint		
3 minutes	Warm-down		

KEYWORDS

Arterioles: small blood vessels into which arteries subdivide, taking blood into the capillaries

Artery: Large blood vessel taking oxygenated blood from the heart to the body. (Exception: the pulmonary artery takes deoxygenated blood from the heart to the lungs)

Blood pressure: force of blood against artery walls caused by heart pumping blood around the body

Capillaries: microscopic blood vessels which link arteries with veins

Cardiac output: amount of blood ejected from the heart in one minute

Cardiovascular: relating to the heart and blood vessels

Circulatory system: The heart, circulation of the blood and composition of the blood (also known as the cardiovascular system)

Haemoglobin: oxygen-carrying substance in red blood cells

Heartbeat: one complete contraction of the heart

Heart rate: the number of times the heart beats each minute

Pulmonary circulation: carries deoxygenated blood from our heart to our lungs and oxygenated blood back to the heart

Stroke volume: the volume of blood pumped out of the heart by each ventricle during one contraction

Systemic circulation: carries oxygenated blood from the heart to the rest of our body and deoxygenated blood back to the heart

Veins: large blood vessels taking deoxygenated blood from the body to the heart. (Exception: the pulmonary vein takes oxygenated blood from the lungs to the heart)

Venules: small blood vessels that take blood from the capillaries to the veins.

Key to Exam Success

For your GCSE you should be able to:

- explain how the heart works
- understand how the heart, blood, and blood vessels work together
- know how the circulatory system links with the respiratory system to provide an energy source for physical activity
- describe the composition and functions of the blood
- know how the circulatory system responds to exercise and training.

❝ KEY THOUGHT ❞

'Our circulation system is a delivery service in perpetual motion.'

The circulatory system in action

Our **circulatory system** (sometimes called our **cardiovascular system**) is made up of our heart, blood and blood vessels.

Our circulation system has two parts, our **systemic circulation** and our **pulmonary circulation**. Our systemic circulation carries oxygenated blood from the heart to the rest of our body and the oxygen is used by the cells. Deoxygenated blood returns to the heart with waste products, which have to be removed from our body.

Our pulmonary circulation carries deoxygenated blood from our heart to our lungs. Here carbon dioxide is exchanged for oxygen. Oxygenated blood is then carried back to the heart.

This is called a double circulatory system which means that at every heartbeat blood is pumped out of the heart to both the lungs and the body at the same time.

Our circulatory system:

- takes oxygen and **nutrients** to every cell

- removes carbon dioxide and other waste products from every cell

- carries **hormones** from the hormonal (**endocrine**) glands to different parts of the body

- maintains temperature and fluid levels

- prevents infection from invading germs.

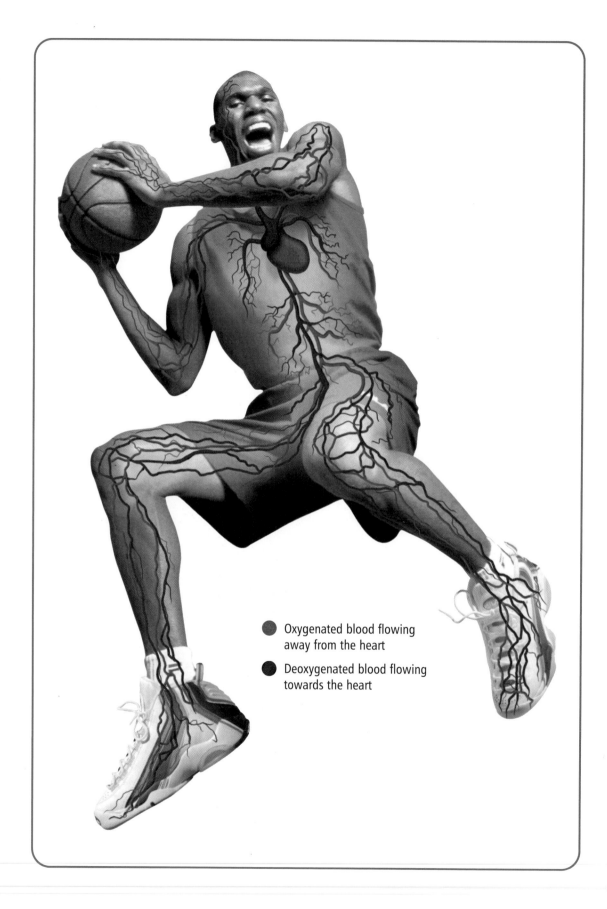

Oxygenated blood flowing away from the heart

Deoxygenated blood flowing towards the heart

How does our heart work?

The heart is a muscular pump. It is made of special cardiac muscle which contracts regularly without tiring. It pumps blood first to the lungs, to exchange carbon dioxide for oxygen. Then blood with the new oxygen is returned to the heart to be pumped out around the body.

The three stages of heart action are shown on page 68.

- Our cardiac cycle is one complete cycle of these three stages.

- Our **heartbeat** is one complete contraction of the heart.

- Our **heart rate** (pulse) is the number of heartbeats per minute.

At rest, our heart pumps between 50 and 80 times a minute. It pumps about 4.7 litres of blood around the body. At rest this journey takes about 20 seconds.

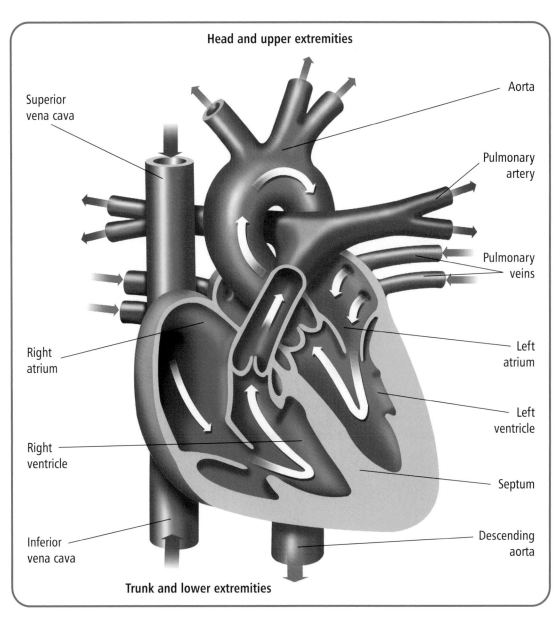

Head and upper extremities

Superior vena cava

Aorta

Pulmonary artery

Pulmonary veins

Right atrium

Left atrium

Left ventricle

Right ventricle

Septum

Inferior vena cava

Descending aorta

Trunk and lower extremities

Stage 1

- Blood flows into the heart when it is between beats and relaxed.
- Deoxygenated blood from our body enters the right atrium through the two vena cava veins.
- At the same time newly oxygenated blood from our lungs enters the left atrium through the pulmonary veins.

Stage 2

- Our right atrium muscles contract to pump blood through the tricuspid valve into the right ventricle.
- At the same time, our left atrium muscles contract to pump blood through the mitral valve into the left ventricle.

Stage 3

- Our right ventricle muscles contract to pump blood through the semilunar valves into the pulmonary artery to travel to the lungs.
- Our left ventricle muscles contract to pump blood through the semilunar valves into the aorta, to travel around the body again.

How does blood move around the body?

The heart is a double pump divided into two parts by a muscular wall called the septum.

The right-hand side of the heart deals with blood returning from our body through the vena cava. During its journey, our blood has given up much of its oxygen. It has picked up waste products, including carbon dioxide. It is now a dull red colour. The heart pumps this blood to our lungs in our **pulmonary artery**. This is the only artery which carries deoxygenated blood.

Our blood vessels include **arteries**, **veins**, **venules** and **capillaries**. These carry blood to all parts of the body and back again to the heart.

The left-hand side of the heart deals with the blood returning from our lungs in our **pulmonary veins**. These are the only veins that carry oxygenated blood. In our lungs the blood releases carbon dioxide and other waste products, and is

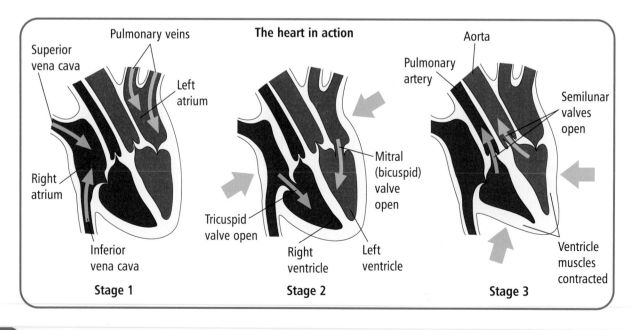

The heart in action

Stage 1 — Superior vena cava, Pulmonary veins, Left atrium, Right atrium, Inferior vena cava

Stage 2 — Tricuspid valve open, Mitral (bicuspid) valve open, Right ventricle, Left ventricle

Stage 3 — Aorta, Pulmonary artery, Semilunar valves open, Ventricle muscles contracted

supplied with fresh oxygen. When blood returns to the heart it is bright red. The heart pumps this blood into our largest artery, the aorta, to travel around the body.

The thickness of the walls of the heart vary according to the task which they carry out. The atria are both thin-walled, because they only pump the blood to the ventricles below. Both ventricles have much thicker walls.

The left ventricle has very thick, muscular walls. This is because the blood leaving the heart must be pumped out very powerfully at high pressure to travel the long distance around the body. In contrast, the right ventricle only pumps blood a short distance to the lungs and is therefore not so thick-walled.

The arteries carry freshly oxygenated blood from the heart. They become smaller and smaller. The smaller arteries are called **arterioles**. They take blood into the tissue where they join up with our smallest vessels – the **capillaries**. In turn the capillaries join up with venules, which increase in size to

become veins. Our veins return deoxygenated blood to our heart.

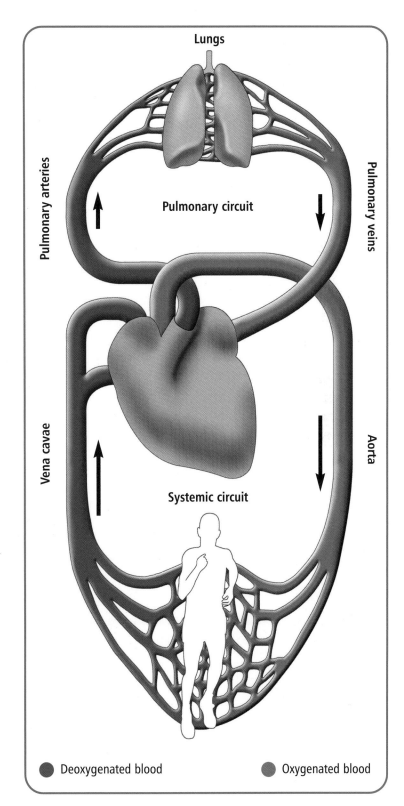

Lungs

Pulmonary arteries

Pulmonary veins

Pulmonary circuit

Vena cavae

Aorta

Systemic circuit

● Deoxygenated blood   ● Oxygenated blood

Our heart and exercise

As we work harder, our muscles need more oxygen and we breathe in and out more deeply and quickly in order to get the oxygen to the lungs. These increased supplies of oxygen are picked up by the blood in our lungs and transported more quickly back to the heart. The double circulatory system ensures that the increased supplies of oxygen collected from the lungs are transported at an increased rate to the working muscles. At the same time, carbon dioxide and other waste products are removed at an increased rate.

The right type of training can increase the size and pumping ability of the heart – that is, the **stroke volume** and **cardiac output** of the heart. Like all muscle, heart muscle responds to training by becoming stronger as its walls thicken. In this way we can increase the amount of blood going to the lungs to pick up oxygen and therefore increase the amount of oxygen going to our working muscles. This helps us to work harder and for longer periods in our sport. During hard physical activity, our heart rate can increase to over 200 beats per minute. The heart of a trained athlete can pump up to 45 litres of blood a minute. Training will reduce the resting heart rate of an athlete considerably.

How well does our heart pump?

Our heart is made up of cardiac muscle and we cannot control its action voluntarily. Fortunately cardiac muscle never tires. The speed and force of each heartbeat are controlled by our brain. Our brain is affected by what we are doing. If we start running, our brain tells our heart to pump more blood to supply our working leg muscles with more oxygen. Like any other muscle, heart muscle can get stronger when exercised. The amount of blood pumped by the heart depends on heart rate and stroke volume.

Heart rate

Heart rate is the number of times the heart beats each minute.

At each heartbeat, blood is pumped out of our heart into the arteries. Our arteries are forced to expand and then contract, which is called our pulse. The number of pulses in one minute is our heart rate. For a normal adult when resting this will be about 70 beats per minute.

A pulse can be felt at pressure points in the body where arteries are near to the skin.

Resting heart rate

Resting heart rates can vary between people, due to factors such as sex, age and health. For a healthy resting adult it is about 70 beats per minute. Endurance sportspeople will have a much lower heart rate – perhaps as low as 30 beats per minute. This is because their hearts are stronger and are able to pump more blood in fewer beats than an unfit person. Their stroke volume is therefore greater.

Resting heart rate can be one way to measure fitness. The speed at which heart rate returns to normal after exercise is called the recovery rate. This can also be used to measure fitness.

Stroke volume

Stroke volume is the volume of blood pumped out of the heart by each ventricle during one contraction.

When we exercise, stroke volume increases for a number of reasons. Working muscles squeeze blood in our veins, forcing more blood back to the heart. The heart stretches as it fills up with the extra blood and in turn it contracts more strongly. This results in more blood being pumped out of the heart for each beat.

Cardiac output

Cardiac output is the amount of blood ejected from the heart in one minute. It is controlled by both heart rate and stroke volume.

> Heart rate × Stroke volume = Cardiac output

In sport we usually want to increase the amount of blood going to the working muscles – that is, our cardiac output. We can do this by increasing stroke volume, heart rate or both.

What happens to our circulatory system when we exercise?

- The hormone adrenaline is released even before we start to exercise. It prepares the body for action.

- Adrenaline in the bloodstream causes the heart to beat more quickly, so heart rate increases.

- The heart contracts more powerfully. It sends out a greater amount of blood with each contraction. Stroke volume increases.

- Blood circulation speeds up, and greater amounts of oxygen-carrying blood reach the working muscles. Cardiac output increases.

- The pumping action of muscles forces more deoxygenated blood back to the heart more quickly.

- Blood flow is reduced to the areas of the body not in urgent need of oxygen, for example the digestive system.

- Blood flow is increased to the areas in greatest need of oxygen, for example, the skeletal muscles.

- Blood vessels to skin areas become enlarged. This allows excess heat from muscles and organs to be lost more easily from the skin.

- During very hard exercise even these blood vessels will be reduced in size. Body temperature will then rise very quickly and can cause overheating and fatigue.

- The oxygen going to the muscles can be up to three times the resting amount.

- Blood flow can be increased up to 30 times. Therefore, the working muscles can receive up to 90 times the amount of oxygen they receive at rest.

Blood circulation and exercise

The body can alter the flow of blood to different areas. At rest our skeletal muscles need little oxygen, so only 15–20% of our heart's output goes to them. During exercise more blood is directed to these working muscles and away from such areas as the digestive system. As much as 80% of the heart's output may go to our working muscles during exhausting exercise. Training actually increases our body's ability to redistribute blood more efficiently.

Within the working muscles the oxygen reaches actual muscle fibres through the capillary network. As a result of training this capillary network increases, allowing more oxygen to be delivered to the working muscles. Blood pressure increases during exercise when massive amounts of blood are forced through the arteries. However, regular exercise leads to lower resting blood pressure.

Blood supply to the skin increases during exercise as the blood vessels beneath the skin expand to allow heat to escape from the skin surface.

activity

Blood circulation

The following activities are designed to reinforce your understanding of how the double circulatory system works.

Begin by selecting members of your group to represent the following:

- Vena cava
- Right atrium
- Tricuspid valve
- Right ventricle
- Semilunar valve
- Pulmonary artery
- Lungs
- Pulmonary veins
- Left atrium
- Mitral valve
- Left ventricle
- Aorta
- Arteries
- Arterioles
- Venules
- Veins.

Each member of the group has a card indicating which part of the circulatory system they represent.

1 You have five minutes to get yourself into the right order in a circle, starting with the vena cava. Now decide whether red, blue or red and blue blood flows through you.

2 A student is chosen to represent a drop of blood, and attempts to circulate through the system. In order to go past each of the various parts of the system they have to correctly answer one or more of the following questions:

  – Are you red or blue blood?
  – Which part of the system have you just come from?
  – Are you carrying oxygen or carbon dioxide?
  – Where are you going next?

3 Repeat Task 2, but with the names of the various parts of the circulatory system hidden. The blood drops have to first name the part of the system which they are visiting before they can proceed.

What makes up our blood?

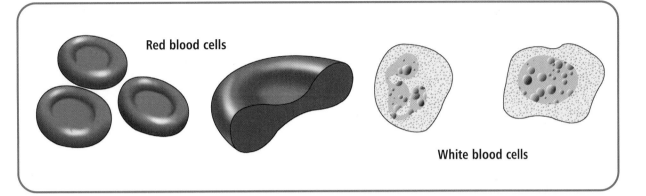

Red blood cells

White blood cells

The total volume of blood in the body varies from person to person and depends mainly on body size. Men on average have 5–6 litres and women 4–5 litres.

Blood is made up of 55% plasma and 45% formed elements. The formed elements are red blood cells (erythrocytes), white blood cells (leukocytes) and platelets (thrombocytes).

- **Plasma** is a pale yellow, watery liquid which contains dissolved substances: salts and calcium, nutrients including glucose, hormones, carbon dioxide and other waste from our body cells.

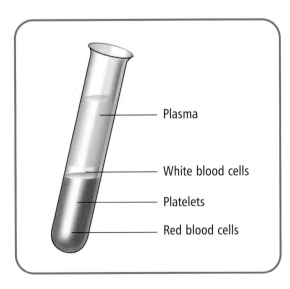

Plasma

White blood cells

Platelets

Red blood cells

- **Red blood cells** give blood its colour. They contain haemoglobin (see below), which carries oxygen from the lungs to all our body cells. Red blood cells are made in the marrow of our long bones, sternum, ribs and vertebrae. They are extremely numerous, have no nucleus, last for about 120 days and are replaced in very large numbers.

- **Platelets** are made in our bone marrow. They stick to each other easily and work with fibrinogen to produce clots when a blood vessel is damaged.

- **White blood cells** are three times the size of red blood cells but far fewer in number. They are made in our bone marrow, lymph nodes and spleen and act as a mobile guard system to deal with infection and disease. Some eat up germs, some produce antibodies to destroy germs.

How do our red cells carry oxygen?

Our red blood cells contain an iron-based substance called **haemoglobin**. When the blood travels to our lungs, the oxygen in the air joins up with the haemoglobin in the blood to form oxyhaemoglobin.

Our blood is now oxygenated and bright red. In this way the oxygen is carried by our blood around our body.

When blood arrives at our capillaries, the oxyhaemoglobin breaks down, setting the oxygen free to pass to our body cells.

Our blood is now deoxygenated and dull red in colour. It is pumped back first to our heart then to our lungs to pick up more oxygen.

What does blood do?

Our blood links all the tissues and organs of the body together. It has four main functions:

Transportation

- carries nutrients from our digestive system to all our body cells

- takes oxygen from our lungs to our working muscles

- removes carbon dioxide from our body in our lungs

- removes waste products and excess water in our kidneys

- takes hormones to where they are needed.

Protection

- carries white cells to sites of infection

- carries antibodies to destroy germs

- carries platelets to damaged areas to form clots.

Temperature regulation

- carries heat away from working muscles to skin

- carries heat away from centre of body to skin

- maintains temperature within the body.

Maintaining the body's equilibrium

- reduces the effect of lactic acid produced in the working muscles

- regulates fluid balance

- enables hormones and enzymes to work.

Our blood and exercise

Our muscles need a continuous supply of oxygen in order to move our body. This oxygen is carried to the working muscles by the haemoglobin in the red cells in our blood. Regular exercise increases the red cells we produce in our bones. This enables a fit person to work harder and for longer periods of time than an unfit person.

At high altitude it is more difficult for people to carry sufficient oxygen in their blood to supply their working muscles. As a result people who live at high altitude have more red blood cells and haemoglobin than those who live at lower altitude. This helps them to take in sufficient oxygen in their activities.

Endurance athletes from high-altitude areas usually have an advantage when they compete at lower altitudes since they can carry extra oxygen in their blood. For this reason, sportspeople will train at high altitude to increase the number of red blood cells and to improve their cardiovascular endurance.

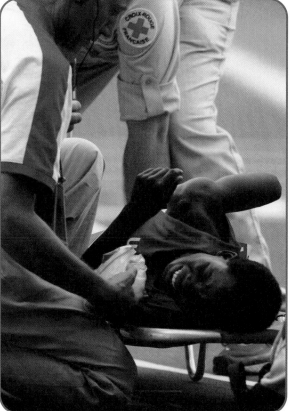

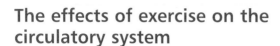
The effects of exercise on the circulatory system

Immediate effects of exercise on the circulatory system

- The hormone adrenaline enters the blood system.

- Adrenaline causes the heart to beat more quickly – increased heart rate.

- The heart contracts more powerfully – increased stroke volume.

- Blood circulation speeds up with more oxygen carried to the working muscles.

- Blood is diverted to areas of greatest need.

- Blood temperature increases, causing sweating response.

- Blood vessels to skin areas enlarge, allowing heat to be lost more easily.

The effects of regular training and exercise on the circulatory system

- Increased amount of blood pumped around the body

- Cardiovascular system copes more easily with increased demands

- Body able to carry and use more oxygen per minute

- Body able to remove waste products (especially carbon dioxide) more efficiently

- Increased recovery rate after exercise.

Long-term benefits of exercise on the circulatory system

- Healthier heart and blood vessels

- Reduced risk of heart disease

- Increased cardiovascular endurance

- Reduced blood pressure

- Lower resting heart rate and quicker recovery after exercise

- Heart muscle increases in size, thickness and strength

- Increased number of capillaries

- Volume of blood increases.

QUESTIONS

4 The circulatory system

1 **Which component of blood carries oxygen?**

(1 mark)

2 **Which blood vessel carries blood from the heart to the lungs?**

(1 mark)

3 **What is cardiac output?**

(1 mark)

4

a Our circulatory system is very important when we exercise.

i It carries out a number of functions. Give three.

(3 marks)

ii Explain what happens to the blood when it reaches the lungs.

(2 marks)

b Give the function of the following three parts of the heart:

i The right ventricle *(1 mark)*
ii The left ventricle *(1 mark)*
iii The right atrium. *(1 mark)*

5 **Andy is about to run in a 1,500-metre race.**

a What effect has the hormone adrenalin already had on his body?

(1 mark)

b The race has now started and his heart contracts more powerfully and quickly. Explain why this happens.

(2 marks)

c Andy has now covered the first 1,200 metres and is sweating a lot. Explain why his body has reacted in this way.

(1 mark)

d Define stroke volume and explain why Andy's stroke volume changes during the 1,500-metre race.

(3 marks)

e The change in Andy's stroke volume can be made in two different ways. Describe these two different ways.

(2 marks)

f Unfortunately Andy had a large meal only an hour before his race. What effect is this likely to have on his performance?

(2 marks)

g **i** Name the four main components of blood.

(4 marks)

ii Explain how one of them is vital to Andy's performance.

(3 marks)

h Andy is a trained runner whilst his friend Bob's only exercise is the occasional game of golf. Explain why Andy's resting pulse rate is likely to be lower than Bob's.

(2 marks)
(Total 31 marks)

5 The respiratory system

Our bodies are made up of millions of cells, all of which use oxygen to break down the nutrients contained in food. This sets free the energy which the cells need in order to work. Our respiratory system takes in oxygen from the air and transfers it to the blood in our lungs. The oxygen travels to the cells in our body, where it is exchanged for carbon dioxide. Our respiratory system then removes the carbon dioxide.

The respiratory system and sport

The respiratory system is important for health and sporting performance, but more so for some sports than for others. For example, in archery, snooker and shot put competitions, the efficiency of the respiratory system is not a factor. However in swimming, running, cycling, major team games and most other sports, performance will be affected by the efficiency of the respiratory system. As sportspeople we should avoid activities which reduce the efficiency of our respiratory system such as smoking cigarettes.

activity

Getting oxygen to our working muscles

Matt and Dwayne are 23-year-old middle-distance runners. When they are resting, their breathing rates are both the same: 16 breaths a minute. However, Matt has an advantage over Dwayne as he is able to get much more oxygen to his working muscles and therefore produces much faster times than Dwayne.

Read the descriptions below and try to think of three reasons to explain the difference in their times. The following questions may help your discussions:

- Body size and lung size are closely linked. Will this have any effect on cardiovascular endurance?
- Can body weight or body type have an effect on cardiovascular endurance?
- What is the importance of aerobic fitness and anaerobic fitness for running the 1,500 metres?
- Do you think the time they have given to training and the way they have trained will affect their performances at 1,500 metres?

Matt is 1.6 metres tall, weighs 61 kg and is of ectomorphic body type. He works as a bricklayer and is able to vary his working hours to fit in his training. He is a member of his local athletics club and trains three times a week on the track. He has a very experienced coach who bases his training on high-quality track work involving interval training.

Dwayne is 1.9 metres tall and weighs 85 kg. He is a call-centre operator and works long, regular hours (9 am to 6 pm) five days a week. He is a member of his local athletics club but trains on his own with some advice from his father, a former athlete. His training consists mainly of long runs and a body-building session in the gym once a week.

KEYWORDS

Aerobic activity: activity when enough oxygen is available to meet the needs of the working muscles

Anaerobic activity: activity performed in the absence of sufficient oxygen from our lungs to meet the needs of working muscles

Expiration: breathing air and waste products out from the lungs

Gaseous exchange: 'the process involved in the exchange of oxygen from the air with carbon dioxide in the body' (OCR)

Inspiration: breathing air into the lungs

Lactic acid: waste product of muscular action that builds up if oxygen is not available

Oxygen debt: 'the amount of extra oxygen needed after exercise or physical activity over and above that which would have been required at rest' (OCR)

Oxygen deficit: build-up of lactic acid during activity when insufficient oxygen is available

Tidal volume: the amount of air breathed in or out of the lungs in one breath

Vital capacity: the maximum amount of air that can be forcibly exhaled after breathing in as much as possible

VO_2 Max: the maximum amount of oxygen that can be transported to the muscles and used in one minute.

Key to Exam Success

For your GCSE you should be able to:

- identify the main parts of the respiratory system and know how it works
- understand how respiration takes place both in the lungs and at the working muscles
- explain the effects of exercise and training on the respiratory system
- know how the respiratory system links with the circulatory system
- explain how oxygen debt occurs and is repaid
- understand the terms aerobic and anaerobic in relation to exercise.

66 KEY THOUGHT 99

'Cell respiration is at the centre of all human activity.'

How do we breathe?

- Air enters through the nose and mouth.

- The **nasal passages** contain mucus and hair. They moisten, filter and warm the air.

- The **palate** separates the nasal cavity from the mouth. It allows us to chew and breathe at the same time.

- The **epiglottis** is a flap at the back of the throat. It closes when we swallow to stop food from going down the trachea.

- The air passes through the **larynx**, or voice box, on its way to the **trachea**.

- The **trachea** or windpipe has rings of cartilage to hold it open. It divides into two **bronchi**. Each bronchus branches out into smaller tubes, which in turn become **bronchioles**.

- The bronchioles split up and end in **alveoli**.

- The **alveoli** are thin-walled, spongy air sacs. Most of our lung tissue is made up of large numbers of alveoli. When we breathe these tiny air sacs fill with air and then empty.

- The **lungs** are two thin-walled elastic sacs lying in our chests, in the thoracic cavity. This is an airtight area with ribs at the back and front and the diaphragm below.

- The **pleural membranes** surround the lungs. They are slippery double skins which keep the lungs moist. They also lubricate the outside of the lungs. The membranes slide against one another as our lungs expand and contract. This reduces friction with the surrounding ribs and diaphragm.

- The **diaphragm** is a sheet of muscle which separates the thoracic cavity from the rest of the body. It is very important for breathing.

- The **intercostal muscles** are found between the ribs and control rib movement. They are very important for breathing.

How do we get oxygen to our working muscles?

The respiratory system needs two stages to supply oxygen to the working muscles and all the other body cells.

Stage 1: External or pulmonary respiration
This part of the process is what we know as breathing. It includes:

- getting air into and out of the lungs

- exchanging oxygen and carbon dioxide in the lungs

- getting oxygen into the bloodstream.

The individual steps are as follows:

- The air we breathe in passes through our trachea into our bronchi and through our bronchi into our bronchioles. The bronchioles end in tiny air sacs called alveoli. There is direct contact between the walls of the alveoli and the capillaries. The capillaries contain deoxygenated blood that has been brought to the lungs in the pulmonary artery.

- The haemoglobin in the blood of the capillaries takes up oxygen from the alveoli.

- Carbon dioxide is exchanged for the oxygen and is breathed out.

- The oxygenated blood is carried in the pulmonary veins to the left side of the heart.

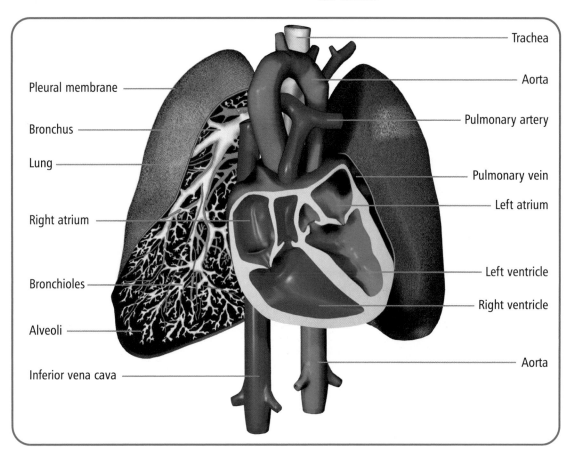

- The oxygenated blood is then pumped through our aorta to muscles and other body cells.

- After exchanging oxygen for carbon dioxide and other waste products in our cells, the deoxygenated blood returns to the heart in our veins.

- In the alveoli the carbon dioxide is exchanged once again for oxygen and is breathed out.

Stage 2: Internal or cell respiration

The respiratory system needs a second stage to supply oxygen to the working muscles and other body cells. This is called internal or cell respiration. It includes:

- getting oxygen into the body cells

- exchanging oxygen and carbon dioxide in the cells

- removing carbon dioxide and waste.

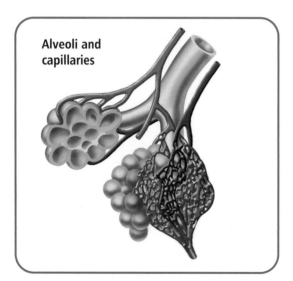

Alveoli and capillaries

The individual steps are as follows:

- The heart pumps the oxygenated blood around the body in the arteries. The oxygen is carried by the haemoglobin in the red blood cells.

- The arteries get smaller and smaller, becoming arterioles. These end in a network of capillaries which cover every part of the body cells. The capillaries are tiny, with walls only one cell thick. It is easy for oxygen and nutrients such as glucose to escape through these walls into the cells.

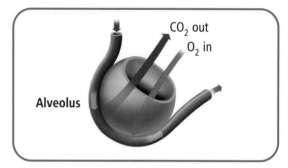

CO_2 out
O_2 in

Alveolus

- At the same time carbon dioxide and other waste products such as water move from the cells to the capillaries. The blood has now lost its oxygen.

- The capillaries join up with small veins called venules. These carry deoxygenated blood to the veins.

- Blood returns to the heart in the veins.

In this process we use oxygen to release the energy from glucose inside our body cells. This can be shown as:

Glucose + Oxygen =	Energy + Carbon dioxide + Water

This glucose is obtained from glycogen stored in our muscles and liver. The glycogen comes from the carbohydrates in our diet. This is why we need to keep our intake of carbohydrates high while we are training and taking part in sport. If activity continues over a long period of time, as, for example, when running a marathon, then glycogen can also be obtained from fat reserves in our body.

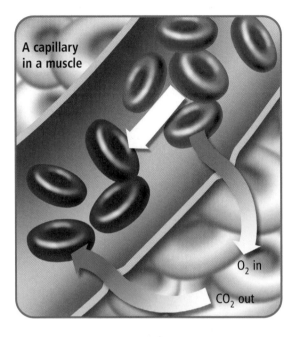

A capillary in a muscle

O_2 in

CO_2 out

As a result of training, more oxygenated blood reaches our working muscles; the exchange of oxygen and carbon dioxide is improved and waste products are removed more quickly. The overall result of training is that internal respiration becomes more efficient, improving our cardiovascular endurance and our sporting performance.

Breathing and sport

When our body is at rest, the movements of the diaphragm alone are enough for breathing. Breathing is automatic. As soon as we start physical activity, we use our intercostal muscles to increase the depth of breathing. As a result of exercise and training, all the muscles involved in breathing (the diaphragm and intercostal muscles) become stronger, allowing us to breathe more deeply and for a longer period of time and to inhale a greater amount of

air in each breath. Exercise and training will also increase the capillary network surrounding the alveoli in the lungs. This improves the process of exchanging oxygen for carbon dioxide. Regular exercise therefore makes our breathing more efficient.

When we are at rest we breathe in and out about 16 times a minute, taking in about 0.5 litres of air in each breath. If we exercise very hard, our breathing rate can increase to 50 times a minute and the amount of air taken in can exceed 2.5 litres in each breath. Therefore the amount of air breathed in can increase from 8 litres to 125 litres a minute.

Some sports performers use nasal strips which they claim help them to breathe better whilst they are playing. However, little evidence has been found to support this claim. Training can certainly improve breathing (see Chapter 13, Training effects, page 244).

Factors affecting respiration

The air we breathe in (called inhaled air) exchanges some of its oxygen for carbon dioxide in our lungs. The air we breathe out (called exhaled air) therefore contains less oxygen and more carbon dioxide. It also has much more water vapour, which is also a waste product from our cells.

The composition of inhaled and exhaled air

Inhaled air	Exhaled air
Nitrogen 79%	Nitrogen 79%
Oxygen 21%	Oxygen 16%
Carbon dioxide 0.04%	Carbon dioxide 4%

Vital capacity and tidal volume

Tidal volume is the amount of air breathed in or out of the lungs in one breath. It can vary a lot. When we are resting, only about 0.5 litres of air moves in and out of our lungs with each breath. Not all of this reaches the alveoli; some remains in our nose and throat. If we start an activity, the body will need more oxygen. We achieve this increase in our tidal volume by breathing more deeply, increasing our rate of breathing, or both.

Vital capacity is the maximum amount of air that can be forcibly exhaled after breathing in as much as possible. It is our maximum tidal volume and is usually about 4.8 litres in adults. Both tidal volume and vital capacity can be improved by a training programme, as exercise will strengthen the muscles involved in breathing. Improved vital capacity will increase the oxygen inhaled and will help improve performance.

Aerobic and anaerobic energy systems

The energy we need for sport can be found by using either of our two energy systems: the **anaerobic** or the **aerobic** system.

In the anaerobic system the body works without sufficient oxygen being supplied to the muscles, while in the aerobic system there is a constant supply of oxygen. Games players need to develop and improve both types of fitness. This can be achieved by training in both the aerobic and anaerobic target zones – that is, keeping heart rates above a certain level during training.

Lactic acid and oxygen debt

We can continue to perform strenuous activity for some time, even when we run out of sufficient supplies of oxygen. This is because we can draw on glycogen stores in the body as an alternative energy supply. However, in the absence of oxygen, **lactic acid** is formed in the working muscles. This makes our muscles hurt and eventually we have to stop the activity.

In the recovery period after exercise, we take in extra oxygen which is used to convert the painful lactic acid into simple waste products. The oxygen required to do this is called our **oxygen debt**. By following a training programme we are able to improve the ability of our muscles to use oxygen better and to cope with extra lactic acid. This means we are able to continue with our activity for longer before fatigue sets in. Through training we are also able to repay our oxygen debt more quickly.

The effects of exercise on the respiratory system

What are the immediate effects of exercise on the respiratory system?

- Increased rate of breathing

- Increased depth of breathing

- Increased blood flow through lungs

- Increased oxygen take-up and use by the body.

What are the effects of regular training and exercise on the respiratory system?

- Increased strength of intercostal muscles and diaphragm allows deeper and faster breaths

- Greater number of alveoli

- Increased amount of oxygen delivered to the body

- Increased amount of carbon dioxide removed from the body.

What are the long-term benefits of exercise on the respiratory system?

- Healthier lungs

- Increased vital and tidal volume

- Increased capacity of lungs to extract oxygen from the air

- Increased capacity of the lungs to remove carbon dioxide and other waste products from the bloodstream

- Increased tolerance of oxygen debt as lungs can work harder for longer.

activity

Checking breathing rates during exercise

Your breathing rate tells you how much air, and therefore oxygen, is entering your lungs and will be passed into the blood and taken to the tissues. You can measure this rate by placing one hand across your chest and counting the number of times your chest rises in 15 seconds.

1 Look at the table below.
2 Perform each activity and check your breathing immediately after the time period ends.
3 Complete the table.

Time period	Activity	Breathing rate (beats per minute)
	Rest	
1 minute	Walk	
3 minutes	Jog	
10–15 minutes	Play game (e.g. basketball)	
20 seconds	Sprint	
3 minutes	Warm down	

4 Now plot the results on a graph to show how breathing rates are affected by exercise. Do not connect the points.
5 What do you notice about the changes in your breathing rate?
6 Can you explain this effect?
7 Calculate the mean breathing rate for your class in each time period.
8 Compare the mean for the class with the breathing rates of individuals.
9 Note and discuss any large differences in breathing rates within your class.
10 How do you explain any differences?

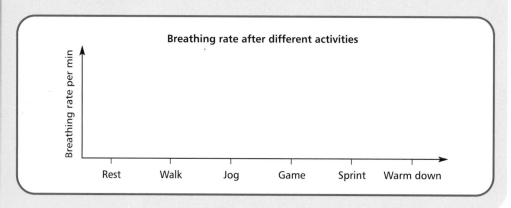

QUESTIONS

5 Respiratory system

1

a Name the thin-walled air sacs in the lungs. *(1 mark)*

b Which two gases are exchanged in the lungs? *(2 marks)*

2 **Which gas has a reduced percentage in expired air?** *(1 mark)*

3 **What is vital capacity?** *(1 mark)*

4 **Which substance makes our muscles tired?** *(1 mark)*

5 **Strenuous exercise will affect tidal volume.**

a Define tidal volume. *(1 mark)*

b Explain why tidal volume is affected by strenuous exercise. *(2 marks)*

6 **Anil is an experienced marathon runner.**

a What part do the following play in his breathing:

 i trachea
 ii alveoli
 iii pleural membranes. *(3 marks)*

b What happens to his breathing rate in a marathon race:

 i immediately after the start of the race
 ii during the middle of the race
 iii when he sprints over the last 100 metres? *(3 marks)*

c Explain why his breathing rate changes at each of these times. *(6 marks)*

d Which words describe the energy system he will be using:

 i during the middle of the race
 ii when he sprints over the last 100 metres? *(2 marks)*

e 'Lactic acid production is the enemy of the marathon runner.'

 i Why is lactic acid produced? *(1 mark)*
 ii Why does it reduce aerobic performance? *(1 mark)*
 iii How can training help to reduce the effect of lactic acid build-up? *(2 marks)*

f Give two possible effects of long-term regular training on the respiratory system. *(2 marks)*
(Total 29 marks)

6 Skill, motivation and mental preparation

Skill is the learned ability to choose and perform the right techniques at the right time, effectively, consistently and efficiently within a competitive game or activity.

We need a basic amount of natural ability in order to develop techniques and skills. We also need a good level of fitness, especially skill-related fitness, to perform skills at a high level.

Our ability to be skilful depends on how efficient our brain is at processing information. To perform a skill, our brain has to receive information from our senses and then use our perception and memory to make sense of it. It then makes a decision. Our muscles respond with movement and our brain gets feedback from our senses, telling us whether or not we have been successful. We can also get feedback from external sources.

Consistent performance relies upon the right mental approach. Top coaches and performers understand the need for mental preparation to ensure the right level of arousal.

activity

Making sense of learning

In this activity you are going to find out how much you depend upon your senses during skilful activities. You will also discover the value of good verbal coaching by working in pairs.

1 Bounce a basketball continuously 20 times on the spot, using your preferred hand. Now repeat this wearing a blindfold. If you do not manage to bounce the ball more than 10 times, try again. Your partner then attempts the task.

In pairs, discuss the reasons why wearing the blindfold makes the task much harder.

2 Wearing the blindfold, once again try to bounce the ball continuously 20 times. However, this time your partner can give you help and advice to try to improve your performance.

Did your performance improve? What was the most helpful advice you were given?

This experiment can be varied by choosing different basic activities. Examples might include bouncing a tennis ball or a shuttlecock on a racket with eyes open and then closed.

Can you think of other ways of taking one or more of your senses out of action – for example, dribbling a basketball wearing wicketkeeper's gloves?

KEYWORDS

Anxiety: level of arousal leading to stress and tension if too high

Arousal: level of motivation and alertness when taking part in sport

Closed skills: skills not affected by the sporting environment

Extrinsic: from outside the performer

Feedback: information about the outcome of a performance

Goal: in psychological terms, an ambition or target that we set ourselves

Information-processing model: theory about how we perform skills, with brain acting as a computer

Intrinsic: from within the performer

Motivation: determination to achieve certain goals

Open skills: skills that are affected by the whole sporting environment

Perception: the way we sort out information we receive, using our memory and past experience

Skill: the learned ability to choose and perform the right techniques at the right time.

Key to Exam Success

For your GCSE you will need to know:

- how different types of feedback improve performance
- how skills are learned, adapted and performed
- the importance of mental preparation for good performance
- the effect of motivation and arousal on performance
- how to set goals to improve performance.

❝ KEY THOUGHT ❞

'Preparation is the key to success in sport.'

How do we learn skills?

We can split the complex process of skill learning into three different periods or phases: **beginner**, **intermediate** and **advanced**. In practice they are not completely separate, but distinguishing them helps us to understand how we learn skills. Knowing about the different phases also helps a coach to plan training activities that match the ability of each player or performer.

The beginner phase

During this phase we need to understand what we have to do. We need a clear mental picture of the movements we need to make. We think carefully about technique and we may talk our way through it. We will often make major errors – for example missing the ball completely. We find it hard to correct our actions. We often feel rushed and have little time to see what is happening. Our teachers need to give us:

- clear demonstrations

- simple instructions

- short periods for practising

- praise for the correct action

- emphasisis on the technique, not the outcome.

The intermediate phase

Having learnt the technique, we now concentrate on practising the skill. Our performance improves a lot. We make fewer errors and begin to analyse our movements and make corrections. We begin to find that we have more time and we play with more consistency. We start to use internal feedback from our senses as well as external feedback from our teacher. Some sportspeople do not move beyond this phase.

The advanced phase

We can now perform our techniques almost automatically so that we can give more attention to decisions about strategies and tactics. In squash we can now focus on where to play the next shot, rather than the shot itself. We use our techniques at the right time and in the

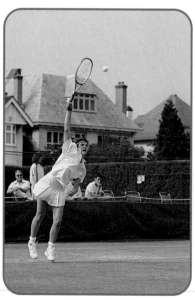

right place. We can often detect and deal with our own errors. We are able to adapt our skills whilst performing. Our coach helps us with the fine detail of the skill, with tactics and with mental preparation.

Skill learning and sport

An awareness of learning phases is important both for players and coaches. Coaches particularly need to understand what phase of learning a player is in. Unreasonable demands placed on novice players create pressure and tension which affect performance and slow down the learning process. All performers must understand that advanced skills require a high level of physical fitness. If fitness levels drop, the speed, range and consistency of performance will decrease.

What helps us to learn skills?

We learn techniques and skills by practising. Our learning is affected by the:

- guidance given to us
- type of practice we use
- what experience we have
- feedback we get.

Guidance
Guidance is given to us in three ways.

- **Visual**: demonstrations show us what we are required to do.
- **Verbal**: explanations must be brief and focus on the most important points.
- **Manual**: support will keep us safe and give us confidence.

All guidance must be easily understood and linked to our phase of skill learning.

Practice
Skills can be taught to us as a whole or broken down into parts (whole or part practice). If all the parts of the action take place at the same time we usually practise them as a whole, as in cycling. Skills that use a number of techniques are usually practised in parts at first. For example, the basketball lay-up shot involves:

- footwork with the bounce
- the pick-up
- the jump
- the shot itself.

Massed practice means using long active sessions without rests. For example, a gymnast might spend an hour repeating the same vault.

Distributed (or **spaced**) **practice** means having rests between shorter practice periods. For example, a gymnast might have three sessions of vaulting practice in an hour, with other activities in between.

Long practice sessions can lead to tiredness and boredom, which may be dangerous for difficult activities.

During practice we may copy the correct techniques when shown them on video or during the training session. On other occasions skills are developed by trial and error, although this is a slow process and will often lead to problems with technique.

Experience

Experience of basic movement patterns can often be transferred from one sport to another. For example a person who has played tennis usually finds some transfer to squash when first learning the game. Teachers can help by pointing out the similarities.

Feedback and sport

Feedback is essential for skill learning. We would find it very difficult to improve without knowledge of how well we are doing. However, when we are coaching we must take care to give the right kind of feedback at the right time if we are to get the best from our performers. The feedback given will mainly depend upon the ability and experience of the performers.

How much feedback?

Beginners only need a small amount of verbal or visual feedback, that is, comments or demonstrations. They find it difficult to use their own internal feelings about their performance and they cannot handle a great deal of detailed information. As performers become more experienced they get the 'feel' of successful movements and they can rely more on internal feedback, backed up by their coach's observations.

Input: our senses tell us what is happening.

Decision-making: our brain decides what to do.

Output: our body carries out the action.

Feedback: we find out whether or not we have been successful.

How do we perform skills?

The **information-processing model** of skill performance is based on the idea that the brain works like a computer. The process has four stages:

1 **Input**: our senses tell us what is happening.

2 **Decision-making**: our brain decides what to do.

3 **Output**: our body carries out the action.

4 **Feedback**: we find out whether or not we have been successful.

Input

- **Receiving information**: During this stage our brain receives information from our senses. In basketball our eyes tell our brain the position of the ball and the players. Our ears tell us what the coach is saying. Messages come from our joints and inner ear to tell our brain about our movements and body position.

- **Selecting information**: We must choose, very quickly, the pieces of information which are important – for example, the sound of the gun in sprint starts. As we become more experienced in our sport, we become better at shutting out information that we do not need. This is helpful, as our brain can only deal with a limited amount of information at a time.

Decision-making

At this stage we must make sense of what is happening and use our past experience to help us decide what to do next.

For example, an experienced batsman can work out the sort of 'ball' to expect by observing the bowler's run-up and delivery.

Output

This is the stage when we react to the situation. Our central nervous system sends messages to our muscles which then contract. Movement is a complex process. Our muscles must work at the right time, in the correct order and with the right amount of force.

Feedback

Feedback is vital information about our performance. By using feedback we are able to analyse and then improve our performance. We receive feedback from two sources.

- **Intrinsic** feedback comes to us from our senses. The proprioceptors in our joints tell us how the shot felt and our eyes tell us whether or not we were successful.

- **Extrinsic** feedback comes to us, for example, by watching ourselves on video, listening to our coach or being given our score.

There are two forms of extrinsic feedback:

- **Knowledge of results**: this tell us the outcome of our performance: whether or not we scored the goal, how many points we were given or our position in the race.

- **Knowledge of performance**: this is about how well we performed rather than the result. For example, a skilled ice dancer will know how good her performance felt and can find out more about the quality of her performance by talking to her coach.

When is feedback given?

Comments should be made at key moments, but not after every attempt. Sportspeople will usually be trying to do the right thing and will know when they have made a mistake. Coaches should always allow a little time for performers to consider their performance. They should also check that performers have understood what was expected of them. It could be that they did not understand earlier instructions, or they might have been trying to achieve something different. Above all, feedback needs to motivate as well as correct the performer.

Types of skill

We all know that different sports involve an amazing variety of skills. Some people describe skills such as throwing a ball as **basic**, and more complicated skills, such as the spike in volleyball, as **complex**. Basic skills are often called **techniques**, with the term **skill** being reserved for complex combinations of movement. It is also possible to classify skills as being **open** or **closed**. We can place them on a continuum from 'open' at one end to 'closed' at the other.

- **Open** skills are affected by the whole sporting environment such as other players and the weather. An example of a sport involving open skills is lacrosse, which is played out of doors with a number of players. This gives it a lot of unpredictability. For example, each player must take account of opponents, team-mates, the speed of the ball, the surface of the pitch and the weather conditions. Players need

open skills because they are not able to control what will happen next.

- **Closed** skills are used in a fixed environment where the performer has the situation under control. An example is a gymnast performing a vault, where the equipment is fixed and there are no influences from other people or the weather.

The skills continuum

We can place skills on a line (called a continuum) which goes from 'open' at one end to 'closed' at the other.

- **Judo** is placed towards the 'open' end, because the player must react to his or her opponent. However, the surface for competition is always the same, there is only one opponent to consider and the weather has no effect. In this sense judo is not as 'open' as lacrosse.

- **Archery** is nearer to the 'closed' end of the spectrum, because the whole action is learned and repeated for competition. However, wind strength and direction will affect the flight of the arrow, so the skill involved is not completely closed.

- **High jump** could be placed near to the middle. The jump itself is a closed skill, but the run-up must take account of the weather, the runway surface and the height of the bar.

In some open sports, closed skills will be used. For example, squash and netball are open sports, but when players serve in tennis or take a free shot in basketball they are in control, and so the skill is a closed one.

Lacrosse

High jump

Gymnastics

OPEN CLOSED

Judo

Archery

Motivation and mental preparation

Sports performers are always under pressure. This is often physical, caused by fatigue or the need to do everything very quickly. Many performers are also affected by mental pressure which leads to anxiety and tension. Mental preparation helps to motivate the performer, reduce anxiety and improve performance.

What is motivation?

Motivation is our determination to achieve certain goals: the driving force which makes us do something.

- **Intrinsic** (or self-) motivation comes from our own inner drives. We may play for fun, for the satisfaction of performing well, for pride in winning or for the enjoyment of taking part with others.

- **Extrinsic** motivation comes from rewards and outside pressures. We may play to win trophies, to please other people who are important to us or to avoid letting our team down.

Most motivation in sport is a mixture of both types. We may play for the school team for enjoyment and to win trophies.

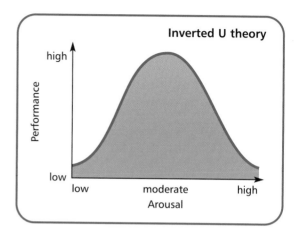

It is intrinsic motivation that will keep us interested in sport when extrinsic rewards are no longer available.

What is arousal in sport?

In a sporting situation the intensity of our motivation is called **arousal**. The link between arousal and performance can be explained using the 'inverted U theory'. This theory suggests that our best performances come when we are moderately aroused. If our arousal level is not high enough, we may feel bored and we will perform badly. This often happens when players or teams

activity

Positive or negative?

Organise four teams of similar ability to play a number of small-sided games against each other such as hockey, netball or football. Each of the teams has a coach who comments on their performance as they play.

Game one: coach gives constant negative feedback and destructive comments to all his or her team players.

Game two: coach gives constant positive feedback and encouragement to all his or her team players.

Game three: coach gives no feedback or comments at all.

Discuss the results. Did the coach affect the team performance? How did the players feel about the different types of comments made by the coach?

meet opposition of a supposedly lower standard. But if our arousal gets too high, we may become anxious and worried. This creates tension, which causes our performance to become less effective.

Coping with anxiety

It is natural to feel anxious about our performance before competition. Anxiety levels are often higher as the level of competition increases. An audience or crowd can also lift levels of anxiety, especially those of inexperienced players. However, we must manage our level of anxiety, or stress, in order to perform to the best of our ability.

Mental preparation involves:

- thinking positively
- using mental rehearsal
- focusing
- relaxing.

Thinking positively

Confidence in our own ability is an essential ingredient for sporting success. Telling ourselves that we are good enough and that we will do well should be part of our thinking. We should gain confidence from the positive expectations of those around us, especially our coach.

Mental rehearsal

We should develop the ability to picture ourselves carrying out successful movements in our sport – for example, successfully clearing the bar in high jump. In our mind we need to have clear pictures of each of the different stages involved: run-up, take-off, movement over the bar and landing. We can then practise the whole activity in our mind and see ourselves being successful.

Focusing

Successful sportspeople are able to identify and focus on the key points of their sporting activity. This involves

cutting out anything at all which distracts them from their goal. This may include the noise of spectators, the weather conditions, personal worries and the threat of opponents.

Relaxing

Our best performances usually occur when we achieve a balance between arousal and relaxation. Both too much and too little arousal will result in a poor performance.

Physical relaxation means reducing the build-up of muscular tension through, for example, a gentle warm-up or massage. Everyone has their own chosen method of relaxation, whether it is listening to music or talking with a coach or advisor.

Goal-setting

In sporting terms, a **goal** is an ambition or target that we set ourselves. For example, a goal might be to reduce your 400-metre time by 3 seconds over the season, or to achieve a regular place in the school volleyball team.

Many of us have long-term ambitions in sport. One ambition, or goal, might be to run a mile in under five minutes. We would call this a **long-term goal**. To achieve this we need to meet **short-term goals** along the way. Short-term goals would include achieving quicker and quicker times as a result of training regularly.

Setting goals is an excellent way to motivate ourselves to work hard. It also helps to reduce anxiety, because we know that we are not expected to achieve everything at once. By giving us confidence in this way goals help our performances.

Which types of goals can we set?

The type of goals we choose and the way we set up our goals are important. We cannot win all the time in sport. It is important for us to focus on our achievements, whatever happens when we compete.

There are two types of sporting goals:

- **Outcome** or **target goals** are linked to the result of a competition, for example, winning a trophy or a league.

- **Performance** or **process goals** are concerned with the standard of our performance compared with previous ones, for example, achieving a better time for a race.

We have more control over our performance goals than over our outcome goals. We can, for example, improve our best time but still not win the race. It is better, therefore, for us to set performance goals, as these give a better chance of success. This in turn can increase confidence and motivation.

How should we set goals?

The National Coaching Foundation (NCF) has developed the acronym **SMARTER** to help sportspeople set performance goals.

- **S**pecific: goals should be as specific as possible to focus attention.

- **M**easurable: they should assess progress against a standard.

- **A**ccepted: they should be accepted by the performer and the coach.

- **R**ealistic: they should be challenging, but within the performer's capacity.

- **T**ime-phased: there should be a specific date for completion.

- **E**xciting: they should challenge, inspire and reward the performer.

- **R**ecorded: they should be written down by the performer and coach to evaluate progress, provide feedback and motivate performers.

An example of a **SMARTER** performance goal in volleyball is:

- **S**pecific: to receive serve and make a controlled underarm pass to the setter

- **M**easurable: one set of ten repetitions

- **A**ccepted: yes

- **R**ealistic: 70% success rate (7 out of 10)

- **T**ime phased: achieved consistently by 31 December

- **E**xciting: yes, especially with varied servers

- **R**ecorded: in performer and coach training diary.

Goal setting and sport

Sporting performance is usually a team effort involving the performer, the coach, other club members and the people who support the performer (e.g. parents). It is important that everyone involved has the same goals.

In an individual sport, the coach and the performer need to agree on goals and share them with the others. If this does not happen it is very easy for confusion, and possibly conflict, to arise. This leads to anxiety, lack of motivation and poor performance.

In a team sport the goals need to be shared by all team members. When this is not the case, conflict on the field of play and in the changing rooms will affect performance. We sometimes see teams in different sports who seem to play beyond their potential. The usual explanation is that they had great team spirit. This is another way of saying that the coach and players had set and agreed their goals and were motivated to achieve them.

2003

QUESTIONS

6 Skill, motivation and mental preparation

1 What do we mean by skill?

(3 marks)

2 Guidance helps us to learn skills. Give two other factors which help us to learn skills.

(2 marks)

3

a Explain the difference between open and closed skills

(2 marks)

b Give an example of each type of activity.

(2 marks)

4

a Feedback is one of the four important stages in the information-processing model of skill performance. Name the other three.

(3 marks)

b Explain the difference between internal feedback and external feedback when playing hockey.

(2 marks)

c Give two reasons why feedback is important.

(2 marks)

5 Nadine plays badminton for her local club.

a How might her performance in a club match be affected by:

  i too much arousal
  ii too little arousal. *(2 marks)*

b Nadine's motivation might be extrinsic or intrinsic.

  i Explain the difference between intrinsic and extrinsic motivation.

  (2 marks)

  ii Give an example of each type of motivation.

  (2 marks)

c Mental preparation will help Nadine cope with her anxiety before club matches. Suggest three ways in which she could prepare.

(3 marks)

6 Kris is 14 and learning to play tennis for the first time

a Give two important rules for his teacher to remember when teaching him at this learning stage.

(2 marks)

b His teacher will give him visual and verbal guidance. Give an example of each.

(2 marks)

c His teacher has explained SMARTER goal setting. He wants Kris to set himself a goal for his serving. Suggest a goal and put it in the SMARTER form.

(7 marks)
(Total 36 marks)

7 Social factors and participation

Sport is popular. Every weekend millions of us take part in sporting activities of one kind or another. Although we all realise that an active lifestyle will help to keep us fit and well, our reasons for taking part are many and varied. Why and how do we come to these decisions about sport? There are usually no simple answers. We are affected by many different factors in our lives.

Sport is not for everyone. Some people take no interest in sport at all. Others decide not to take part but to enjoy watching sport instead. Society is made up of people of all ages – men, women, different ethnic groups, able-bodied people, and people with disabilities. Particular groups of people in society may encounter a number of barriers to taking part in sport. Not everybody enjoys equal access to sport. This is a complex issue. In order to be able to understand it properly, we need to understand why people take part in sports.

activity

Taking part in sport and physical activity

There are many reasons why we take part in sport. These reasons are linked to our particular lifestyle and the influence of our family, school and friends. Read the following pen pictures and then discuss why you think that each individual takes part in sport or physical activity.

John is a 26-year-old accountant and works in the City. His job is very demanding; he works long hours most days of the week, tends to eat out a lot and goes to the pub regularly. He visits the gym three lunchtimes a week and works out on both weights and aerobic machines. He also tries to have a run or a cycle ride each weekend.

Nisha is a freelance graphic designer who works from home. She is single and in her late twenties and has little contact with the outside world during her working week. She tends to eat a lot, has problems controlling her weight and worries about her appearance. As a student she enjoyed dance and has recently joined a modern dance group which meets twice a week.

Martin is 17 years old and has returned to college after failing most of his recent exams. He gets frustrated with his lack of progress and loses his temper quite easily. He has always enjoyed sport without making the school teams, but his PE teacher recommended that on leaving school he joined the local rugby club. He now trains twice a week with the club and plays a match every weekend. He has also started serious weight training at a local gym.

Ellie (18) is quiet and shy and took little part in PE and sport during her time at school. Through a friend at work she met a parascending group who eventually persuaded her to try the sport. To her surprise she not only enjoyed the thrill of the sport but realised that she was quite good. She is now group secretary, taking part every weekend, and has also developed a growing interest in paragliding.

Can you think of any other reasons why people take part in sport? Think of your own experiences.

KEYWORDS

Extra-curricular activities: school activities which take place outside of lessons

Environment: the surroundings in which we live

Gender: Being male or female

Leisure time: Free time after we have taken care of our bodily needs, our work and our duties

The media: all the different channels of communication in modern society

National Curriculum: Basic subjects which have to be taught in school by law

Peers: People who are the same age and same social grouping as ourselves

Physical recreation: recreation involving physical activity

Racism: not treating people of different races equally

Recreation: constructive use of our leisure time

Role model: a person who is seen as a good example for young people to follow

Socio-economic factors: factors related to our income, type of employment and family background

Sponsorship: financial help from a company or business in return for linking the company name with an individual, team or sport

Stereotyping: holding narrow or prejudiced views about a group or groups of people in society.

Key to Exam Success

For your GCSE you should be able to:

- recognise and explain the reasons for increased leisure time and why people participate in physical activities
- describe and explain the role of the school in promoting participation in physical activity
- describe and explain both the positive and negative effects that the following have on participation: age, gender, access, education, family, peer group, environment and climate, disability, the media, sponsorship, politics, tradition and culture.

66 KEY THOUGHT 99

'Sport: available to all, chosen by many'

Sport and leisure

Our leisure time is our free time after we have taken care of our bodily needs, our work and our duties. We usually take part in sport during our leisure time. It follows that the more leisure time we have, the more opportunity we have to take part in sport.

Our day

Most of our daily activities can be classified under the headings of bodily needs, work, duties and leisure time.

- Our **bodily needs** consist of all the things we have to do to stay healthy, including sleeping, eating and washing.

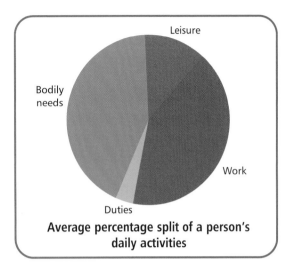

Average percentage split of a person's daily activities

- We also need to **work** to earn a living. Some unemployed people, mainly women, do not earn money but look after their home and children. This is also work. Pupils might consider time at school as work. Some activities are closely linked to work, such as travelling to work.

- There are also various things which we feel we have to do for our family or in the home – these are our **duties**. Many activities may be called duties, for example, washing up or taking the dog for a walk.

If we set aside the time used for bodily needs, duties, work and work-related activities, what we are left with is our **leisure time**. This is the time when we have the greatest choice about what we do. During leisure time we are free to take part in sport and physical recreation.

Work patterns

Although work patterns are changing, most people still work regular hours, and fit their leisure activities into weekends, evenings and holidays.

People who work long hours or large amounts of overtime have little time for leisure. Those who work nights or on shifts may have to take their leisure time when other people are working. Despite this, over the last 50 years there has been a great increase in the amount of time people have available for leisure.

Leisure time will continue to grow for almost all of us. There are many reasons for this:

- **Working lives are shorter**. Today most pupils continue in full-time education after 16 and many continue with their studies in higher education until their early twenties. Early retirement is more and more popular, with many people retiring in their fifties and very few carrying on to 65. Therefore working careers are shorter, starting later and finishing earlier.

- **Retirement lasts longer**. Improvements in medical care and standards of living have resulted in an increased average lifespan for both men and women. Therefore we live longer in retirement and can enjoy our leisure time for many more years.

- **Paid holidays have increased**. A minimum of four weeks' paid annual holiday is now normal for full-time workers. This enables holidays to be taken throughout the year, allowing people to take winter skiing holidays as well as summer holidays.

- **The shorter working week**: over the years the basic working week has gradually been reduced for the majority of workers. This gives people more leisure time. At the same time, job-sharing and part-time working have increased, particularly for women. However, many people spend more time travelling to work today and overtime working has greatly increased.

- **Technological advances**: thanks to technological progress, housework now takes much less time than in the past. Improved technology, especially the use of computers, has made many people far less active in their working lives, thus increasing the need for physical recreation in leisure time.

- **Unemployment**: Increased leisure time is a poor compensation for losing your job. However, unemployment does allow time to take part in physical recreation – assuming that you have the money and motivation.

activity 😊😊

Time for sport

It is recommended that all of us take part in some sport or physical recreation for at least 20 minutes at least three times a week. Using the survey sheet below, interview a working adult in order to calculate how much time he or she actually spent in sport or physical recreation over the last week.

Name and occupation:	Total number of hours per day, to nearest half-hour					
	Work	Bodily needs	Duties	Leisure time		
				TV	Sport	Other (give details)
Monday						
Tuesday						
Wednesday						
Thursday						
Friday						
Saturday						
Sunday						
Total						

Collect all the information obtained by your group and create a database from which you can calculate how much time people actually spend on sport and other activities in their leisure time. From your results, make recommendations that you think would help people to develop a more active and healthy lifestyle.

Leisure time, recreation, physical recreation and sport

There are many different ways in which we can choose to spend our leisure time. Our choice will depend on a number of factors including age, sex, culture, social class, financial situation, upbringing and facilities available. Most people think it a good thing to spend at least some of our leisure time being active and trying to follow a healthy lifestyle.

Why take part in sport?

Each of us makes a decision whether or not to take part in sport or physical activity. This can be based on a variety of different reasons, depending on our personal situation and all the other influences on our life.

Health

We are very health-conscious today and know the benefits of regular physical activity and sport.

In order to keep our bodies fit for the demands of daily life, we need minimum levels of strength, flexibility and stamina. We know that the more active we are, the better our health is likely to be and the more we can enjoy life.

Body shape

Combined with a healthy and balanced diet, regular exercise helps us control our weight and improve our body shape. If we are unfit and overweight, we know we are putting our health at risk.

Feeling and looking good

Physical activity helps us to feel and look good, improving our self-image and our confidence. Following a programme of activity helps us to increase our flexibility and to improve the strength and tone of our muscles.

Coping with stress

Stress is one of the greatest challenges to health today. Sport and physical activity may not solve our worries, but they can help us relax for a while, reduce our tension and take a fresh look at our problems. This can help us avoid stress-related illness.

Enjoyment

For most of us, enjoyment is the main reason why we take part in sport and physical activity. Sport is enjoyable for many different reasons.

Aesthetic

Sporting movement can be and often is beautiful. We can all appreciate the speed and elegance of a sprint hurdler in full flow or the controlled power of a gymnast in a tumbling routine. These activities appeal to our aesthetic sense. Dancers enjoy the experience of moving to the music and performing complex movement patterns.

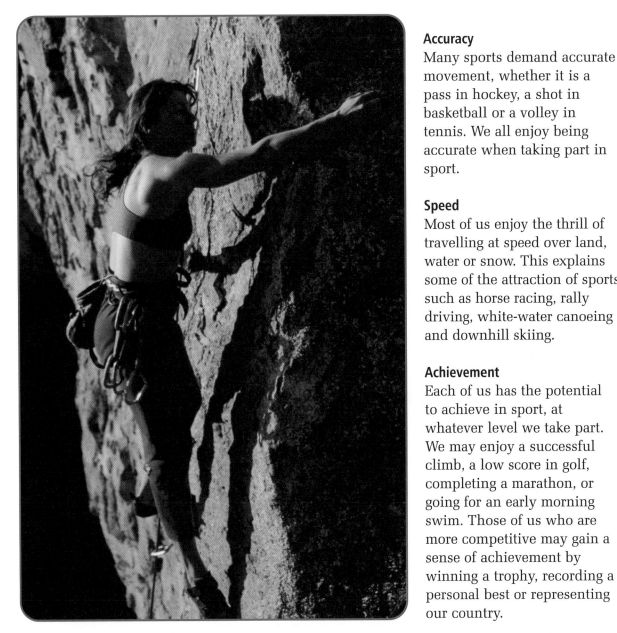

Accuracy

Many sports demand accurate movement, whether it is a pass in hockey, a shot in basketball or a volley in tennis. We all enjoy being accurate when taking part in sport.

Speed

Most of us enjoy the thrill of travelling at speed over land, water or snow. This explains some of the attraction of sports such as horse racing, rally driving, white-water canoeing and downhill skiing.

Achievement

Each of us has the potential to achieve in sport, at whatever level we take part. We may enjoy a successful climb, a low score in golf, completing a marathon, or going for an early morning swim. Those of us who are more competitive may gain a sense of achievement by winning a trophy, recording a personal best or representing our country.

Channelling aggression

Sport can provide an outlet for our natural aggression. Within the rules of sport it is possible for us to test our physical power against others in a controlled environment. We can see obvious examples of aggressive actions in sports such as rugby, judo and wrestling.

Physical challenge

Sport enables us to test our physical and mental strength and endurance to the limit. We can compete against our own best performance in running, swimming or cycling, or pit ourselves against the natural environment when climbing, caving or sky diving.

Competition

Sport provides a perfect opportunity to test ourselves against others. We can compete directly in matches and tournaments in a variety of sports from lacrosse to water polo, and from basketball to sailing. Competition can take place at a variety of levels, from Sunday football in the park to the Olympic Games.

Co-operation

Many activities take place in sports centres and clubs. We may attend

regularly and develop an interest in a group or a club. Many people like being part of a team and choose to play together. Others co-operate with one another to run a sports club.

Friendship

We all need daily contact with other people. Sport and physical activity give us the opportunity to meet and talk to others. In clubs or classes, sport provides a common bond, helping to stimulate conversation and encouraging friendships and social mixing.

Sport as a career

Most of us take part in sport as amateurs, purely for enjoyment. We train and compete in our own time and are not paid.

Professionals are paid to compete in sport. They train full-time and winning is all-important to them. Sport is their work and they are bound by contracts of employment.

Only a very few people can earn a living as professional sportspeople. Some are able to make money from sport as part-time professionals. This means that they have regular jobs, but earn income from sport in

their spare time. However, they have to spend quite a lot of leisure time training and competing in order to maintain their fitness and ability.

There are many careers in sport apart from performing. These include: teacher, coach, team manager, physiotherapist, leisure centre manager, sports development officer, journalist, commentator, sports retailer and groundsperson.

Sport in school

We are all affected by our experiences of Physical Education (PE) lessons and also by sport in school generally. Schools play an important part in promoting and encouraging participation in sport and physical recreation.

PE has the same aim as other subjects on the school curriculum, i.e. to help in the general education of children. As a **National Curriculum** subject which schools are legally required to teach, PE offers a wide range of educational benefits. It:

- educates children through physical activities

- helps to develop personal fitness and good health

- encourages a positive attitude towards health, fitness and lifelong physical recreation

- teaches skills which enable pupils to take part in a variety of sports and physical recreation

- provides information about the world of sport, health and fitness.

The National Curriculum

The National Curriculum was established by the government to ensure that all pupils are taught a common group of essential subjects. PE has always been a foundation subject in the National Curriculum, enjoying equal status with other subjects. Targets for achievement are set for each age group. Particular sports are chosen by the school PE department, and checks are made to ensure that pupils achieve their targets. PE teachers decide on the best teaching methods.

Skill development is at the centre of a good PE programme. A wide variety of activities, well taught in a structured programme, develop skills and motivate pupils to continue taking part in sport beyond school.

PE in the curriculum

The PE department has day-to-day responsibility for PE and sport in school. PE lessons are timetabled, and extra-curricular sporting activities take place at lunchtime, after school and at weekends.

Timetabled lessons include:

- practical PE lessons for all pupils

- examination courses, such as GCSE and A level

- cross-curricular links with other subjects, for example, respiration in science.

Extra-curricular activities include:

- team practices for different age-groups

- matches, competitions and tournaments for school teams

- clubs open to all abilities

- visits to sporting events, including international matches

- visits to specialist facilities, for example, indoor climbing walls

- visits to local sports clubs

- activities leading to sporting awards

- courses arranged under the Sports Leaders' Awards Scheme

- adventure activities and skiing holidays.

Exams in sport

Most pupils today have the opportunity to study PE at GCSE level, and an increasing number take PE at A level. Many continue with PE and sports studies at GNVQ, BTec and degree level. Within school, pupils usually have the opportunity to gain achievement, coaching and leadership awards in a variety of physical activities.

School sports co-ordinators

Sports co-ordinators work in both primary and secondary schools to help improve the teaching of PE in primary schools and to develop extra-curricular activities in secondary schools. The work of sports co-ordinators is overseen and controlled by specialist sports colleges.

The benefits of PE in school

Good PE lessons and enthusiastic teachers have an important part to play in encouraging pupils to take part in sport in later life. The following factors significantly affect pupils' motivation to continue with sporting activity after leaving school.

Skill levels

Through PE, pupils learn the basic skills of a variety of different sporting activities. These are developed during their time at school so that they can take part confidently in sporting activities as adults. While at school pupils also have the opportunity to:

- take on roles such as performer, coach, official, observer, captain, leader and choreographer

- improve their abilities through coaching and training during after-school practices

- visit local sports clubs or centres of excellence

- try for achievement awards in different sports.

Attitude

An important aim of PE is to develop a positive attitude towards health and fitness and make pupils aware of the advantages of lifelong involvement in physical recreation. Teachers themselves often provide a positive **role model** for pupils by demonstrating the benefits of an active lifestyle.

Health

Through PE lessons, pupils can learn:

- the value of regular exercise for health and fitness

- the principles involved in training for different sports, both in theory and practice

- the importance of safety and safe practices in sport

- how to avoid and treat sporting injuries.

Ideally, by the time pupils leave school they should have:

- a sound basis of sports skills

- wide experience of different activities

- good understanding of the link between health and exercise

- positive attitude towards physical recreation

- knowledge of local sporting opportunities.

One of the most important aims of any PE department is to encourage pupils to continue with sport and physical recreation after leaving school. Schools can:

■ bring local club members, leisure centre managers and others involved in community sport into the school to talk to pupils

■ arrange for pupils to visit clubs, centres and other facilities in the area

■ explain how to find out about other sports not taught at school.

Clubs and centres can:

■ run special introductory courses for young people at school

■ ensure that clubs and centres are welcoming to young people

■ provide coaching and training for young people.

'In The chair'

In small groups, prepare three questions to ask either your PE teacher, the head/director of PE, or the headteacher in your school, as part of an imaginary TV discussion programme.

To avoid repetition, each group should focus on one of the following areas:

■ The amount of time given to PE and sport in schools.
■ The importance of PE and sport in the curriculum.
■ The range of sporting activities offered in your school and others.
■ Reasons for the government's interest in PE and sport.
■ The future of PE and sport in schools.

You have ten minutes to prepare your questions. Select one student to be the compére for the programme. He or she will invite the person selected to take the chair and then invite a representative from each group in turn to ask a question, allowing follow-up questions if appropriate.

One member of each group will act as a local reporter and make notes of the answers provided to each question.

Sport and society

As we have seen, school is a very important factor in our decisions about physical recreation. But there are many other factors which may have positive or negative effects on participation in sport, including age, access, gender, education, family, peer group, environment and climate, disability, the media, sponsorship, politics, tradition and culture.

Age

In general people become less physically active as they get older.

While at school, children of all ages will follow a PE programme as part of the National Curriculum. They will learn the skills of a wide variety of sports. At secondary school they will be encouraged to join local clubs and to continue with their sport and physical recreation beyond their schooldays.

However, young people in their twenties have many demands on their time, and work and social pressures may squeeze sport out of their weekly routines. Married people with young families often have to put their children before their own need to keep fit and healthy.

By middle age, people who have not made a habit of physical activity may decide that the effort of getting into shape is simply too daunting. But often those who have managed to maintain their involvement in sport and physical recreation throughout their lives find they can still enjoy sporting activity in retirement.

Old people may lack the skills, the physical health and the money to enjoy an active physical life. However, there are signs that an increasing number of the over-sixties are continuing with physical recreation. This may be as a result of their early positive PE experiences at school.

Access

Access to sport is limited not only by the physical location of sports facilities, but also by a range of personal, social and economic factors. We can only take part in sport and recreation in our free time. The amount of free time we have depends on all our other commitments.

Are sports facilities within easy reach?

Local authorities provide sports facilities for the community, including leisure centres, swimming pools and recreation grounds. If you live in the country, you are more likely to have to travel some distance to find the facilities and coaching you need. If you live in a city, there are likely to be facilities in your neighbourhood.

For activities requiring specialised equipment or facilities – for example, high board diving – you may still have to travel some distance. Living by the sea or a river will give you the opportunity to take up water sports. Similarly, a more remote area may offer opportunities for climbing and canoeing.

Are facilities affordable?

Although local authorities provide basic leisure facilities, the better and more specialised facilities may be privately run. Golf courses, racket clubs and fitness centres are often run as clubs, with membership restricted to those who can afford to pay. People with disabilities may also find physical problems of access to local facilities.

Access therefore also depends on money as well as location. People who are unemployed or poorly paid may not be able to afford to take part in sport. Playing sport outside school will involve costs of travelling, training and competition as well as paying for equipment, clothing, hire of facilities and club membership.

If we live by the sea, we may have access to the water, but the cost of buying a racing sailing boat may be beyond us. Some sailing clubs encourage young people to join by making the boats belonging to the club available to members and by offering coaching.

Gender

It is now accepted that women should be able to take part in the sport of their choice without limitation. Social changes have given women more and more opportunity to control their own lives. But this is a relatively recent development, and the history of sport is mainly the history of men's sport.

Gender stereotyping

In the past girls were encouraged to play with dolls, to learn to cook and to keep themselves clean, while boys were encouraged to play ball games and allowed to climb trees and get covered in mud. Children were, and some still are, brought up to fit these gender stereotypes. As a result, girls often have fewer opportunities to develop sports skills and to acquire the confidence which goes with them.

For boys, sport has high status, whilst many girls are turned off PE at school and do not consider sporting achievement to be important.

Some sports are still seen as unsuitable for women. Many young women think that playing sport makes them unattractive to men. Married women are often expected to take on the major responsibility for the home and children and to give a low priority to sporting activity. Coverage of sport on television and in the press focuses overwhelmingly on the activities and achievements of men.

How is the situation changing?

Statistics show that many fewer women take part in sport and physical recreation today than men. However, the gender stereotypes are gradually being broken down.

Women certainly have greater opportunities to take part in physical recreation today. The reasons include:

- the emphasis in the media on fitness and health

- women's greater economic independence

- availability of more childcare facilities and more women-friendly activities at leisure centres, e.g. aerobics and swimming

- more female sporting role models in the media, e.g. Denise Lewis and Paula Radcliffe

- increased media coverage of women's sport, e.g. the women's FA Cup Final and international rugby union

- more female presenters and reporters on television sports programmes, such as Sue Barker presenting Wimbledon and 'A Question of Sport'.

Today women play rugby, throw the hammer and box – all activities that would have been unthinkable in the past. Women are also gradually moving into coaching, management and organisational roles in sport. This will give them more influence in the future development of sport. At present, however, there are still fewer opportunities for top sportswomen, with fewer events, smaller prize money and less media attention than for top sportsmen.

Education

As we saw earlier school is an important influence on our decision to take part in sport and physical recreation. A good PE experience will equip us with the skills and positive attitude towards physical activity to make it a lifelong commitment.

Sports colleges have played an important part in raising the standards in school PE and extra-curricular activities and in supporting pupils with sporting talent.

Not all schools are able to offer the ideal PE experience. Some do not have high-level sports facilities and can only offer a narrow range of activities. In recent years playing fields have been sold by local authorities to raise money, reducing the facilities available. In some schools, the demands of the National Curriculum have also led to a reduction in curriculum teaching time for PE. An increase in the administrative workload of teachers has left less time and enthusiasm for extra-curricular activities.

However, for most people education continues beyond school in some form, and universities and colleges continue to offer good opportunities for sport. Local authority youth services and adult education programmes also offer recreational and sporting activities.

Family

The family is a very important influence on us. If our parents play sport regularly, then the chances are that we will be brought up in a sporting atmosphere. Sporting parents and older brothers and sisters will give us role models to follow. Sporting parents will also be willing to provide transport and pay for sports equipment and sports clothing.

Sometimes children with famous sporting parents follow in their parents' footsteps (although many decide to do something completely different – for example Ian Botham's son is a professional rugby player, not a cricketer). Family influences can also be negative if there is little interest or encouragement to do sport.

Friends and peers

Our **peers** are the people who are the same age as us and share the same social background. Our friends are often also our peers. What our friends do in their leisure time will usually affect us. Friends often have similar interests. We all need friends, and if our friends are not interested in sport, we may drop out of sport too. On the other hand, if our friends enjoy taking part in sport, we may be encouraged to give it a try. In school, **peer pressure** – the pressure to conform with whatever our peers are doing – can be very strong.

Disability

In the not-too-distant past, people with disabilities were not expected to play a full part either in sport or in society in general. It was widely thought that people with disabilities were not able or motivated to take part in sport.

In sport recently, great efforts have been made to give people with disabilities every opportunity to take part.

Wheelchair athletes have been given a high profile in major events such as the London Marathon. The Sydney Paralympic Games showed the outstanding achievements of disabled sportspeople. It is now accepted that the benefits of sport apply just as much to people with disabilities as to able-bodied sportspeople.

Sport allows everybody to stay healthy and mix socially. Equality of opportunity must be seen to apply to all citizens. The law now insists on wheelchair access to buildings such as sports centres and swimming pools. Many governing bodies of sport have formed sections for disabled sportspeople and some sports have combined championships for able-bodied and disabled competitors.

In practice, however, sportspeople with disabilities still face serious obstacles to taking part:

- It is not always possible for disabled competitors to get to events because of transport problems.

- Buildings still present problems because of a lack of suitable doors and ramps at entrances.

- Staff at sports centres are not always trained to cope with sportspeople with disabilities.

- Sports centres do not always offer activities for sportspeople with disabilities.

- People with disabilities may not have had the opportunity to develop sports skills. They may not know of activities that are available and may not be able to afford them.

Sport for all?

Working in pairs, carry out a survey of your local sports centre. Find out which particular sporting activities are provided for people with disabilities and how many people with disabilities attend the centre.

Contact the manager before you visit and ask for permission to carry out the survey. Offer to give him or her a copy of the results.

Using your survey, draw up a number of proposals to make the sports centre even more helpful for the people with disabilities. Remember it is often the small, simple and cheap modifications that provide the most benefits to the largest number of people. Also, remember that improvements for people with disabilities are often improvements for all users.

The government and sport

In the past in England, individual sportspeople, groups and clubs developed their sport in their own ways. This freedom meant that there was no overall pattern for the development of sport. Sports clubs and governing bodies always protected their independence, and the government rarely became involved.

Today sports clubs and governing bodies are still at the heart of sport in England. However, the government now controls much of the finance for sport through National Lottery grants and funding for Sport England. The government also helps to fund the local authorities, who are responsible for most of the public facilities for sport, as well as those in schools.

In 2002, the government published Game Plan, a strategy for delivering its sport and physical activity objectives. These are to:

- increase participation
- improve success in the popular sports
- improve the hosting of major events
- simplify the distribution of funding
- reform the organisation of sport.

The government is committed to sport, especially to the sporting needs of young people. Sport is seen not just as a good thing in itself but is increasingly linked to aspects of social policy, such as health, crime prevention, social cohesion and community problems.

The sport national governing bodies receive grants from Sport England. To do so they must show that their plans are in line with the government's aims. They

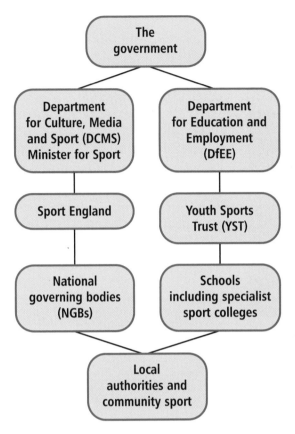

The government

Department for Culture, Media and Sport (DCMS) Minister for Sport

Department for Education and Employment (DfEE)

Sport England

Youth Sports Trust (YST)

National governing bodies (NGBs)

Schools including specialist sport colleges

Local authorities and community sport

must also set out their targets in detail and ensure they are achieved.

The government also influences sport through education. It is rapidly expanding the number of sports colleges and the role of the Youth Sports Trust (YST). The YST was founded in 1994 to develop quality physical education and sport programmes for all young people in school and the community. The Trust has since developed a number of TOP programmes to help young people's sports development.

Tradition and culture

Ethnic background

In our multicultural society, people of all races and ethnic backgrounds take part in sport at all levels. As a result of this, we often assume that they face no problems in sport. However, there is still discrimination and disadvantage in sport, as there is in everyday life.

Racism means not treating people of different races equally. Racists often hold stereotyped views about people from different ethnic backgrounds. Stereotypes lead to sporting myths about what different people can and cannot do. One example of a racist sporting myth is that 'black people can't swim'. This is nonsense.

- **Personal racism** is seen when black and ethnic minority sportspeople are made to feel unwelcome by individuals at a sports club.

- **Institutional racism** is seen when an organisation lacks understanding or the willingness to understand and respond to the needs of black and ethnic minority sportspeople.

There are many different cultures in Britain, each with its own set of beliefs and practices. Amongst some groups, for example, women may not be able to take part in sport for religious reasons. Some people think this needs to change; others believe it is for individuals to decide.

The most extreme example of racism in sport was seen under the apartheid system in South Africa prior to 1994, when people who were classified as non-whites were treated as second-class citizens both in society and in sport.

The media

When we talk about the **media**, we refer to all the different channels of communication that are used to bring us stories, news, action and information. Examples include magazines, books, newspapers, radio, television, film, video, DVD, CD-ROMs and the Internet.

Magazines
If you walk into any newsagent you will find dozens of magazines about individual sports, from major activities like tennis to minority sports like the triathlon. General sports magazines are very much rarer, although a number focus on health and fitness.

Books
Successful books on sport usually consist of biographies of current sports stars. At regular intervals, the histories of individual sports or their clubs are published in great detail. Coaching and training books can help us to improve our sporting performance.

Newspapers
The national newspapers devote several pages to sport and employ large numbers of sports journalists. Sunday newspapers now have separate sports sections.

The aim of editors is to sell more newspapers. This is reflected in the content of the sports pages. Some carry more details about the private lives of the sports stars than they do about the sport itself.

Newspapers are good at building up stars when they are successful. However, they are even better at knocking them down when they fail! Today, newspapers play a major part in forming our views about sport.

Radio

In spite of television, radio still has its place. For broadcasters, it is much cheaper to report on radio and requires a much smaller team of people.

Radio Five Live is a national radio station which concentrates on news and sport.

For the listener, radio is a much cheaper and more mobile medium than

television. It also allows us to do other things while we listen to the match, race or competition, and to keep in touch with the action while we are on the move.

Film, video and DVD

Being dramatic, full of heroic triumph and tragic tears, sport should make excellent material for films. However, successful fims about sport are relatively rare. Video and DVD collections of great sporting occasions and outstanding individual performances are very popular, as are instructional videos for improving our sporting performances.

CD-ROMs and the Internet

CD-ROMs contain a wealth of information about a whole range of sporting subjects. Much of the information in this book is also available on CD-ROM, together with interactive tests and animated diagrams of the body in action. From The World of Sport Examined website at **www.worldofsportexamined.com**, you can go directly to a number of other sport-related websites.

activity 😊😊😊

Sport interactive

As one of a team of four journalists, you have been given the task of creating a new TV sports channel.

The new channel must:

- provide news and information about a wide range of popular sports
- cater for minority sports interests
- aim to attract 16–30-year-olds
- appeal to both men and women
- meet the sporting needs of people from different ethnic groups and people with disabilities
- satisfy the needs of sports performers as well as spectators
- provide links to viewers' favourite sports, teams, players, etc.
- include a 24-hour sports news service
- make it easy for viewers to influence future programmes and how they are shown
- be at the cutting edge of technology by using links between mobile phones, televisions, computers and future ICT developments.

You have one week to prepare a presentation which will be shown to the management group of the television company (your PE class). You will need to use a variety of sources of information. For example, check the sport currently available on television and radio, research the sports coverage in newspapers, use the Internet for further information. Do not limit yourself to what is currently on offer. Try to be creative and think ahead. Technology is moving very quickly.

Make sure that your presentation is lively and persuasive. Try to use music and pictures, perhaps even video, to enhance your delivery.

Television

Whether you love sport or hate it, you certainly cannot get away from it on television! An ever-increasing number of hours are devoted to sports of many different kinds. This is because sport is immensely popular and relatively cheap to produce. Sport also overcomes language barriers, making it easier for sporting events to be screened around the world.

Sport on television can be seen on terrestrial channels and satellite channels, some of which are now also available via cable. The five terrestrial channels include BBC1 and BBC2, which are funded by the television licence fee, and the independent companies who rely on money from advertising in the same way as the satellite companies. The BBC and these companies must bid for the right to show sport on television – that is, they must negotiate with the national governing bodies of the individual sports or the organisers of specific events. This leads to fierce competition for the rights to televise popular events such as Premier League football matches.

Satellite television

Satellite television has had a great impact on sport, allowing us to watch a wide variety of sports events in this country and live from around the world. It also gives us the choice of a large number of channels, including Sky Sports and Eurosport. As a result, many minor sports are now seen regularly on television. However, satellite sport is only available if you can afford to buy the equipment and make monthly payments to the satellite network.

How does television affect sport?

It is difficult to say whether or not televised sport influences us to take part in sport. Certainly it increases our interest and makes us more knowledgeable about sport. On the other hand many people would rather watch sport in the comfort of their homes than go to an event or actually take part in sport.

Television undoubtedly benefits sport in a number of ways:

- Sport increases in popularity through exposure on television. This is especially true when a national team or individual does well in international sport. Minor sports may also become more popular when covered on television.

- Large amounts of money flow into sport from sponsors and television companies. This can be used to pay sports performers and to help develop the sport.

- Some sports have been saved from economic collapse by money from sponsors and television companies.

- Television increases the rewards for both individuals and teams. This in turn raises the standards of performance.

However, it is also true that television has changed sport – and not always for the better:

- Many sports such as football have come to rely on television money. When this money is reduced or withdrawn, the sport suffers major problems.

- Rule changes have been introduced to make sports more exciting for TV audiences. Examples include one-day cricket, tie-breaks in tennis and penalty shoot-outs in football.

- Changes have been made in clothing. For example, in some competitions cricketers wear multicoloured clothes instead of the traditional white.

- Starting times of events have been altered to increase the number of viewers – for example, Premier League football matches now take place on Sunday and Monday.

- Complete control and reorganisation of rugby league has passed to the sponsors, with the sponsoring company forming new league teams and arranging for the game to be played in the summer.

- The authority of officials can be undermined when their decisions are examined in detail by TV commentators. Umpires and referees have to make decisions instantly without the help of replays and different camera angles. Constant criticism of officials is not good for sport.

- Domination of television by a few of the most popular sports can lead to the impression that others are of little importance.

- The emphasis on winning has produced sportspeople and teams who are desperate for success. This

can encourage sportspeople to take part too often, to play when injured, to resort to unsporting play or to cheat by using drugs.

Sponsorship

Sports **sponsorship** takes place when a company gives financial help in return for linking its name with an individual or team, or a sport in general.

Sponsorship is a form of investment. Companies exist in order to make profits. They do not have to make donations to charity or to sponsor sport, although many do so. When sponsoring a team or individual, the company expects to get something in return. Sponsorship helps the company by:

- allowing it to promote a sales message

- enhancing its image.

Both of these are good for the company's business.

Promoting a sales message

At its simplest, sponsorship gives a company a chance to put its name in front of the public and to communicate a simple sales message. This can be done in a number of ways:

- Sports stars are linked with a particular company's product.

- A team wears shirts with the company's name for all to see.

- Advertising hoardings at a televised sports event are caught by the cameras.

- A competition may carry the sponsor's name, for example the 'Barclaycard Premiership'.

Promoting an image

At a more subtle level, sponsorship aims to promote the company by making the potential customer feel happy about the company and its products.

For example, if the name of the company is worn by our favourite player, we may, without realising it, also start to feel warmly towards the company.

In this way, a company can transfer some of the values of the team or player to its own products. If the player or team is successful then this success also reflects on the sponsoring company. By winning the Rugby World Cup, both the England team and the sponsor achieved their goal!

Who receives sponsorship in sport?

Today, sponsorship is available throughout the sporting world, and it is not only star performers who are sponsored. Local teams and individuals can also find sponsors, often among the local business community.

Sponsorship is received by individual sportspeople, sports teams and groups, national governing bodies, coaching and achievement schemes and sporting events:

- For **professional sportspeople**, sponsorship is an important way of adding to their income from sport.

- **World champions** and Olympic gold medallists can usually take their pick of sponsors. Successful sportspeople are in great demand because sponsors want the name of their product to be associated with sporting excellence. We forget sometimes that players advertise one product rather than another because of the money they are paid.

- For **younger up-and-coming sportspeople**, sponsorship is a means to buy the best equipment and to meet all the costs of training, competition and travelling.

- **Top amateurs** rely on sponsorship to pay their living expenses so that they can give up work or only work part-time. Money is also available for equipment, clothing and travel, accommodation and the expenses of training and competition.

- **Successful sports teams** attract a lot of sponsorship. Sponsorship received by a team is used by the organisation responsible for the team.

- **Amateur teams** who are sponsored may have their equipment, clothing, training and travelling expenses paid for by the sponsor.

- Sometimes sponsorship is given to teams at different age levels. Sponsorship of **junior teams** usually results in very favourable publicity for the sponsor.

- The **national sport governing bodies** receive various forms of sponsorship, both to develop their sport generally, and to pay for events and special projects.

- **Coaching and achievement schemes**: Most children are very happy to win a competition or achieve a standard in sport, and many sponsors support achievement schemes for young people. Sponsors pay the costs of running the scheme, including badges and certificates, and receive publicity when the children take their badges and certificates home.

- **Sporting events**: international matches and championship finals are very popular with sponsors. These events are televised and the sponsor is guaranteed good publicity. Sponsors pay for the administration, organisation and expenses of the event and the sport keeps any profit from television fees or gate money.

- Sometimes companies sponsor a **league** or a **cup competition** which takes place over a period of time. Most major events depend on sponsorship to take place.

- **Local events** are also sponsored, with companies benefiting from local publicity.

Unacceptable sponsorship

Although sport has undoubtedly benefited from sponsorship in many ways over the years, some forms of sponsorship remain controversial. For example:

- Tobacco companies sponsor sport, yet smoking is a proven health risk. Sport keeps us healthy, so smoking and sport cannot go together. Young people should not be encouraged to smoke.

- Companies making alcoholic drinks sponsor sport, yet alcohol is known to cause both health problems and problems involving anti-social behaviour. Alcohol and sport do not go together. Young people should not be encouraged to drink alcohol.

There is no doubt that sponsorship has raised the profile of sport in society. This has come about because of the vast sums of money invested by companies in order to improve their profits. But it is very difficult to assess the impact of sponsorship on ordinary people. Young people have been encouraged to develop their sporting skills through training, coaching and achievement schemes which are funded by sponsorship. The sponsorship of professional sport largely benefits professional sportsmen and women. National governing bodies have used sponsorship money to provide coaching schemes which have in turn encouraged participation.

SportsAid!
The Charity for Sport

A similar argument is now being used against sports sponsorship by manufacturers of high-fat products such as chocolate, biscuits and cakes which may raise cholesterol levels and contribute to obesity. Young people should not be encouraged to eat unhealthy foods.

activity

Link the sponsor

Below you will find details of four companies who are considering sponsoring sport in some form or another. You will also find information about a number of sporting individuals and groups who are seeking sponsorship.

Your task is to see if you can match the sponsors to these individuals or groups. You should consider:

- whether the company and the individual or sport will make good partners
- what will be the advantages and disadvantages of a sponsorship agreement between them.

Companies considering sponsorship

1 The **Coopersale Brewery** is a long established company providing a range of popular beers and lagers. The company is trying to increase sales, particularly to younger adults, and believe that sponsoring sport or sportspeople could improve their image and raise awareness of the brand.

2 Future is a clothing company which specialises in selling fashionable clothes to people within the 15–25 age range. It currently has 20 shops, mainly in the south east of England. It has had a very good year for sales and is now looking to expand its business throughout England. It is looking at sponsoring sport and its team of designers gain much of their inspiration from sportswear.

3 WH Jones is a bookseller and stationer known throughout the country. The company is facing fierce competition from other similar stores. Its last venture into sponsorship was a disaster as it involved professional footballers whose careers were shortened because of involvement in a drink and drugs scandal. They wish to be involved in sport but are looking at a different form of sponsorship.

4 Peabody & Nurden are traditional cricket bat manufacturers who have recently taken over a smaller company making a range of cricket goods, including clothing. They are based in Berkshire and are looking to link their name with sport in general and cricket in particular.

Sporting individuals and groups seeking sponsorship

A Carlos is an 18-year-old skateboarder who has represented Great Britain in the World Junior Championships. He is a full-time student and finds it difficult to fit in his heavy training schedule with his studies. His coach lives 50 miles away, near the skateboarding training facilities, and he does not have a car. He does not have time to take a part-time job and finds it difficult to make ends meet.

B Pieta has had a very successful career as a speed skater. She has won a bronze medal at the European championships and looks destined for even greater things at the next Olympics. Her partner who is a top swimmer has recently been found guilty of taking a performance-enhancing drug and has been banned from competition for two years. He has retired from the sport in order to coach Pieta. Her sponsorship contract with a well-known cosmetics company has just come to an end and the company has taken the decision not to renew it.

C Carlton is director of a charity which helps people with learning handicaps to take part in competitive sport. The charity is based in a major city and organises evening classes at sports centres, swimming pools and other venues. The charity has decided to hold an international event in their city and Carlton has been given the task of raising funds through sponsorship. The event will feature athletics, swimming and gymnastics. It is expected that 2,000 competitors will take part ,and up to 10,000 carers and spectators will attend. It is hoped that full television coverage will be available.

D The **Old Swan football club** in the village of Appledom, in Berkshire, has entered a team in the local Sunday football league. The new owner of the pub is an ex-professional footballer who is not only enthusiastic about the team, but is also a very good coach. The team are very keen but of mixed age, experience and ability. In the past, they have raised a great deal of money for local charities.

E The **county organisers for archery** have decided to launch an achievement scheme to promote archery in schools. The scheme will give badges and certificates to children who achieve set standards when shooting at a target from different distances. At present only 50 schools take part, but the organisers hope to double this number within two years. If sufficient sponsorship is available, they would hope to subsidise the cost to schools when buying archery equipment.

Advantages and disadvantages of sports sponsorship

Advantages for sport

- For professional sportspeople and organisations, sponsorship is another source of income.
- For amateur sportspeople, sponsorship may:
  - allow them to give up their jobs and train full-time
  - pay day-to-day living expenses
  - pay for clothing and equipment
  - pay for costs of training and competition.
- For amateur organisations, sponsorship money can be used to:
  - fund the running of events
  - improve facilities
  - organise coaching, training and award schemes.

Disadvantages for sport

- Once sponsorship is accepted, the sport comes to rely on it. If sponsorship is removed, there may be financial problems for sport. This gives the sponsor a powerful hold on the sport.
- Sponsors may be able to change the sport. For example, professional rugby league has been changed to a summer game and completely reorganised.
- The national governing bodies make agreements with sponsors without necessarily consulting their sportspeople. As a result players may find themselves forced to wear their sponsor's clothing or use the sponsor's equipment, and have their name linked to the sponsor without their agreement.

- Sponsors need successful people. Regular losers and weak teams attract few sponsors.

Advantages for the sponsor

Sponsorship:
- advertises the name of the company's product, linking it with a popular activity or person
- provides exposure on television whenever the sport is seen
- ensures the use of the sponsor's name in the media
- improves a company's reputation because the company is seen to be supporting British sport
- transfers the spectators' good feelings about the sport to the sponsoring company's product
- can reduce the company's tax liability, depending how they give the money to sport.

Disadvantages for the sponsor

- Sponsors have to decide if the sponsorship has been good value for money. They must consider the success of the sportsperson, team or event, the publicity received and any improvement in business.
- Sponsors sign agreements which may last for a long time. The action of some sportspeople may bring bad publicity because of their behaviour in their private lives or in their sport. In some cases the sponsor may want to withdraw its sponsorship.

Sports sponsorship organisations

Sportsaid

Established in 1998, Sportsaid is a charity managed by trustees and governors which aims to educate young people through sport and to encourage those with social or physical disadvantage to improve their lives through sport.

Sportsaid raises money through fundraising and sponsorship and gives grants to talented young sportspeople nominated by sport national governing bodies.

A major supporter of people with disabilities, Sportsaid is funded by the Foundation for Sport and the Arts, by sponsorship from companies and by donations from individuals and organisations.

The Institute of Sports Sponsorship (ISS)

The Institute of Sports Sponsorship is a national non-profitmaking organisation founded in 1985 in order to promote sports sponsorship by bringing together sponsors and sports. It consists of a group of companies who support sport and is run by a committee made up of member companies. It also runs the Sportsmatch scheme for the government.

The Sportsmatch scheme

Sportsmatch was started by the government in 1992 and is run by the ISS. It is a grassroots sponsorship scheme which encourages new sponsors of sport. The government gives the same amount as the sponsor, doubling the amount received by the grassroots sports club or organisation.

Environment

Where we live affects some of the sports in which we can take part.

- If we live near the sea, a large lake or river, there will be greater opportunities to learn water sports.

- Country areas provide good opportunities for outdoor activities, but have fewer leisure centres and swimming pools.

- Inner-city areas are often short of open space, but indoor sports facilities are more likely to be within easy reach.

- Because of their high population, cities and towns can attract both commercial and private sports clubs.

- Particular parts of the country often have localised sporting traditions – for example, Highland wrestling in parts of Scotland.

Depending on where we live, it is often necessary to arrange transport to get to and from sports facilities. If we do not have access to a car, this means finding money for public transport.

Climate

The climate can affect our participation in sport. For example, winter sports need low temperatures, and activities such as skiing depend on heavy snowfalls.

Many athletes like to train in a warm climate. Some British teams and individuals travel to training camps abroad, rather than train through the British winter. The recent hot British summers mean that sportspeople must take extra precautions to avoid sunburn and dehydration in long-lasting outdoor activities such as marathon running.

QUESTIONS

7 Social factors and participation

1

a Explain what we mean by leisure time.

(3 marks)

b Give three detailed reasons why leisure time has increased in recent years.

(6 marks)

2 **We all take part in sport for different reasons. Give four reasons and explain why each might be important to different sportspeople.**

(8 marks)

3

a Describe three different ways in which schools provide for physical education.

(3 marks)

b Give three reasons why PE teachers are important in encouraging young people to take part in lifelong sport and physical activity.

(3 marks)

c Suggest three ways in which schools encourage pupils to take part in sport and physical activity.

(3 marks)

4 **List three benefits which television can bring to sport.**

(3 marks)

5 **Leon is a sportsperson who uses a wheelchair as he has a disability.**

a Suggest three problems which Leon might encounter at leisure centres.

(3 marks)

b Suggest ways in which leisure centres might deal with each of these problems.

(3 marks)

6 **Kim is a good footballer, but is married with two young children and has no time for her sport.**

a Explain what we mean by 'gender stereotyping' in sport.

(3 marks)

b Give three ways in which Kim is disadvantaged in sport and physical recreation compared to boys and men.

(3 marks)

7 **Jessica likes playing hockey very much. Her peer group is also very important to her.**

a Explain what we mean by Jessica's peer group, with an example.

(3 marks)

b Suggest three ways in which Jessica's peer group might affect her participation in sport.

(3 marks)

8 **Wayne is an outstanding young athlete who is sponsored by a travel company.**

a Individuals are sponsored in sport. Name three other groups or organisations who receive sponsorship.

(3 marks)

b Give three advantages of sponsorship for Wayne.

(3 marks)

c Give three disadvantages of sponsorship for Wayne.

(3 marks)
(Total 56 marks)

8 Local and national facilities

England has a history of strong, independent national governing bodies which controlled and developed sport successfully for more than a century. Today the government has a strategy for sport and uses Sport England to achieve its aims.

activity

Planning a sports facility

In groups of 6–8, study the following extract from a local newspaper. Imagine this is your town. Find out what facilities already exist before you decide on new and improved facilities. Use the information from your survey to complete each of the tasks below.

Local Sports Council scoops the jackpot

Glenwood's sports centre manager, Brian Blake, received the shock of his life when he heard on Friday that the centre had taken first prize in Sport England's 'Centre Management' national competition. This means that the local Sports Council will receive a grant of £2 million to improve the town of Glenwood's sports facilities. The only condition is that the plans are acceptable to Sport England.

1 Use maps of your town and surrounding area to produce a radial chart showing the direction and distance of sporting facilities from the centre of town.

2 Use a separate map to shade in housing areas, playing fields, parks and recreation grounds.

3 List the major sports facilities in your town and comment on the ease of access using a chart like the one below:

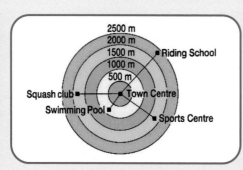

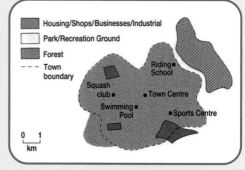

Facility	Travel by car including parking facilities	Travel by public transport	Proximity to town centre	Access (Easy–difficult, scale 1–5)
Swimming pool	On the main road. A large car park.	Regular bus service. 5 minutes walk from station.	15 minutes walk	1
Squash club	Minor roads, long queues in early evening. No car park; difficult to find parking in early evening.	10 minutes walk from nearest bus stop. 30 minutes walk from station.	45 minutes walk.	4

activity

😊😊

4 Compile a summary of the sports facilities in the town and comment on the standard of each facility and possible improvements as in the chart below. Take photographs, video, or make sketches of the facility if possible.

Facility	Number	Comments	Possible development
Tennis courts	20	6 in good condition at private club, 14 in two recreation grounds in poor repair.	Improve facilities at one site, convert other courts to all-weather surfaces for 5-a-side football, etc., in association with local youth club.

5 Prepare a presentation to explain your recommendations, preferably using Microsoft Powerpoint and including drawings, photographs, video, etc. Your teacher may be able to arrange a representative from your local Sports Council to attend your presentation.

KEYWORDS

Funding: the way finance (money) is provided

Local authority: the organisation responsible for public services in a particular area

National centres of excellence: high-level sports facilities run by Sport England

Public sector: the part of the economy that is run by government and local authorities

Private sector: part of the economy that is run by business for profit

Voluntary sector: local sports clubs and national governing bodies.

66 KEY THOUGHT 99

'Sport reflects society'

Key to Exam Success

For your GCSE you should be able to:

▪ describe and explain how the range of sporting facilities and opportunities, both locally and nationally, affects participation in physical activities
▪ describe the range of facilities provided nationally, including the role played by the national centres of excellence
▪ describe the range of facilities provided by the local authority, private enterprise and voluntary organisations.

The structure of sport in England

The original Sports Council was founded in 1972. Now we have five independent sports councils.

- The UK sports council, now known as **UK Sport**, looks after issues at UK level.

- The four councils of England, Scotland, Wales and Northern Ireland are each responsible for sport in their own countries.

In this book we will look at the work of **Sport England**, the brand name of the English Sports Council.

The national governing bodies of each sport work with the international sports federation for their sport to arrange fixtures and championships.

- The **British Olympic Association (BOC)** is responsible for the British team for the Olympics.

- The **International Olympic Committee (IOC)** is all-powerful in Olympic rules and organisation.

- The **Central Council of Physical Recreation (CCPR)** is an independent body which enables the many different governing bodies to speak with one voice.

UK Sport

UK Sport deals with high-performance sport at the UK level. It aims to achieve sporting excellence for Britain. To do this it:

- gives full support to our world-class performers through the World Class Performance Programme and the UK Sports Institute
- extends the UK's international sporting influence
- encourages the world's major sporting events to come to the UK
- promotes ethical standards of behaviour
- is the UK's national anti-doping agency.

The role of the Central Council of Physical Recreation

The CCPR:

- aims to improve and develop sport and physical recreation at all levels
- enables NGBs to meet to discuss common problems and the best way to develop their sports
- runs campaigns, for example against the loss of school playing fields
- advises government, local authorities and Sport England on sporting matters
- gives advice on sport sponsorship through the Sports Sponsorship Advisory Service
- runs the Sports Leader Award scheme with the British Sports Trust.

Sport national governing bodies

The role of the NGBs is to:

- promote development of their sport
- organise competitions and events
- select teams at all levels

- arrange coaching and training
- organise award schemes
- enforce rules and laws
- negotiate with television and sponsoring companies
- distribute funds for the World Class programmes.

The British Olympic Association

The BOA:

- develops interest throughout the UK in the Olympic movement
- runs the British Olympic Medical Centre to support Olympic sportspeople
- helps the NGBs of sport to prepare their teams for the Olympics
- organises the British team for each Olympic Games, taking care of travel, transport, insurance, health care, accommodation, food, training, publicity, documentation and all aspects of teams' behaviour at the Games.

What is Sport England?

Sport England is responsible for sport in England and putting into action the Government's strategy for sport.

The Sport England strategy

Vision: to make England an active and successful sporting nation

Mission: to work with others to create opportunities for people to get involved in sport, to stay in sport, and to excel and succeed in sport at every level.

'Start, stay and succeed in sport.'

Objectives

1 **Opportunities to play sport**: to increase participation in sport in order to improve the health of the nation, with a focus on priority groups.

2 **Opportunities to stay in sport**: to retain people in sport and active recreation through an effective network of clubs, sports facilities, coaches, volunteers and competitive opportunities.

3 **Opportunities to achieve success in sport**: to make sporting success happen at the highest level.

Sport England consists of a main board appointed by the Secretary of State for Culture, Media and Sport and a London head office with full-time staff and nine regional offices across England.

The regional offices:

- promote Sport England policy through Regional Sports Boards

- keep Sport England in touch with needs at grassroots level

- have close links with local authorities, local sports councils, national governing bodies and other organisations involved with sport, education, recreation and environment.

The local sports councils are encouraged by Sport England, but act independently. Their role is to:

- bring together local people, clubs and groups interested in sport

- discuss problems, exchange views and plan for the future

- promote developments in local sports in the best interests of the community.

The role of Sport England

The objective of Sport England is to lead the development of sport in England. Its aims are:

- to make England more active
- to influence decision makers on sport
- to distribute funding.

Sport England uses its money to start, stay and succeed in sport.

Funding

In 2003, Sport England changed the way it funded sport. Its money is now used for:

- Community investment – the money is distributed through the regional sports board. They provide the money for the active England campaign. The money comes from both the National Lottery and the Government grant. The aim is to develop sporting facilities and activity projects in local communities across England.

- National investment – the money is distributed through the national governing bodies of sport. There are 30 sports that receive priority for support and development.

Active England Campaign

An ambitious new campaign, based on the Government's plans, aims to get 70% of the population doing 30 minutes activity a day by 2020. This is intended to improve the health and happiness of the nation.

Who pays for Sport England?

Sport England currently receives a government grant of £35 million and distributes £200 million of National Lottery money.

Who provides sports facilities?

Sports facilities are provided by the **public sector**, the **private sector** and the **voluntary sector**.

The public sector

The government gives grants to the regional sports councils to run the national sports centres. Sport England runs five national sports centres, each equipped with special facilities for particular sports:

- **Crystal Palace**; athletics, swimming and diving

- **Bisham Abbey**; judo, powerlifting and tennis

- **Lilleshall Hall**; football and gymnastics

- **Holme Pierrepont**: water sports

- **Plas-y-Brenin**: outdoor activities.

Each centre has facilities and support services for top sports performers and aims to provide them with the best possible training environment. Priority is given to:

- sportspeople participating in the World Class Programme

- national team training and competition

- training of leaders and officials.

The National Lottery Fund
The government distributes National Lottery funds to the five sports councils for a variety of projects, including facilities. Through Sport England, the National Lottery fund has provided money for a large number of schemes throughout the country. A total of

£13 bn has been raised and 150,000 projects supported to date. Sport is one of the six 'good causes' to receive money.

The new English National Stadium at Wembley
The site of the former Wembley football stadium was bought by Sport England from Wembley plc and has received £120 million of National Lottery money. With 90,000 seats, the new Wembley will be the largest football stadium in the world, with no obstructed views and every seat under cover. It is scheduled to open in 2006.

The Countryside Agency
The government funds the Countryside Agency, which is responsible for the eight national parks of England – the Broads, Dartmoor, Exmoor, the Lake District, the North Yorkshire Moors, Northumberland, the Peak District and the Yorkshire Dales. The New Forest has a similar status. These areas provide a wide range of opportunities for outdoor recreation.

Local authorities

Local authorities provide a variety of services such as education, street-cleaning and leisure. In large cities, these services are usually provided by a single authority, but in other areas a county council may be responsible for major services such as education, with district or town councils providing leisure and recreation services.

In all areas there are small town or parish councils which are responsible for halls, play areas and open spaces.

Leisure and recreation departments

Each local authority has separate departments to deal with their services, including leisure and recreation. Local authorities are not obliged to provide facilities for general leisure, but sports centres, swimming pools and recreation grounds are usually provided, as well as halls, play areas and open spaces. All facilities need qualified staff, good equipment and regular maintenance.

Leisure and recreation departments provide facilities for all sections of the community and costs must be kept as low as possible so that programmes are attractive, accessible and affordable. Local authorities usually employ sports development officers whose job is to develop local sport and to encourage links between schools and local sports clubs.

Sport in schools and colleges

- Schools and colleges are required by law to provide facilities for sport and physical education.

- Local authorities also provide sports facilities for colleges, youth clubs and adult education.

- Some schools have dual-use sports facilities which are shared by the school and the local community.

The private sector

Where there is a need that is not met by the public sector, specialist sports facilities may be provided on a commercial basis. Commercial sports facilities can be expensive, but are usually friendly and welcoming and offer good value for money, combining social activities with up-to-date facilities and equipment.

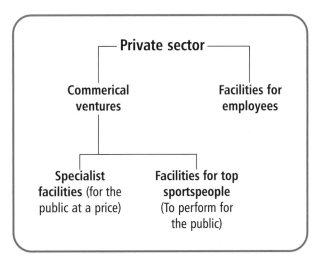

Examples include health and fitness centres, golf driving ranges, riding centres, tenpin bowling halls, ice-rinks and tennis courts. Purpose-built activity holiday centres are often well-equipped for sport, and some hotels and country clubs offer high-class sports facilities as an extra attraction for members.

Company sports and social clubs

In the past, large companies had social clubs which provided a range of sports and social facilities for employees and their families. This not only helped to create a healthy and contented workforce, but encouraged employees to be loyal to the company.

Although sports facilities were provided free of charge to employees, the cost of upkeep of the buildings, courts, pitches and greens was considerable. Today companies are more likely to make arrangements with sports centres to offer special rates or introductory fitness courses for employees.

The voluntary sector

Sports clubs

For many adults, taking part in sport means belonging to a local club. Most towns have their own sports clubs, which are usually run by enthusiasts and concentrate on one sport.

Those that are well established may own their own facilities – for example, golf, tennis and cricket clubs. Clubs that are new or do not have the money often have to hire facilities from the local sports centre, school, playing field or church hall.

Community associations

Sometimes groups of people in a village or neighbourhood get together to provide a variety of physical recreation for the local community.

In rural areas, the village green may be available for cricket in the summer and hockey in the winter. Village and church halls can also provide facilities for a number of indoor sports, such as table tennis and badminton. Other facilities may be available for hire if necessary.

National governing bodies

Some national governing bodies (NGBs) have magnificent facilities – for example, the Rugby Football Union's ground at Twickenham. Most of the newer NGBs have no facilities of their own and have to use the facilities provided by the national sports centres.

Some NGBs have close historical links with an established club and use their facilities for major events – for example, the Marylebone Cricket Club (MCC) uses Lords cricket ground. The Football Association does not own its own ground and has used Wembley Stadium, which used to be owned by a private company before it was acquired for redevelopment by Sport England.

Athletics and swimming do not have their own national facilities, and neither do many other major sports.

Sports facilities and participation

Sports facilities vary greatly. A local badminton club might play in a church hall with one court, faded markings and a low ceiling. In the past, swimming pools were usually built as facilities on their own, but are now more often part of modern leisure centres. Running tracks were originally used only for running, with other field events neglected. Nowadays they may include a stand, changing rooms and indoor training facilities such as a weights room or fitness suite, with a range of equipment to monitor fitness.

Many playing fields, especially for Sunday football, still have very poor changing facilities – and little else. Teams that are able to use school playing fields may benefit from the use of the school's facilities on match day and also for training.

Sports facilities can be grouped into two main categories:

- **Indoor facilities**: these include general-purpose facilities such as sports and leisure centres together with specialist facilities, such as swimming pools, squash centres, fitness suites or ice rinks.

- **Outdoor facilities**: these include pitches for major games, golf courses, hard areas for tennis, netball and five-a-side football, water sport centres and parts of the countryside used for sport, such as climbing areas, stretches of river, sea or lakes, walking or jogging trails.

User needs

Sports centres must be able to cope with the needs of a variety of different user groups. including the elderly, active retired groups, people with disabilities, mothers with small children, ethnic minority groups and

the unemployed. They must also meet the needs of individuals, teams, clubs and advanced groups.

These different user groups may include different ages, single or mixed-sex groups and the able-bodied or people with disabilities.

In order to tempt us away from our sofas in front of the television and into the sports centre, we need facilities for our sport which are available locally, easily accessible at a convenient time and an affordable price.

Sport at local level

Local sports clubs exist because enthusiastic people have met together in the past to enjoy their sport. However, enthusiasm is not enough to keep a club going. To be successful, a club needs members, a committee, a constitution, facilities and finance.

Members should be:

- enthusiastic about their sport
- happy to take part with others
- willing to pay their share of the costs
- able to accept club rules
- available to play, organise, coach or officiate at competitions.

Committee members should be:

- willing to take on jobs
- ready to work as a team

- able to make decisions for the club
- elected by the club's Annual General Meeting (AGM).

There are three essential jobs:

- **Chairperson**: controls committee meetings and acts as the club's representative
- **Secretary**: deals with the day-to-day business, arranges meetings
- **Treasurer**: deals with all the club's finances.

The **constitution** sets out the rules of the club. It explains:

- how the club is organised
- how to become a member
- how people are elected to jobs
- how fees can be charged
- what happens if members break the rules
- how the club can be changed.

Facilities are needed for playing and training, as well as for meetings and social events. The needs of the club will depend on the type of activity and the number of members. Facilities might be hired or owned.

A club will need to pay for:

- hire or upkeep of facilities
- team clothing and equipment
- training and competition costs
- office expenses.

It can raise money through:

- fees and subscriptions
- fundraising
- grants and sponsorship.

Under new management

Read the report from the Daltringham Echo about the problems facing Daltringham Sports Club. Then read the letter from Mr Sweetingham to Trevor Woodhouse. Working in groups of four, imagine that you are Trevor Woodhouse. Draft a letter of reply in which you agree to take on the role of chairperson. Put forward your plans and ideas for reorganising the club and boosting membership.

You might like to use the following headings:

- Immediate action
- Finance
- Fixtures
- Clubhouse
- Proposals for improvement for next season
- Pitches
- Meetings
- Committees
- Publicity
- Fundraising
- Clubhouse
- Social events.

Club's Dive to Disaster

For many months the people of Daltringham have wondered what has happened to their sports club, once the pride of the town. Founded just ten years ago it quickly established a reputation in junior rugby with players winning county caps and one an England trial. As soon as a Sunday football section was formed, the club won the local league three times in the first five seasons.

However, times have changed dramatically. Last Saturday only one rugby side took the field and, composed largely of veterans and youngsters, it crashed 66–7 as expected. Only two seasons ago five sides were fielded regularly. The two Sunday football teams withdrew from their leagues at Christmas as they were unable to raise full sides each week.

Off the field, the club has been plagued by apathy and financial mismanagement. Although the club still has a long lease on its council pitches, the severe financial problems have cast doubt on its future beyond this season.

Our reporter, Tracy Binns, has been talking to a number of officials who have left the club recently and has established the following facts:

1. The club's dire financial situation first came to light last month when Rex Whaker, the Treasurer, left the club, his wife and family to join his secretary, Amanda Prior, in the Canary Islands.
2. The players lost faith in the Selection Committee after a number of controversial decisions in October last year. This resulted in an exodus of players to Redhouse Park just before Christmas.
3. The pitches and the clubhouse have gone to wrack and ruin since old Fred Lane, a founder member of the club, unofficial groundsman, steward and handyman, died suddenly in January.
4. The general management of the club this season has been appalling. Dates of meetings and agenda have not been publicised in advance and it is claimed that important decisions have been made without the necessary majority. Social events have been virtually non-existent, the annual dinner-dance was cancelled and the bar is often closed even on match days. The number of players attending training has fallen dramatically. The disciplinary record is unacceptable. Plans to build squash courts and to develop activities to attract women members and families have been shelved indefinitely.

The people of this town must decide whether or not they want a sports club. Time is running out fast. A special meeting has been called for next week to decide the club's future.

The Clubhouse
Daltringham Sports Club
Ringland Road
Daltringham.

25 March 2004

Mr Trevor Woodhouse
27 The Glebe,
Daltringham

Dear Mr Woodhouse,

Thank you very much for the detailed notes you sent me giving guidelines for the management of clubs such as ours. I am writing to you now in the hope that you might be able to rescue the club from its desperate plight. We understand that you have had many years experience with the Sports Council and that your book *Club Guidelines* is highly recommended.

Currently there are only three officials left in the office — myself (Vice-Chairman), Mr Brian Mount, the acting Secretary and Mr Dean Smart, the manager of the Colts rugby side. We intend calling an Extraordinary General Meeting next week and would like you to consider nomination as Chairman. I do hope you will be willing to help us. It would be tragic for the town if the club went under.

Yours sincerely,

T J Sweetingham

Thomas J. Sweetingham
Vice Chairman DSC.

QUESTIONS

8 Local and national facilities

1 Make a list of six different sports facilities and put them under the heading of indoor or outdoor facilities.

(6 marks)

2

a Give four examples of facilities likely to be provided by the local authority.

(4 marks)

b Give two examples of facilities likely to be provided by private enterprise.

(2 marks)

c Give two examples of facilities likely to be provided by voluntary bodies.

(2 marks)

3

a Give the three main ways in which the government provides for sport.

(3 marks)

b Name three of the five national sports centres run by Sport England.

(3 marks)

4 Local sports clubs need to be organised to survive.

a Name three important officials in any sports club.

(3 marks)

b Describe the main responsibility of each official.

(3 marks)

c Suggest three ways the club might raise money to meet its running costs.

(3 marks)

5 Many organisations provide for sport. Explain briefly the role of each of the following;

a Sport England *(2 marks)*

b UK Sport *(2 marks)*

c CCPR *(2 marks)*

d British Olympic Association *(2 marks)*

6

a Name the local authority department responsible for sport and physical recreation.

(1 mark)

b Name the officers who have the responsibility to develop sport for the local authority

(1 mark)

7 Voluntary organisations play an important part in providing sport at a local level. Describe what they do and why it is important to the community.

(8 marks)

8 Explain how the national sports centres play a role in the development of sporting excellence.

(4 marks)
(Total 51 marks)

The relationship between health, fitness and practical activity

9 Components of fitness

- What is physical fitness?
- Components of fitness
- Skill-related fitness

10 Factors affecting fitness

- Why do we need a balanced diet?
- Food for sport
- Drugs

11 Fitness training principles

- Training for success
- Thresholds of training
- Planning a training programme

12 Training methods

- How do our muscles work?
- Training options
- Your Personal Exercise Plan (PEP)

13 Training effects

- The effects of exercise and training on our body systems
- Anaerobic and aerobic activity in training
- Training thresholds and target training zones

Components of fitness

Being fit is central to our health and helps us to feel good about ourselves. Fitness is vital for success in sport.

Physical fitness circuit

Working in groups of three, complete a circuit of tests designed to help you experience the different factors involved in fitness.

Fitness circuit	
Tennis ball pick-up	Place three tennis balls on the floor two metres away. Run, pick up the first ball and return both feet behind the starting line. Repeat with the second and third ball. Finish as quickly as you can. Record the time taken to complete the test.
Balancing ball	Extend your arm at right angles to the ground, fist clenched, back of the hand facing upwards. Place a volleyball on the back of your hand and time how long it can be balanced up to a maximum of 60 seconds. Your arm may be moved but not your feet.
The pinch	Have a partner pinch a fold of fat on the back of your upper arm, halfway between the elbow and the tip of the shoulder. Measure the thickness of the fold in centimetres.
Two-ball juggle	Hold two tennis balls in your preferred hand. Juggle them up to 10 times without dropping either ball. Score one point for each catch up to maximum of 10.
Shoulder raise	Lie face down on the floor with your arms stretched out in front. Hold a metre rule with your hands shoulder-width apart. Raise your arms as high as possible, keeping your chin on the ground at all times and the rule parallel to the floor. Hold the highest position for three seconds. A partner measures the height reached from the floor.
Grip test	Squeeze a hand grip dynamometer as hard as possible with one hand. Record the reading.
Standing broad jump	Start with your feet comfortably apart and your toes immediately behind the start line. Then bend your knees and jump forward as far as possible. Measure the distance from your rear heel or any other part of the body which is nearest to the start line. You are allowed two attempts.
Press-ups	Complete as many press-ups as possible in 60 seconds. Girls can perform press-ups from the kneeling position.
Metre rule drop	Ask a partner to hold a metre rule so that the side edge is between your thumb and index finger at a point 30 cm from the end. When your partner releases the rule, catch it before it slips through your thumb and finger. Do not move your hand lower to catch the rule. Record how far the rule has fallen.
Double heel click	With feet apart, jump up and tap your heels together twice before you hit the ground. You must land with your feet at least 10 cm apart. Make three attempts. Record the number of successful attempts.
Shuttle run	Complete a 10-metre shuttle run as many times as possible over a one-minute period.

KEYWORDS

Agility: the ability to change the direction of the body quickly and control its movement

Balance: the ability to maintain equilibrium, whether stationary or moving

Cardiovascular endurance: the ability of our heart and lung systems to cope with activity over a relatively long period of time

Components of fitness (health-related fitness): are the five basic factors which provide the level of fitness necessary for good health

Co-ordination: the ability to carry out a series of movements smoothly and efficiently

Flexibility: the range of movement possible at a joint

Health: a state of mental, physical and social well-being

Muscular endurance: the ability to use voluntary muscles many times without getting tired

Muscular power: ability to contract muscles with speed and strength in one explosive act; the combination of speed and strength

Muscular strength: the amount of force a muscle can exert against a resistance

Performance: how well a task is completed

Physical fitness: the ability of our body to carry out everyday activities with minimum fatigue and with enough energy left over for emergencies

Skill-related fitness: the level of physical fitness necessary for regular sporting activity

Speed: ability of the body, or part of the body, to move quickly

Speed of reaction (reaction time): the ability to respond quickly to a stimulus

Timing: ability to coincide movements in relation to external factors.

Key to Exam Success

For your GCSE you will need to be able to:

- describe and explain the different components of fitness
- describe and explain the components of skill-related fitness
- understand that fitness is related to particular activities
- describe and explain suitable tests for each type of fitness
- describe and explain how tests of fitness can be used to identify strengths, weaknesses and suitability for an activity.

❝ KEY THOUGHT ❞

'Health-related fitness is essential for life. Skill-related fitness is good for performance.'

What is physical fitness?

Physical fitness is the ability of our body to carry out everyday activities with little fatigue and with enough energy left for emergencies. Fitness means different things to different people. A man who is fit for his work as a taxi driver may be dangerously unfit for a game of squash. A marathon runner may be quite unfit for lifting weights.

Physical fitness consists of two parts:

- **Components of fitness** are the five basic factors which provide the level of fitness ncessary for good health

- **Skill-related fitness** is the level of physical fitness necessary for regular sporting activity.

We will look at skill-related fitness in detail in the latter part of this chapter.

What are the components of fitness?

We all need a minimum amount of physical fitness to be healthy and to cope with everyday life. This fitness protects us from stress, accidents, injury, disease and other health problems. To have enough physical fitness for good health we need the five components of fitness:

- **Cardiovascular endurance** is the ability of our heart and lung systems to cope with activity over a relatively long period of time.

- **Strength** is the amount of force a muscle can exert against a resistance.

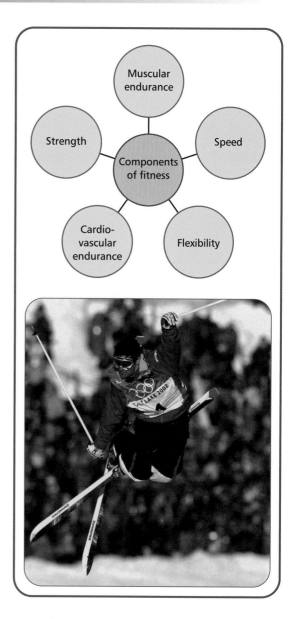

- **Muscular endurance** is the ability to use voluntary muscles many times without getting tired.

- **Speed** is the ability of the body, or part of the body, to move quickly.

- **Flexibility** is the range of movement possible at a joint.

Component of fitness presentation

Working in pairs or small groups, your task is to prepare and deliver a brief presentation explaining one of the five components of fitness (see above). Include the following in your presentation:

- a definition of the fitness component
- an explanation of the component
- the importance of the component in sport
- how the component can be measured
- how the component can be improved.

You may wish to use Microsoft Powerpoint for your presentation.

It is important to link your presentation to your Personal Exercise Plan (PEP). Use the appropriate sections of this chapter to gather your information. You will also be able to obtain more information from the internet. Be sure to include the analysis of the results obtained by your group in the fitness testing. You will be expected to explain your results.

Components of fitness

Endurance

There are two types of endurance – **cardiovascular endurance** and **muscular endurance**. We will deal with muscular endurance in the section on strength.

Cardiovascular endurance

Cardiovascular endurance is the ability of our heart and lung systems to cope with activity over a long period, It is also known as aerobic fitness, stamina or cardiorespiratory endurance. It is essential for work and play in our everyday lives. In order for our body to work hard for a long period we must supply our working muscles with energy and get rid of waste products. To do this, our heart, lungs and circulatory system must work well.

VO$_2$ Max

Our maximum cardiovascular fitness or aerobic capacity is also called our **VO$_2$ Max**. This is the maximum amount of oxygen that can be carried to, and used by, the working muscles during exercise, and it is often used to measure fitness (see below). A person with a high VO$_2$ Max can use more oxygen, work harder for longer, and will have less fatigue, than someone with a lower VO$_2$ Max.

How do we improve our cardiovascular endurance?

We can improve our cardiovascular endurance by taking part regularly in any continuous whole-body exercise, for example, running, swimming or cycling.

We must keep our heart rate between 60% and 80% of our maximum heart rate for our cardiovascular endurance to improve.

We should exercise at first for a minimum of 12 minutes, increasing this to 40 minutes as we become fitter.

We can use continuous training, interval training and circuit training to improve our cardiovascular endurance.

How do we measure our cardiovascular endurance?

We can measure our cardiovascular endurance by finding out our VO_2 Max. This is the amount of oxygen we can use in one minute of maximum exercise.

We can estimate our VO_2 Max by using tests such as the Multistage (Bleep) Fitness Test and the Cooper 12-Minute Run.

Multistage (Bleep) Fitness Test

A pre-recorded tape plays 'bleeps' at regular set intervals while you make 20-metre shuttle runs in time to the bleeps.

After each minute, the time intervals between the bleeps get shorter so you have to run faster. You keep going until you can no longer keep up with the speed set by the bleeps. At this point you stop and record the level. You can then work out your VO$_2$ Max using published tables.

British National Team Scores in Multistage Fitness Tests

Sport	Male	Female
Basketball	11–5	9–6
Hockey	13–9	12–7
Rugby league	13–1	
Netball		9–7
Squash	13–3	

You can get an instant VO$_2$ Max score by using the VO$_2$ Max calculator at
http://www.brianmac.demon.co.uk.
Look for the links to 'Multistage Fitness test'.

Cooper 12-Minute Run

The aim is to run as far as you can in 12 minutes around a marked area. The total distance you run is recorded. You can work out your aerobic capacity using this table:

Cooper 12-Minute Run: comparative scores

	Males 15–16 years	Females 15–16 years
High score	Above 2,800 m	Above 2,300 m
Above average	2,799–2,500 m	2,299–2,000 m
Average	2,499–2,300 m	1,999–1,900 m
Below average	2,299–2,200 m	1,899–1,800 m
Low score	Below 2,200 m	Below 1,800 m

The importance of cardiovascular endurance

Cardiovascular endurance is essential for an active lifestyle. It also enables us to cope with unexpected physical demands like running away from a dangerous situation. It is essential in all sporting activities lasting more than a few seconds. The better our cardiovascular endurance, the longer we can continue our activity, whether it is swimming, running, cycling or rowing. Our skill level declines as we get tired. This can be seen in team games when more goals and points are scored towards the end of matches as a greater number of mistakes are made. A player with a high level of cardiovascular endurance will be able to maintain his skill level for longer. It is often said that 'When fatigue sets in, skill goes out of the window.'

Speed

Speed is the ability of the body or part of the body to move quickly.

For our bodies to achieve speed, we have to supply energy to our muscles very quickly. The muscles then have to contract in the shortest possible time. We use our anaerobic energy supply system for speed work. If we have a high percentage of fast-twitch fibres in our active muscles, then we will have a natural advantage.

How do we improve our speed?

We cannot increase the percentage of fast-twitch fibres in our bodies, but we can improve our speed in sport in other ways, such as:

- increasing our strength through a programme of weight training and plyometrics. Stronger muscles will give more power and therefore more speed.

- improving our reaction time

- improving our ability to change speed and direction when moving quickly (see page 169)

- improving our ability to cope with lactic acid (see page 86)

- improving our skill in sport; for example, a more efficient swimming stroke will create less resistance and increase speed in the water.

How do we measure our speed?

Speed can be measured simply by recording the time it takes us to run a certain distance – for example, 50 metres – using a stopwatch. Reaction time, speed off the mark, time to reach top speed and deceleration times can all be measured as part of a training programme.

50-metre speed test: comparative scores (seconds)

	Males 15–16 years	Females 15–16 years
High score	Faster than 7.2	Faster than 7.8
Above average	7.2–7.8	7.8–8.4
Average	7.9–8.4	8.5–9.0
Below average	8.5–9.0	9.1–9.6
Low score	Slower than 9.1	Slower than 9.7

Why is speed important?

Children develop the ability to move quickly through play. Although adults do not need speed for everyday tasks, the ability to move quickly can be important in emergencies. Examples include moving out of the way of falling objects or moving to help another person at a time of need.

Speed is important in sports that require a great deal of effort over a very short period of time. Sprinters, speed skaters and sprint cyclists all need to develop speed. It is also important in many team games, when a sudden change of pace and direction is needed. Some sports require speed for the whole body, for example, long jumping; while for the javelin, shoulder and arm speed are of major importance.

Strength

In everyday terms, we think of **strength** as being the ability of our muscles to carry out our daily tasks easily. This type of muscular strength is one of the components of physical fitness. However, our muscles work to produce three different types of strength:

- **muscular strength**: this is also called static strength or maximum strength

- **muscular endurance**: this is also called endurance strength

- **muscular power**: this is also called explosive strength or power.

Many sports and many everyday activities demand a combination of muscular strength, muscular power and muscular endurance.

What is muscular strength?

Muscular strength is the amount of force a muscle can exert against a resistance. It can be improved by training with heavy weights (80–100% of our maximum), using a low number of repetitions. In order to build up muscular strength it is necessary to exercise through the full range of joint movements and to work slowly when lifting.

How do we measure our muscular strength?

To measure our muscular strength, we need to find out the maximum force that a muscle group can apply.

The Repetition Max Test

We can carry out a Repetition Max Test using free weights or multigym equipment. The aim is to find out the maximum weight we can lift just once, by gradually adding weights. This is called our one repetition max. We must allow at least 2–3 minutes between each lift for recovery.

Hand Grip Strength Test

To test the strength of your hand grip, you can use a hand grip dynamometer. You simply squeeze the handle as hard as possible with your hand and record the reading on the dynamometer.

Hand Grip Strength Test: comparative scores

	Males 15–16 years	Females 15–16 years
High score	Above 56 kg	Above 36 kg
Above average	56–51 kg	36–31 kg
Average	50–45 kg	30–25 kg
Below average	44–39 kg	24–19 kg
Low score	Less than 39 kg	Less than 19 kg

The importance of muscular strength

We use our muscles to move ourselves and everyday objects. Without strong muscles normal life would become very difficult. We need muscular strength to lift shopping and to move furniture. Attempting these kinds of activities without sufficient strength could lead to injury.

Muscular strength is extremely important in most sports. For example, a judo player needs strength when attempting to throw an opponent; a rugby player needs strength when pushing in the scrum, and an archer when drawing back the bow.

Muscular endurance

Muscular endurance or endurance strength is also called anaerobic endurance. It is the ability to use voluntary muscles many times without getting tired. It refers to the efficiency of the anaerobic system within the working muscles when engaged in high-intensity, repetitive or even static exercise.

A person who has a high percentage of slow-twitch fibres will have an advantage in events involving muscular endurance. Muscular endurance is also closely linked with muscular strength.

You can improve your muscular endurance by training with light weights (40–60% of your maximum). The exercises need to be done at speed and with a high number of repetitions (20–30).

How do we measure our muscular endurance?

To measure muscular endurance you can perform repeated exercises such as press-ups or sit-ups for a given time or to exhaustion. Then you can compare your score either with those of others or with your own previous best.

The NCF Abdominal Curl Test

This test measures the muscular endurance of our abdominal muscles.

1 Lie on the mat with your knees bent, feet flat on the floor, hands resting on your thighs and the back of the head on your partner's hands. Your feet should not be held down to the floor.

2 Curl up slowly using the abdominal muscles and slide your hands up the thighs until your fingertips touch your kneecaps.

3 Return slowly to the starting position.

A complete curl should take 3 seconds, allowing 20 repetitions per minute. Repeat as many curls as you can at this rate and record the result.

NCF Abdominal Curl Test: comparative scores

	Males 15–16 years	Females 15–16 years
High score	60 and above	50 and above
Above average	45–59	40–49
Average	30–44	25–39
Below average	20–29	10–24
Low score	Below 20	Below 10

The importance of muscular endurance

Muscular endurance is important in a wide range of everyday activities, whenever the same muscle groups are used over and over again. Examples include ironing, cleaning the car and washing windows. It is particularly important in sports such as rowing, canoeing and other sporting activities where the same muscle groups work continuously with near-maximum effort.

Muscular power

Power is the ability to contract muscles with speed and force in one explosive act:

Power = Strength × Speed

Power, or explosive strength, is the combination of strength and speed of movement. The energy for our power comes from the anaerobic system.

How can we improve our power?

We can improve our power by improving our strength, our speed of movement or both. We can train with medium weights (60–80% of our maximum), but the repetitions need to be performed at speed. Plyometrics training (see page 230) is also an excellent way of improving power. As power is a combination of strength and speed, it is important to develop both these areas of fitness.

How do we measure our power?

There are two simple ways to measure the power of your legs: the Standing Broad Jump and the Standing Vertical Jump.

Standing Broad Jump

Stand with your feet comfortably apart and your toes immediately behind the start line. Then bend your knees and jump forward as far as possible. Measure the distance from your rear heel back to the start line. You are allowed two attempts.

Standing Vertical Jump

Stand next to a wall and reach up with whichever arm is nearest to the wall. Mark the highest point you can reach with your fingers. Both feet must remain flat on the floor at this stage. Now chalk your fingers and perform a vertical jump, marking the wall at the highest point you can reach. The distance between the two marks gives a measure of how high you can leap from the ground from a stationary start. It takes into account your height and so is a fairer test than the standing broad jump.

Standing Broad Jump: comparative scores (metres)

	Males 15–16 years	Females 15–16 years
High score	Above 2	Above 1.65
Above average	2.00–1.86	1.65–1.56
Average	1.85–1.76	1.55–1.46
Below average	1.75–1.65	1.45–1.35
Low score	Less than 1.65	Less than 1.35

Standing Vertical Jump: comparative scores (centimetres)

	Males 15–16 years	Females 15–16 years
High score	Above 65	Above 60
Above average	65–56	60–51
Average	55–50	50–41
Below average	49–40	40–35
Low score	Less than 40	Less than 35

The importance of power

Although power is not used a great deal in our everyday activities, we need it for certain physical tasks such as digging a hole or swinging a sledgehammer. Children often use power in their play, when they run, throw and jump.

Power is used a great deal in activities such as sprinting, throwing and jumping or when we try to move an object or ourselves as far and as fast as possible. Athletes need a lot of power, as do games players, racket players and gymnasts.

Flexibility

Flexibility is the range of movement possible at a joint. Flexibility is also known as mobility and **suppleness**.

Flexibility is necessary to stay healthy and avoid injury, and does not depend on our shape.

How can we improve flexibility?

We can improve our flexibility by stretching our muscles and tendons and by extending our ligaments and supporting tissues beyond their normal range of movement – for example, by holding an extended position for 20 seconds and repeating the stretch after a short rest period.

When exercising in this way it is important not to overload your muscles unless you feel comfortable. You should also stretch the prime movers and then the antagonist muscles – for example, stretching the quadriceps followed by the hamstrings. This helps your muscles recover and adapt in a balanced way.

The effects of flexibility exercises are very specific. We can, for example, be very flexible in our shoulders and yet show little flexibility in our lower limbs.

Flexibility exercise, or stretching, should be part of all training programmes.

What are the different types of stretching?

There are four main types of stretching which can be used to improve flexibility. In each case you extend your limbs beyond their normal range and hold the position. How you get to the stretch position varies:

- **Static stretching**: you use your own strength

- **Passive stretching**: a partner or coach applies external force

- **Active stretching**: you move rhythmically and under control to extend the stretch

- **PNF stretching**: you contract the muscle before stretching it.

How do we measure flexibility?
The tests used depend upon the joints that are being measured.

Sit and Reach Test
This test measures the flexibility of the hamstrings. Sit on the floor, legs straight, feet flat against the table with shoes removed, fingertips on the edge of the top plate. Bend your trunk and reach forward slowly and as far as possible, keeping the knees straight. Hold this position for two seconds.

Measure the distance from the edge of the table to the position reached by the fingertips. Be sure you make a number of warm-up attempts before the actual measurement is taken. As the 'sit and reach' table has an overhang of 15 cm, a person who reaches 5 cm past their toes scores 20 cm.

Sit and Reach Test: comparative scores

	Males 15–16 years	Females 15–16 years
High score	Above 28 cm	Above 35 cm
Above average	24–28 cm	32–35 cm
Average	20–23 cm	30–31 cm
Below average	17–19 cm	25–29 cm
Low score	Less than 17 cm	Less than 25 cm

Shoulder Hyperextension Test
This test measures your ability to stretch the muscles of your chest and shoulders.

Lie face down on the floor with your arms stretched out in front. Hold a metre rule with your hands shoulder-width apart. Raise your arms as high as

Shoulder Hyperextension Test: comparative scores

	Males 15–16 years	Females 15–16 years
High score	41 cm and above	46 cm and above
Above average	31–40 cm	36–45 cm
Average	21–30 cm	26–35 cm
Below average	11–20 cm	16–25 cm
Low score	0–10 cm	0–15 cm

possible, keeping your chin on the ground at all times and the stick parallel to the floor. Hold the highest position for three seconds while your partner measures the height reached.

The importance of flexibility

We need a full range of movement in our joints for such everyday activities as putting on our shoes, reaching up to cupboards and twisting round as we work in the kitchen or garden. Without flexibility our movements will be limited and we are more likely to injure our joints and muscles.

All sports need a flexible body. Sports such as gymnastics and hurdling need a great deal of overall body flexibility. Other sports – for example, javelin and volleyball – need flexibility in particular parts of the body. Flexibility exercises should form a part of all training programmes, as flexible joints are less likely to be injured when put under stress.

Sportspeople often need a combination of flexibility and strength. Flexibility allows us to use our strength through a full range of movement. Strength is needed to stabilise joints and avoid injury.

Skill-related fitness

Skill-related fitness is the level of physical fitness necessary for regular sporting activity. Although we may be fit from a health-related point of view we may not be fit for sport. There are many different kinds of sporting activities and each makes its own particular demands on our body. For example, the fitness needed to be a high jumper is totally different from the fitness necessary for a triathlete.

To be successful in any sport good health is essential. We need the five components of fitness to give us health-related fitness. On top of this we need to have fitness related to our own sport. This skill-related fitness will include some or all of the following:

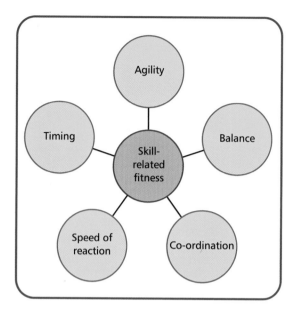

- **Agility** is the ability to change the direction of the body at speed.

- **Balance** is the ability to maintain equilibrium, whether stationary or moving.

- **Co-ordination** is the ability to carry out a series of movements smoothly and efficiently.

- **Timing** is the ability to coincide movements in relation to external factors.

- **Speed of reaction (reaction time)** is the ability to respond quickly to a stimulus.

activity

Skill-related fitness presentation
Working in pairs or small groups, your task is to prepare and deliver a brief presentation explaining one of the components of skill-related fitness. Include the following in your presentation:

- a definition of the fitness component
- an explanation of the component
- the importance of the component in sport
- how the component can be measured
- how the component can be improved.

You may wish to use to use Microsoft Powerpoint for your presentation.

It is important to link your presentation to your Personal Exercise Plan (PEP). Use the appropriate sections of this chapter to gather your information. You will also be able to obtain more information from the internet. Be sure to include the analysis of the results obtained by your group in the fitness testing. You will be expected to explain your results.

 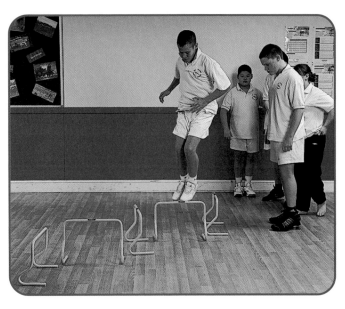

Agility

Agility is the ability to change the position of the body quickly and to control its movement. It is a combination of speed, balance, power and co-ordination.

Agility can be developed by training, and by rehearsing the movements made in our chosen sport. This needs to be done at full speed and under conditions similar to those in a competitive situation. We must also improve our speed, balance, power and co-ordination, as all these fitness aspects affect our agility.

How do we measure our agility?

An expert watching us play our particular sport can make a very good assessment of our agility. We can also assess our general agility using a test such as the Illinois Agility Run.

Illinois Agility Run

Begin by setting up a course as shown in the diagram (left). Lie face down on the floor at the starting line. When told to start, leap to your feet and complete the course in the shortest time possible.

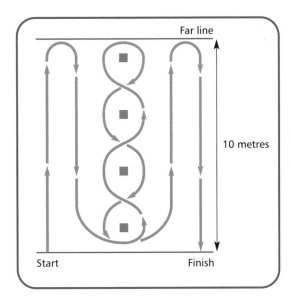

Illinois Agility Run: comparative scores (seconds)

	Males 15–16 years	Females 15–16 years
High score	Faster than 15.9	Faster than 17.5
Above average	15.9–16.7	17.5–18.6
Average	16.8–18.6	18.7–22.3
Below average	18.7–18.8	22.4–23.4
Low score	Slower than 18.8	Slower than 23.4

The importance of agility

We need a basic amount of agility to carry out our everyday tasks – for example, moving through a crowd of shoppers, getting on a train or bus or getting into a car. We need to maintain our agility as we get older, or it will deteriorate. Agility is closely linked to flexibility as it requires us to have a good range of movement of our joints.

Agility is important for most games and sports. Gymnasts, basketball players and skiers all need specific agility if they are to be successful. Only in static activities such as archery and shooting is agility of no importance.

Balance

Balance is the ability to maintain equilibrium whether stationary or moving.

To maintain our posture we must keep our equilibrium.

- **static balance** is the ability to maintain our equilibrium when stationary

- **dynamic balance** is the ability to maintain our equilibrium when moving.

Maintaining equilibrium means keeping the centre of gravity over the area of support. Our base of support is the area formed by those parts of the body which are in touch with the ground. For example, in a handstand we have a very small base of support, whereas in press-ups we have a very large base of support. If we do not keep our equilibrium we fall over. We maintain our balance through the co-ordinated actions of our eyes, our ears and the proprioceptive organs in our joints.

We can improve the balance needed in particular sports through practice and training. We can then put these skills to the test under the stress of competitive situations.

How do we measure our balance?

Dynamic balance is best measured by an expert watching us play our particular sport. Static balance can be measured in a number of ways. The Stork Stand described below is a test of static balance.

The Stork Stand

Stand comfortably on both feet and place your hands on your hips. Then lift one leg and place the toes against the knee of the other leg. On command, raise the heel and stand on your toes, balancing for as long as possible without letting either heel touch the floor or the other foot move away from the knee. Time your balance in seconds.

The Stork Stand: comparative scores (seconds)

	Males/females 15–16 years
High score	Above 49
Above average	40–49
Average	26–39
Below average	11–25
Low score	Below 10

The importance of balance

Without the ability to keep our balance, life would be impossible. Fortunately loss of the ability to balance is rare and few of us ever have to worry about it. It is only when taking up a new activity such as skiing that we realise that we have to learn how to balance.

Static balance is only seen in a few sports such as gymnastics – for example, when holding a handstand. But dynamic balance is very important in most sports; for example, snowboarders and surfers who have to move very fast over uneven surfaces and who have to constantly adjust their positions need very good dynamic balance.

Co-ordination

Co-ordination is the ability to carry out a series of movements smoothly and efficiently. This will happen if the nervous and muscular systems work well together. We talk about hand–eye co-ordination being necessary to catch a ball, and foot–eye co-ordination being necessary in football. Most of us are better co-ordinated on one side of our body and favour it in sport, for example, using a racket or throwing a ball with a particular hand.

Co-ordination improves with practice. Many of the toys we play with when young help to develop our hand–eye, foot–eye and whole-body co-ordination. Early PE lessons further develop our co-ordination through gymnastics and playing with balls, hoops and skipping ropes.

How do we measure co-ordination?

An expert watching us play our particular sport can make a very good assessment of our co-ordination.

Observers can also assess our hand–eye co-ordination using a test such as the Alternate Hand Wall Toss Test.

The Alternate Hand Wall Toss Test

Stand two metres away from a smooth wall. With your right hand throw a tennis ball against the wall and catch it in your left hand. Then throw it with your left hand and catch it with your right. Do this as quickly as possible for 30 seconds.

Alternate Hand Wall Toss Test: comparative scores

	Males/females 15–16 years
High score	Above 35
Above average	35–30
Average	29–25
Below average	24–20
Low score	Below 20

Juggling test

A fun way to test co-ordination is to try juggling with first two and then three balls. Some people are able to achieve the three balls juggling much more quickly than others.

The importance of co-ordination

We need to be well co-ordinated to cope with everyday life. Co-ordination is involved in every movement we make, from picking up a cup to cutting down a tree.

Good co-ordination is also essential for skilful performance in sport, from movements in gymnastics such as triple somersaults to saving penalties in football. We become only too aware of poor co-ordination when we try to learn a new sporting skill.

Timing

Timing is the ability to coincide movements in relation to external factors. It combines decision-making, co-ordination and reaction time, enabling us to be in the right place at the right time. Once there, we are able to control our body and the ball or implement that we are using. Sportspeople with good timing always seem to be unhurried when playing. As a result they are able to play consistently well. The mistimed movements of beginners are less likely to be as consistently accurate as those of experienced players.

How do we improve our timing?

Practice in drills and in competitive situations is the only way to improve our timing. Regular practice develops our ability to anticipate where we need to be. Anticipation helps us to improve our timing as we begin to move into position earlier.

As our timing improves, the speed with which we perform will increase. In net games, players can practise beating the ball/shuttlecock to where it is going. As their timing improves, they will find themselves in position waiting to play their shot.

How do we measure our timing?

There is no objective measure of good timing in sport. However, success rates in drills which include movement are a good indicator – for example, a hockey drill such as running to meet a cross and shooting first time. Eight shots on target out of every 10 attempts would indicate good timing. If a player misses the ball, or slices it wide on a number of attempts, this would suggest that his or her timing needs to be improved.

In many sports good timing is shown when the player is in position before the ball arrives. This can be practised (see above) or observed as a measure of timing.

Why is timing important?

Good timing reduces effort, improves performance and reduces the risk of injury. After a break from performing, sportspeople often report that they are 'off the pace' when they play. This refers to the fact that they are mistiming their movements. Once they are training regularly, their timing returns and they play far more effectively.

Speed of reaction (reaction time)

Speed of reaction (reaction time) is the ability to respond quickly to a stimulus.

A reaction can be simple, or it can involve choice.

- **Simple reaction time** is the time taken between the stimulus and our movement – for example, between the gun going off in a sprint race and a runner's first movement off the starting block.

- **Choice reaction time** is the time taken between the stimulus and an action which involves making a choice – for example, when we receive a ball from an opponent in a tennis match.

In both cases we have to react quickly; but in the first case, no choice has to be made. In the second case, we have to decide where and how to hit the ball. These decisions depend on where the ball is about to land, in which direction our opponent is moving and many other factors. We are therefore involved in making choices. The more skilled and experienced the player, the more likely he or she is to make the right choice and to hit the most appropriate type of return.

It is not possible to improve our simple reaction time through training. Speed of reaction to a single stimulus is due mainly to the efficiency of the nervous system. If we are lucky, our sensory and motor nerves will be capable of transmitting messages efficiently, and our muscles will get the message from our brain very quickly.

However, we can improve our choice reaction time a great deal through practice and experience. In a game like hockey, players will be receiving stimuli from their:

- **eyes**: about the position of the ball, other players and goal

- **ears**: from players, spectators and referee

- **kinaesthetic sense**: about their own body position and their options to pass, shoot, etc.

Skilled players can reduce their choice reaction time by focusing on important information. They can anticipate the action of other players and the movement of the ball. This skill is developed mainly through training and experience.

Movement time

Movement time is the time that we take to move once the decision to move has been made. If we have a high percentage of fast-twitch fibres, we will be able to respond faster than people with a high percentage of slow-twitch fibres. We can improve movement time by improving our power.

How do we measure our reaction time?

A number of computer programmes are available to measure reaction time.

The importance of reaction time

All of us have to respond quickly to situations in everyday life. Examples include driving a car, riding a bike and crossing the road. Quick reactions can often prevent accidents – sometimes even save lives.

Simple reaction time is very important in sporting activities such as the 100-

metre sprint on the track or in the pool. Choice reaction time is important in all games where we have to respond rapidly and effectively to the movements of other players, a ball, or both. However, movement time is critical in all sports and is most easily improved through training.

Fitness factors in sport

Study the photographs below, then write down the sport or sports in which you can see examples of the following fitness factors:

A Basketball

B Wrestling

C Fencing

D Hammer

E High jump

F Marathon

G Sprinting

H Gymnastics

- Good dynamic balance
- High level of cardiovascular fitness
- Extreme flexibility
- Appropriate body composition
- Muscular strength
- High level of power

- Muscular endurance
- Exceptional speed
- Considerable agility
- Skilful co-ordination
- Reaction time

activity

Fitness match

For this activity you will need to refer to the fitness match grid which links fitness testing with the planning of your PEP. If you do not have this, ask your teacher for a copy.

Using the grid, decide the fitness requirements of your chosen sport, test your levels of fitness and analyse your results.

Component of	Definition	Importance in sport	Measured by	Improved/developed by

The effect of fitness on performance and how to assess it

For your OCR examination there are seven tests of fitness that you should understand. These are:

1. The Multistage Fitness (Bleep) Test
2. The Cooper 12-minute Run
3. Sprint tests
4. The Sit and Reach Test
5. Press-up/NCF Abdominal Curl Test
6. The Illinois Agility Run
7. The Stork Stand Test.

In order to match fitness with activities, it is helpful to include more tests of fitness in any assessments made. Tests of co-ordination, muscular strength and muscular power will provide data that is essential when assessing suitability for activities that require those types of fitness.

Q QUESTIONS

9 Components of fitness

1 **What do we mean by:**

a   physical fitness?   *(3 marks)*
b   components of fitness?   *(3 marks)*
c   skill-related fitness?   *(2 marks)*

2 **Strength can be split up into:**

a   muscular endurance
b   muscular strength
c   muscular power.

Link these terms with the following definitions:

i   the amount of force a muscle can exert against a resistance

ii   the ability to contract our muscles in one explosive act

iii the ability to use our voluntary muscles many times without getting tired.

(3 marks)

3 **Give one test used to measure the following fitness components:**

a   balance
b   cardiovascular endurance
c   agility.

(3 marks)

4 **Consider the following three sporting actions:**

a   a sprinter starting a race
b   a high jumper at take-off
c   a surfer riding a wave.

For each action, state the main component of skill-related fitness required and explain why it is important to the performance.

(6 marks)

5 **Grace is a footballer who wants to improve her performance. She knows about the components of fitness.**

a   Explain what each of the following components mean when applied to football:

i   speed
ii   reaction time
iii co-ordination
iv   power.

(4 marks)

b   Suggest one method for measuring Grace's:

i   flexibility
ii   speed
iii muscular endurance
iv   power.

(4 marks)

c   Suggest one way in which Grace could improve her:

i   cardiovascular endurance
ii   flexibility
iii speed
iv   agility.

(4 marks)
(Total 32 marks)

10 Factors affecting fitness

Our sporting performance is influenced by many factors, including our ability and our training programme. We can influence our performance by the way that we live. A healthy lifestyle will help us to perform to our full potential. Our diet must be balanced and should match our sporting needs.

activity

Different sports, different people

All the sportspeople pictured here are performing well in their chosen sports. They have trained hard, but their body build and their lifestyle also help them. Working in small groups, look at the pictures and discuss the following questions:

- What is it about the body build (shape and size) of each person that helps them to excel at their sport?
- How will their training differ?
- Which person is likely to eat more food each day?
- Would you expect their diets to be different?

KEYWORDS

Carbohydrate loading: eating a large amount of carbohydrates before endurance events in order to increase the amount of glycogen available to working muscles

Cholesterol: fat-like substance found in blood which can build up on artery walls

Energy equation: term to describe the link between diet, weight and energy needs

Glycogen: chemical substance used to store glucose in the body

Nutrients: basic elements of food that provide nourishment for the body.

Key to Exam Success

For your GCSE you will need to know:

- the components of a balanced diet
- how our diet provides energy for sport
- why diet is important for sport
- how and what we should eat for our specific sports.

66 KEY THOUGHT 99

'Food for sport is food for thought.'

Why do we need a balanced diet?

To be healthy and successful in sport, we need to know about different food types, what makes a healthy diet and how food can provide us with the right energy for sport.

Why do we need food?

We need food for:

- energy
- repair
- growth
- good health.

We get energy from food in order to make our muscles work. Food contains the basic materials needed for growth and repair. We need many different **nutrients** for good health, and a balanced and varied diet will provide them. If we are following a regular training programme for our sport, we must plan our diet accordingly. We will need extra amounts of energy-producing foods, as well as sufficient foods to allow repair of tissues.

What is a balanced diet?

A balanced diet contains seven essential components:

- carbohydrates
- fats
- proteins
- vitamins
- minerals
- fibre
- water.

We should limit the amounts of the three main food types: carbohydrates, fats and proteins. The Department of Health recommends that a healthy diet should contain:

- 50–60% carbohydrates (mainly from starch and natural sugars)
- 25–30% fat (mainly from unsaturated fat)
- 10–15% protein (mainly from lean meat, fish, poultry and plants).

We should also:

- decrease the amount of salt that we eat
- increase the amounts of fibre, calcium and vitamin C that we eat.

Nutrients that provide energy

What are carbohydrates?
Carbohydrates are broken down in the body into different sugars. There are two types of carbohydrate:

- **Sugars** (simple carbohydrates): these are found in:
  - fruits
  - cakes
  - honey
  - biscuits
  - jam
  - beer
  - sweets
  - table sugar.

Highly processed food such as sweets will give us a quick supply of energy but no other nutrients. Biscuits and cakes often contain a lot of fat.

- **Starches** (complex carbohydrates): these are found in:
  - vegetables
  - rice and cereals
  - bread
  - pasta.

It is better to take most of our carbohydrates in the form of starches rather than sugars.

Why are carbohydrates important for exercise and energy production?

Carbohydrates give us the energy needed for our working muscles. We can also get energy from fats and proteins, but not as quickly or as efficiently as we can from carbohydrates.

Large amounts of carbohydrates are stored as **glycogen** in the liver and muscles. Small amounts are stored as glucose in the blood. Intense exercise quickly uses up these stores, so active sportspeople need plenty of carbohydrates in their diet. Extra carbohydrates can be stored as fat around the body.

Fats

Fats are broken down in the body into saturated and unsaturated fatty acids. There are two types of fats:

- **Saturated fats**: these are found in animal products, and in foods made from them. These include:
  - milk
  - meat
  - cheese
  - cream
  - butter
  - cakes
  - biscuits
  - chocolate.

Saturated fats can raise our cholesterol levels.

- **Unsaturated fats**: these are found in:
  - fish
  - nuts
  - corn
  - soya beans.

Why are fats important for exercise and energy production?

Fats provide energy, although much more slowly than carbohydrates. Fats need extra oxygen supplies to provide energy. Fats are the main source of energy when we are resting or asleep. They keep the skin in good condition, help to keep us warm and protect our vital organs. Extra fat is stored just under the skin. However, this extra weight will not help sportspeople. Too much fat can also lead to obesity and high cholesterol levels.

Cholesterol is a fat-like substance found in the blood. It is present in some foods, especially fatty animal products. Cholesterol which is not needed by the body builds up on our artery walls and may cause circulatory and heart problems.

Proteins

Proteins are broken down in the body into amino acids. There are two types of amino acids:

- **Non-essential amino acids**: for our bodies to function properly, we need 21 different amino acids. We can make 13 of these, which are called non-essential.

- **Essential amino acids**: these are the eight amino acids that we have to take from our food because we cannot make them for ourselves. They are found in both animal and plant foods.

Proteins are found in:

- fish
- meat
- milk
- cereals
- poultry
- beans
- eggs
- cheese
- peas
- nuts.

Proteins from animal products contain all the essential amino acids. However, plant proteins (with the exception of soya beans) lack some essential amino acids.

Why are proteins important for exercise and energy production?

Much of our body tissue is made up of protein, including our skin, bones and muscles. Proteins are needed for the repair, growth and efficient working of our tissues. Protein is only rarely used as an energy source, when no carbohydrate or fat is available. Excess proteins cannot be stored in the body as protein. They are either used as an energy source, stored as fat or excreted.

Nutrients that do not provide energy

Vitamins

Vitamins enable our bodies to work normally and efficiently. We cannot make vitamins. They must be supplied in our food. Some vitamins are water-soluble (vitamin C and the B vitamins). We need these vitamins in small regular amounts. Unfortunately, because they are water-soluble, they are washed out of foods during cooking.

Fat-soluble vitamins (such as vitamins A, D and E) can be stored by our body. We need to eat some foods containing fat in order to get these vitamins.

Sources of vitamins

Vitamin	Contained in:
A	Deep orange or yellow fruits and vegetables, dark-green vegetables, liver, codliver oil, dairy products
B1	Cereals, whole-grain bread, yeast, milk, potatoes, fish, sunflower seed
C	Most fruits and vegetables; high concentration in citrus fruits
D	Oily fish (mackerel, salmon, tuna), liver, codliver oil, butter, eggs
E	Beans, nuts, seeds, green, leafy vegetables, egg yolk, codliver oil

Why are vitamins important for exercise?

Vitamins do not provide energy. They regulate the activities of the body. They help in the working of muscles and in the release of energy from food. They also play a role in the growth and repair of body tissues.

The function of vitamins

Vitamin	Function
A	For good vision and healthy skin
B	Energy production, stress reduction
C	Fights viruses, keeps skin and gums healthy, heals wounds
D	Helps to build bones and teeth
E	Protects cells, helps immune system, aids growth

The function of minerals

Mineral	Function
Calcium	Strengthens bones and muscles
Iron	Aids production of red blood cells, helps get oxygen to the muscles, prevents fatigue
Magnesium	Helps muscles to contract and relax
Potassium	Aids muscle contraction, maintains normal blood pressure
Sodium	Maintains body fluid levels, aids muscle contraction

Minerals

Minerals are substances found in a variety of foods which enable the body to work normally and efficiently. They do not provide energy, and the body cannot make its own minerals.

Sources of minerals

Mineral	Contained in:
Calcium	Milk, sardines and salmon with bones, vegetables, beans
Iron	Spinach, dark-green vegetables, liver, red meat, beans, peas, nuts
Magnesium	Dark-green vegetables, nuts, soya products
Potassium	Bananas, dried fruit, meat, vegetables, sunflower seeds
Sodium	Table salt, soy sauce, preserved meat, crisps, canned foods

We need small but regular amounts of minerals, and a balanced diet can provide them all. Too much of some minerals can be harmful: for example, sodium in the form of salt can cause increased blood pressure.

Why are minerals important for exercise?

All minerals have their own function in helping the body to work well.

Fibre

Fibre is also called roughage or dietary fibre. Fibre is the part of a plant that cannot be digested. It does not contain any nutrients. Fibre is found on the outside of seeds, in vegetables, fruits and nuts.

Why is fibre important for exercise?

Fibre does not provide energy but adds bulk to our food. This helps the food to move through our digestive system and prevents constipation. Fibre is also involved in food absorption. It slows down the release of sugars from our food so that we get a more even release of energy. Dietary fibre adds bulk without adding extra kilojoules. A high level of fibre helps us to lose weight and to maintain good health.

Water

Although water does not provide energy, it is essential for living. It comes from the fluids we drink and the food we eat. We lose water in our sweat, urine, faeces and in the air we breathe out. About two-thirds of our body weight is made up of water. It is the main component of blood and cells. As part of the blood, water carries nutrients, electrolytes, blood cells and waste products around the body.

Water in our blood also helps to control our body temperature by absorbing heat produced during exercise. This heat is then carried to the skin where it is lost to the air. Water helps to cool the body when it evaporates on the surface of the skin in the form of sweat. Heat is also lost in the water vapour in the air that we breathe out. Loss of water can lead to dehydration and heatstroke. An adequate supply of water is vital during training, especially for strenuous exercise in the heat.

How do overeating and undereating affect sporting performance?

Imagine that you have been asked to compete in a sports tournament, but that you have to carry your rucksack when playing! You would be very quick to complain that your chances of success were being harmed by the extra weight you had to carry.

It is easy to see that being overweight or obese will slow you down when sprinting, make you less able to twist and turn in a games situation and will prevent you from doing well in a long-distance race. Long-distance runners keep their weight down to reduce the load they have to carry. The lighter the load, the further and faster they can run.

Some sports such as wrestling, boxing and weight lifting have fixed weight categories. Despite being able to compete when very heavy, top performers will have much more muscle than fat, because whilst eating a lot of food they will also be training very hard.

Other sports such as gymnastics, long-distance running and horse racing require

athletes to be very light. Controlled diets are essential for these athletes to avoid problems caused by rapid weight loss through crash diets. Although they need to be light, they must make sure that they have enough energy reserves to compete and enough vitamins and minerals to stay healthy.

What is an ideal body size?

The ideal body size for sport depends on the needs of the individual sport or the position the person plays in the game. For example a height of 1.9 metres would be short for a top basketball player but very tall for a gymnast. In rugby, we see players of various heights and weights.

Scientists are able to work out how much of our body is fat. The rest of our body weight is called fat-free and includes bone, muscle, organs and connective tissue.

In most sports, the higher the percentage of a participant's body is fat, the poorer the performance. Therefore most sportspeople try to keep their body fat low and their fat-free weight (i.e. muscle weight) high. However, this is not the case for long-distance runners. They must keep both their fat and non-fat weight as low as possible as they have to carry all extra weight for the length of the race.

Standard height–weight tables suggest a range of weights for a particular height but they do not help sportspeople to estimate their optimum weight because they do not allow for body composition. Being 'overweight' is not a problem if it is composed of extra muscle. Some people are 'heavily built'. Their bone structure is large and they have bigger muscle girth. This is often an advantage in sport. However, being overfat can certainly reduce sporting performance.

Food for sport

How do we get enough energy for sport?

When we work hard, the energy we use comes from stores of **glycogen** in the body. Glycogen is made from carbohydrates and also from fats. Our stores of glycogen are limited. To have enough energy for endurance activities we need to eat extra carbohydrates, which build supplies of glycogen. This is called **carbohydrate loading**. When carbohydrate-loading, we reduce our level of exercise for at least three days before competition. At the same time we increase the amount of carbohydrate (pasta, rice, etc.) in our diet.

Carbohydrates or fats?

Our bodies use carbohydrates, in the form of glycogen, and fats to produce energy. The mixture used depends on the length and intensity of the activity.

For example:

- When resting we use mainly fats.
- On a long walk we will also 'burn' mainly fat.
- If we start jogging we will begin to use glycogen.
- If we jog for a couple of hours, our glycogen stores will be used up and we will begin to utilise fats.
- Sprinting will lead to our muscles using glycogen.

Endurance training teaches our body to use more fat during exercise. This helps our limited supplies of carbohydrates to last longer.

Proteins are only rarely used as an energy supply. This happens when all other energy supplies have been used.

Eating for sport

We need to plan how we eat before, during and after exercise.

Before exercise we should:

- eat our main meal at least three to four hours and our snack meal at least one to two hours before exercise, to allow time for digestion
- include starches such as bread, cereal and fruit, to give a slow, steady release of energy
- avoid simple sugars (sweets) because they increase our insulin level, which in turn reduces our blood glucose and makes us feel tired
- avoid foods which are high in fat and protein as they take longer to digest
- include plenty of fluids to avoid dehydration.

During exercise we should:

- continue to drink water, not waiting until we feel thirsty, but taking small sips regularly
- drink a glucose-based sports drink if the activity lasts for more than one hour.

After exercise we should:

- eat foods rich in carbohydrates within an hour of exercising, even if we do not feel hungry, to restore glycogen stores quickly
- drink plenty of water to replace lost fluids.

Which sports foods will improve performance?

Food supplements for athletes are widely available and sports drinks are heavily advertised. Creatine monohydrate is becoming popular as it can help in the production of energy and in the recovery process. When we are trying to perform at our peak we are easily tempted to buy these products. However, we need to look at the scientific evidence and decide for ourselves if the product will really help us.

Drinks

We only need to drink plain water before and during activities lasting 60 minutes or less.

Sports drinks containing carbohydrates and electrolytes (sodium, potassium, chloride and magnesium) can enable us to work hard for longer if our activity lasts more than 60 minutes.

Sports drinks can help after exercise as they help to restore lost fluids, energy and minerals. They also provide useful nutrition during whole-day tournaments. But there is no need to buy sports drinks containing extra vitamins. We do not lose vitamins when we sweat and a balanced diet should supply all the vitamins we need.

Food and food supplements

A high-carbohydrate diet will allow us to work hard for longer, but we must also train well in order to do this. If we are training very hard, our diet should consist of 65–70% carbohydrates, but we should not increase fat consumption even if we are training very hard.

What does it say on the label?

Collect a label from a sports energy drink and a snackbar. The labels will contain details about energy levels and other nutritional information. Compare a sports energy drink with an 'ordinary' fruit-based drink, or compare an energy bar with an ordinary snackbar.

Investigate and compare the claims made for each product. Some products have their own websites, but other information is also available on the internet. Decide whether or not you think the energy drink or snackbar will improve your sporting performance.

Remember also:

- Extra protein in the diet does not help to make extra muscle: it is broken down and stored as fat or used for energy. Using correct training techniques is the only way to increase muscle size.

- High-protein foods are difficult to digest and we should not eat them before training or competing.

- Creatine is found in large quantities in red meat. Our bodies can make it from amino acid.

Body type

Using a method of body typing known as **somatotyping**, it is possible to classify the enormous range of different body types into three main categories: **endomorphs**, **mesomorphs** and **ectomorphs**.

In practice, these extreme body types are rare. We are all part-endomorph, part-mesomorph and part-ectomorph. We can be given a score (from 1–7) for each of these basic body types. For example: 2, 6, 3 means: low endomorphy (2 out of 7); high mesomorphy (6 out of 7); and low ectomorphy (3 out of 7). In this way

we can compare our body type with that of other people. Height is not taken into account in working out our body type.

Somatotyping is too lengthy and complicated a procedure to carry out in college and school. But it is interesting to look at our athletics team and sort the athletes into approximate body types. The throwers are likely to be endomorphs, the long-distance runners ectomorphs and the sprinters mesomorphs.

Body type and sport

Most successful sportspeople are high in mesomorphy. They are suited to sports requiring explosive strength and power. Their muscular bulk also helps them in contact sports.

Those who are high in endomorphy are likely to do well in sports needing power but only limited movement, such as weight lifting and wrestling.

People who are high in ectomorphy may be successful at long-distance events such as running or cycling. By developing muscular strength they may also do well in many non-contact sports. Tall ectomorphs may find that they are suited to basketball and high jump.

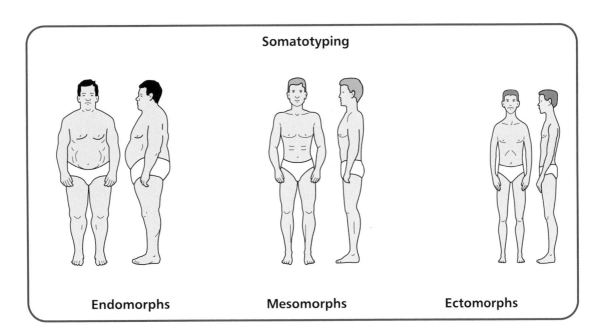

Somatotyping

| Endomorphs | Mesomorphs | Ectomorphs |

How does age affect performance?

Childhood and adolescence

We grow very quickly in the first two years of our lives. Our rate of growth then slows down until we reach puberty. We then grow very rapidly, with girls reaching full height at about 16 and a half years, and boys reaching full height at about 18 years.

If we exercise regularly during childhood and adolescence, we are likely to establish a healthy pattern of activity for the rest of our life. Exercise also helps our bones to grow properly.

As our nervous system grows, our balance, agility and co-ordination improve. Children have much more control over their movements as their body systems develop.

Their performances in most sports will improve as they approach physical maturity. However, in some sports, for example women's gymnastics, a mature body may not necessarily be an advantage.

Training can improve the strength, aerobic capacity and anaerobic capacity of young sportspeople. Training programmes must be designed for specific age groups. During childhood, strength can be increased by careful resistance training. But care must be taken not to damage the growth areas at the end of our long bones by, for example, heavy weight training before our bones are fully formed.

Physical maturity and beyond
Sports records suggest that we are in our prime for most sports during our twenties. After this age, our physical powers in both strength and endurance activities decline by about 1–2% a year.

From our mid-twenties:

- Our MHR decreases at about the rate of one beat per minute per year. As a result the training threshold is lowered.

- Our arteries gradually lose their elasticity. This increases our blood pressure and reduces the blood flow to our working muscles.

- Our maximum stroke volume, heart output and the vital capacity of our lungs all steadily decrease. These changes mean that less oxygen is carried to our working muscles and our VO_2 Max decreases.

- Our maximum strength decreases because our muscles reduce in size.

- Our muscle fibres change to slow-twitch rather than fast-twitch.

- Our body fat builds up steadily over the years, leading to increased weight. We exercise less, eat more and are less able to make use of fat for energy.

Our steady decline in physical ability is due mainly to a reduced amount of regular aerobic activity. However, we can slow down the effects of ageing on our cardiovascular and muscular systems by continuing to exercise.

How do gender differences affect performance?

Boys and girls mature at a similar rate and have similar body shapes and similar amounts of bone, muscle and fat until the age of about 9 or 10. Sporting competition between the sexes is quite fair at this stage.

Body size and shape
At puberty, boys develop larger bones and there is a big increase in their muscle size. This is due to the release of the hormone testosterone, an anabolic (growth-producing) steroid. Adolescent boys are larger and more muscular than girls.

For girls, the release of oestrogen results in breast development, broadening of the hips as well as increased body fat. Women have more fat in the hips and lower body, whilst men carry more fat in the abdomen and upper body.

Women have narrower shoulders, broader hips and smaller chest diameters. Women need wide hips for childbearing. As a result their legs are in a less mechanically efficient position for running.

None of these differences need affect the training programmes for girls and women, but they do have an effect on overall sporting performance.

Strength

Women are generally weaker than men. However, when their body size is taken into account, the differences are not significant. Men are much stronger in the upper body than women. When women train with weights, it is body tone which is increased rather than body size. With men, weight training helps muscles become larger and stronger because of their high levels of testosterone.

Aerobic capacity

Up to the age of 10, girls and boys have the same oxygen-carrying capacity. But while boys' capacity develops throughout puberty, girls stop improving after the age of 12. The best male competitors in endurance events are better than the best females by at least 30%. The differences are due to women's smaller lungs and hearts, as well as their smaller amount of blood. Women also have up to 30% less haemoglobin in their blood. This means that less oxygen reaches their working muscles.

None of these differences need affect the training programmes for girls and women. However, it is important that women take sufficient iron in their diet, as they lose iron in blood during menstruation.

The differences in times and distances achieved in sport between men and women are becoming smaller. It is vital that women have equal opportunity to take part in sporting activities and are given every encouragement to do so.

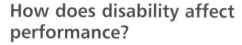

How does disability affect performance?

We can use the word disability to describe very many different physical and mental conditions. These can affect our ability to take part in sporting activities. Many sportspeople with disabilities are able to take part in equal competition with able bodied sportspeople. For some sportspeople their disability means that they must take part in a modified form of the sport. What is disability?

The term 'disability' usually refers to something that disables, or prevents, a person from taking part in an activity. However, disabilities need not prevent anyone from taking part in sport. Wheelchair athletics, tennis and basketball are examples of sports which have highly skilled and physically fit competitors throughout the world. Many sports have events which make them accessible to people who are blind, have learning difficulties or have physical impairments such as paralysis or loss of limbs.

Some of the effects of ageing can be considered to be disabilities. Our eyesight gets worse as we get older and we lose mobility. Older people may also suffer from diseases such as arthritis which causes inflammation and pain in the joints. These are part of the natural ageing processes but need not prevent sportspeople continuing to be active into old age.

What kinds of fitness do sportspeople with disabilities need?

Sportspeople with disabilities need to be just as fit as their able-bodied counterparts. Technology has provided state-of-the-art sports wheelchairs and artificial limbs which aid performance. Other disabilities are overcome through a range of modifications to their sport. For example, blind skiers hurtle down mountainsides following guides who call out instructions. Blind sprinters, runners and high jumpers compete with the aid of sighted 'callers' or guides. Nathalie Du Toit is a swimmer who continues to compete at the highest international level despite losing a leg in a road accident. These athletes need to train as

intensively as able bodied athletes. They
need high levels of the appropriate skill-
related components of fitness.
Paralympic and other disability sports
events are often fiercely competitive and
in many cases disability is not a
hindrance to sporting excellence.

ugs

Drugs are chemical substances that can affect our bodies. Medical drugs are made to fight illness and disease. The use of banned drugs in sport is known as **doping**. As sportspeople we need to know about the potential dangers of social and performance-enhancing drugs.

activity

Guilty or not guilty?

Name: Alain Baxter

Sport: Slalom skiing

Event: 2002 Winter Olympics (bronze medal)

Tested positive for: Methamphetamine, a banned stimulant

Defence claim: Baxter regularly uses a nasal inhaler which does not contain any banned substance. He bought the same brand of inhaler in the USA without realising that it contained the banned stimulant methamphetamine.

Name: Kelli White

Sport: Athletics

Event: 100 and 200 metres World Championships, Paris 2003 (gold medallist for 100 metres and 200 metres)

Tested positive for: Modafinil, a stimulant

Defence claim: Drug is not on the IAAF banned list. It was prescribed to her to treat sleepiness caused by narcolepsy (sleeping sickness).

Name: Mark Bosnich

Sport: football

Event: Random testing

Tested positive for: Cocaine, an illegal banned stimulant

Defence claim: He took the drug unwittingly as his drink had been spiked on a night out.

Discuss the drug abuse cases above. Imagine you are one of the panel members meeting to decide whether or not the athlete should be banned from sport. In making your decision you should consider the effects on:

- the athlete who has tested positive
- other athletes in the same competition
- athletes in the sport worldwide
- young people who may see the athlete as a role model.

Social drugs

Name of drug	Type of drug	General effect
Alcohol	Depressant	Slows down how body works
Amphetamines	Stimulant	Speeds up nervous system. Fights fatigue
Caffeine	Stimulant	Increases heart rate. Increases alertness
Cannabis	Depressant	Reduces worry but slows down responses
Cocaine	Stimulant	Speeds up the nervous system. Creates feeling of well-being
Ecstasy	Stimulant	Increases confidence and sense of well-being
LSD	Hallucinogen	Changes way we see and understand things
Nicotine (tobacco)	Stimulant	Increases heart rate. Increases concentration level

When we play sport we often become part of a social group that meets after training and after competition. Adult sportspeople often meet in bars. Many sports clubs earn money from running a successful clubhouse bar. The drugs that are available within social situations are known as **social drugs**. Some are legal and are widely used. Other social drugs are illegal, but are still used by a number of people.

Social drugs are usually taken to help people to relax or to give users an enjoyable experience. We need to know about each social drug and how social drugs can affect sporting performance.

There are many different social drugs and each has a different effect. The most common are listed above. Of the drugs listed above, only alcohol, caffeine and nicotine are legal in the UK.

Social drugs and sport

Alcohol

Alcohol has a number of effects on our sports performance.

- **Reduced co-ordination, slower reaction time and poorer balance**: these changes affect our movements and skills, especially where catching and balance are involved, and reduce the steadiness needed in sports such as archery, gymnastics and shooting.

- **Dehydration**: alcohol is a diuretic and increases urine production. This leads to water loss from the body. Dehydration seriously affects performance in endurance events and on hot days.

- **Lower muscle glycogen levels and slower removal of lactic acid**: muscle glycogen is needed during endurance events. Lactic acid is produced during exercise and must be removed quickly. Drinking alcohol before any sport involving endurance will reduce performance and delay recovery afterwards.

- **Rapid loss of heat**: alcohol causes the blood vessels in the skin to open up. We lose heat quickly through our skin, which reduces our body temperature, although we feel warm. If we are in a cold environment, hypothermia can develop.

- **Longer injury recovery time**: RICE (see page 270) is used to reduce the blood flow to an injured area. Alcohol has the opposite effect. Recovery time will be increased. If you receive an injury during a match you should not drink alcohol afterwards.

- **Reduced size of arteries**: alcohol reduces the size of the arteries, so that less blood can flow along them. Heart rate and blood pressure both increase.

Alcohol also affects our:

- thinking, judgement, vision and hearing

- stomach (and can cause vomiting)

- liver, as it takes a long time to process

- weight, as it is very high in kilojoules.

Nicotine

Smoking has many effects on our sporting performance:

Smoking and sport do not go together.

- **Reduced lung efficiency**: the smoke damages the hairs lining the bronchial tubes. Dust is not removed from the air so our lungs become clogged and do not work efficiently. We need efficient lungs for all sport.

- **Reduced oxygen-carrying ability**: carbon monoxide is taken into the lungs in cigarette smoke and passes into the blood. It attaches to red blood cells, reducing the amount of oxygen we can carry in our blood. This affects endurance activities.

- **Reduced fitness level**: even if we train hard, our fitness level will be reduced because of the damage to our lungs and circulatory system caused by smoking.

- **Lowered resistance to illness**: colds are caught more often and smokers take longer to recover from chest infections. Smoker's cough is a special hazard, as is bronchitis. Sportspeople need to keep well to train and compete.

- **Raised blood pressure**: nicotine causes our brain to release hormones which make the heart beat faster and the blood vessels in the skin to contract. This causes an increase in blood pressure and a feeling of being cold.

Smoking also affects our:

- **life expectancy**: smokers are at much higher risk of cancer and cardiovascular disease.

- **social standing**: we breathe harmful and unpleasant fumes on people around us. We also smell of stale tobacco.

- **senses**: by dulling our sense of taste and smell.

- **appetite**: by reducing it.

Other social drugs

- **Amphetamines** increase heart rate and blood pressure. They hide symptoms of fatigue and reduce feelings of pain. They are addictive and can cause anxiety and aggression.

- **Caffeine** is a mild stimulant found in tea, coffee and many soft drinks. It increases heart rate and blood pressure. This is not useful to endurance athletes.

- **Cannabis**, or **marijuana**, can result in lack of motivation and poor judgement. Since it is smoked, it causes the same problems as cigarette smoking. It has no role to play in sport.

- **Cocaine** is a highly addictive stimulant. It encourages us to think that we are doing better than we are. This is no help in sport, where good judgement is essential.

- **Ecstasy** is a stimulant with mild hallucinogenic properties. It is not useful in sport because it affects our perceptions. Performance can also be affected the day after Ecstasy has been used, because of the negative effects of the 'come down'.

- **LSD** distorts reality and affects the ability to perceive situations and make decisions. The effects of LSD can often be felt in the form of 'flashbacks' long after the drug has been taken. This drug has no place in sport.

Performance-enhancing drugs

Some sportspeople try to gain an unfair advantage by using banned drugs. This is illegal and sometimes dangerous. We need to know how **performance-enhancing drugs** work and how they can affect sporting performance.

Performance-enhancing drugs take many forms. In the table below, drugs that have similar effects are grouped together:

Some drugs are restricted in certain sports, but are not completely banned. These include all the illegal social drugs and alcohol.

Other restricted drugs

Drug	General effect
Beta blockers	Keep heart rate and blood pressure low, reduce tremble in hands; banned in archery and shooting
Corticosteroids (Cortisone)	Reduce inflammation and pain, masking effects of injury
Local anaesthetics	Reduce pain, masking effects of injury

Other proscribed methods of enhancing performance are:

- blood doping (see page 204)

- changing blood samples, or interfering with them in any way

- using masking agents to hide the use of a performance-enhancing drug.

Doping class	Examples	General effect
Anabolic agents	Nandrolone, Testosterone, Stanozolol, Clenbuterol THG	Reduced recovery time allows users to train harder and for longer. Increased muscle bulk and endurance when combined with regular exercise
Analgesics (narcotic)	Morphine, Methadone, Heroin	Pain-killing effect allows training and competing to continue even in times of injury
Diuretics	Frusemide, Probenecid	Rapid weight loss as result of reduction of fluid levels in body
Peptides, glycoprotein hormones and analogues	Human Growth Hormone (HGH), Erythropoietin (EPO)	Decreased fat mass. Thought to improve performance Increased number of red blood cells, more oxygen carried to body, endurance improved
Stimulants	Amphetamines, Cocaine, Ephedrine	Speeds up nervous system, quickening reactions. Masks fatigue and feelings of pain

Prohibited drugs in sport

All the performance-enhancing drugs and methods described are banned throughout sport. Even nicotine and caffeine levels have to be below a prescribed limit in most sports.

The list of prohibited drugs contains over 1,000 substances and is regularly updated. Sportspeople must check the list before taking any medicine because some banned drugs are contained in standard medicines. These include the steroid clenbuterol, which is used in asthma treatment.

In January 2004 caffeine and pseudo-ephedrine (contained in many over-the-counter cold remedies) were removed from the banned substances list.

Sports performers must be aware that drugs can sometimes be found in the food supplements given to athletes by coaches. These include the steroids nandrolone and THG. A breakthrough in testing enabled the authorities to identify THG, and a number of athletes including world indoor 1,500 metres champion Regina Jacobs and British sprinter Dwain Chambers tested positive for it.

As a result of a number of positive drugs tests in 2003, UK Sport issued the following statement:

> 'No guarantee can be given that any particular supplement is free from prohibited substances as these products are not licensed and are not subject to the same strict manufacturing and labelling requirements as licensed medicines.'

In May 2003 Czech tennis player Bohdan Ulihrach was suspended after testing positive for nandrolone, an anabolic steroid. He was the first of a number of professional tennis players to test positive during 2002/3. He has now had his punishment cancelled, as the food supplement was supplied to him by trainers belonging to the ATP (Association of Tennis Professionals).

UK Sport's Nandrolone Review Group have given this advice:

> 'Competitors are strongly advised that using dietary supplements carries the potential risk of unknowingly taking a banned substance.'

Michele Verroken, Director of Drug-Free Sport at UK Sport, commented: 'Athletes should look at suitable alternatives to taking supplements, the main one of course being to eat a balanced and healthy diet.'

Steroids

Anabolic agents, or steroids, can be taken orally or by injection. They have positive effects upon performance because, when combined with extra exercise, they increase strength, muscle growth, body

Greg Rusedski was cleared of deliberately taking performance enhancing drugs in 2004.

weight and endurance. They enable sportspeople to train more often and harder. However, they have serious side-effects which, for men, include:

- increased aggression
- impotence
- kidney damage
- baldness
- development of breasts.

Disadvantages for women include:

- increased aggression
- development of male features including facial and body hair
- irregular periods.

Narcotic analgesics

Morphine, methadone and heroin are members of the opiate family. They have a positive effect on sporting performance by reducing the feeling of pain. By doing this they mask injury or illness and allow sportspeople to compete when they should not.

The dangers of taking narcotic analgesics are that:

- injuries can be made much worse and even permanent
- they are highly addictive.

Diuretics

Diuretics are mainly used by sportspeople in sports where they have to 'make the weight' – that is, to fit into a weight category. These include horse racing, boxing, weight lifting and martial arts. The diuretic works by removing fluid from the body as urine, so the result is rapid weight loss. They are also used to remove other drugs from the body in order to beat the drug-testers.

The side-effects of diuretics include:

- dehydration
- cramps
- dizziness
- headaches
- nausea.

These conditions seriously affect the ability to play sport.

Jockeys must make the weight.

Peptide and glycoprotein hormones and analogues

These hormones are produced naturally in the body. Analogues are the same hormones produced artificially.

Erithropoietin (EPO) improves endurance by increasing the number of oxygen-carrying red blood cells. The disadvantages of using this type of drug are that it may:

- thicken the blood, so increasing the risk of a stroke and heart problems

- cause oily skin, acne and muscle tremors.

Blood testing for EPO has been introduced, in addition to taking urine samples, at many endurance events as the authorities have sought to keep sport drug-free.

Human Growth Hormone (HGH) encourages muscle growth, increases the use of fat and improves the body's ability to cope with fatigue. The dangers of this type of drug are that it may cause:

- abnormal growth, including enlargement of internal organs

- atherosclerosis and high blood pressure

- diabetes, arthritis and impotence.

Stimulants

Drugs such as amphetamines, ephedrine and cocaine can lead to an improvement in performance because they give a 'lift', keeping us awake and competitive, speeding up reflexes and reducing feelings of fatigue.

The dangers are that they:

- increase heart rate and blood pressure

- hide symptoms of fatigue, putting high levels of strain on the body that can even be fatal

- reduce feelings of pain with the risk of making injuries worse

- can lead to acute anxiety and aggressiveness

- are addictive.

Blood doping

Blood doping does not involve the use of drugs, but requires blood to be injected into the body to increase the number of red blood cells. Athletes usually inject their own blood, which has been removed earlier and stored, but blood can also come from another person. Blood doping makes the blood able to carry more oxygen to the working muscles. This increases aerobic endurance, an effect that can also be gained by training at altitude. Blood doping has a similar effect to the use of EPO.

Blood doping has several dangers:

- overloading the circulatory system, increasing blood pressure and causing difficulties for the heart

- kidney failure

- risk of transmission of AIDS and other diseases.

The campaign against doping in sport

The desire to win is very high amongst competitive sportspeople. If they believe that a drug will help them achieve their goal, they may be tempted to use it – and the temptation is even higher when success will lead to great financial rewards. The pressure to succeed, from the media and public as well as from coaches and managers, can be very great.

Many sports performers rationalise their decision to use drugs by arguing that other competitors are using drugs, and that without them they will have no chance of winning. Some use anabolic agents while being treated for injury in order to speed up the recovery process. To them, the practice is risky but acceptable. Although out-of-competition testing may catch them and lead to a ban, they believe that they will not get caught and are prepared to cheat in order to win.

The case against doping

The International Olympic Committee (IOC) does not allow doping for three main reasons:

- to ensure that competition in sport is as fair as possible

- to protect the health of sportspeople

- to protect the image of sport.

Drug rules: who decides?

Each sport has its own international sports federation (ISF) which controls its

All samples must be provided under supervision.

minimum of two years. The competitor will also face a loss of earnings from competition and sponsorship and will have to live with the personal disgrace of being revealed as a cheat.

The continuing battle against drugs in sport

THG (Tetrahydrogestrinone)

As we have seen, anabolic steroids can improve a sportsperson's ability to train and compete at the highest level. They reduce the tiredness linked with training and the time required to recover after physical exertion. Steroids also promote the development of muscle tissue in the body which leads to an increase in strength and power.

Doping tests for steroids have been in place for a number of years, but recently a 'designer drug' based on the steroid THG (tetrahydrogestrinone) has been uncovered. This drug remained undetectable by the usual tests, until the United States Anti-Doping Agency (USADA) were given a syringe containing THG by an anonymous athletics coach. From this they were able to develop an effective test for the substance. Urine samples taken during an out-of-competition test conducted by the IAAF in August were re-tested using the new method, resulting in a number

activities worldwide. The ISFs make their own rules about doping. In the case of Olympic sport, the sport must also follow the drug code of the International Olympic Committee (IOC). Each governing body in a country has the responsibility for testing sportspeople in and out of competition. In Britain, drug-testing is co-ordinated at the London office of UK Sport, with the support of national administrators in England, Northern Ireland, Scotland and Wales.

What penalties do drug-takers face?

Competitors who are found guilty of taking banned drugs are often banned from competing in their sport for a

activity

Looking for doping offences

Imagine that you are a member of the UK Sport drug-testing team.

1 List all the banned and restricted types of drugs.

2 Make a list of sports in which you would be likely to encounter each type of drug. Conduct an internet search to confirm that each of the drugs on your list has been found in the sports that you have indicated.

Dwain Chambers tested positive for the designer steroid THG and in February 2004 was banned from competition for two years.

Rio Ferdinand (Manchester United and England), was found guilty of failing to turn up for a drugs test. He received an eight-month ban from the game in 2004.

of positive tests, including that of the British sprinter, and European 100-metres champion, Dwain Chambers.

The International Anti-Doping Code

A world conference on doping in sport in 2003 agreed an Anti-Doping Code which came into force at the start of the 2004 Olympics in Athens.

The code works on the principle of strict liability, whereby sportsmen and women are responsible for any prohibited substances found in their system, regardless of whether or not they have performance-enhancing capabilities. The main reason for this new code is to protect those athletes who do not cheat.

QUESTIONS

10 Factors affecting fitness

1 Name the component of a balanced diet which is:

a essential for growth and tissue repair
b an aid to digestion
c the main source of energy for exercise.

(3 marks)

2

a Which mineral is used in the formation of bone?

b Which vitamin helps healing and fights viruses?

(2 marks)

3 Which somatotypes are usually found competing in the following events:

a sprinting
b marathon running
c Sumo wrestling?

(3 marks)

4 Ross is a keen rugby player who wants to increase his strength and body weight. He has changed his diet and started a weight-training programme.

a Name two food types that Ross should eat regularly to provide the energy for his new training programme.

(2 marks)

b Why should Ross's diet include protein?

(2 marks)

c Explain what fibre is, and why it is important in any diet.

(2 marks)

d A man at the gym has suggested that Ross should take a drug to gain weight and strength more quickly. Name the type of drug that is likely to have been recommended.

(1 mark)

e List two side-effects that might result from regular use of the drug.

(2 marks)

f Name the type of drug that might be offered to Ross to mask the use of the first drug.

(1 mark)

g The use of banned drugs is a problem in many sports. Give three reasons why sportspeople might be tempted to use banned drugs.

(3 marks)

h Describe the effects of EPO on the body and explain how this drug improves performance in endurance events.

(3 marks)
(Total 24 marks)

11 Fitness training principles

To be successful in sport, we need our energy systems and sporting skills to be at their highest possible level. We can reach these high levels by training. Training is a regular programme of exercise to improve performance. There are many different methods of training and ways of organising a training programme. We need to be sure that the training programme we follow is right for our sport and for our levels of fitness and skill.

activity

Training plans

The sportspeople below have made plans for their training programme. Read their plans and discuss positive and negative aspects of each.

- **Haythem and Saiful** live in the same street and have decided to train together throughout the summer holidays. Saiful is preparing for the rugby season. He is a prop forward in the school team. Haythem plays badminton for a local club and hopes to play for the district during the next season.

- **Carrie and Alexandra**: Carrie works at a local restaurant for three evenings a week. She and Alexandra play in the same netball team. They plan to train together every Thursday. Alexandra does not have a job. She will also train on Sunday and Tuesday each week.

- **Colin and Christopher**: Colin has been running for the county cross-country team for two years. Chris has decided to take up cross-country running, but has never played any other sport. He and Colin have agreed to train together four times a week for the next month.

- **Oliver** wants to improve his stamina. He is planning to go to a circuit training session at the local sports centre every Wednesday afternoon.

KEYWORDS

Aerobic activity: working with sufficient oxygen for the muscles

Anaerobic activity: working without sufficient oxygen for the muscles

Fartlek: 'speed play' – a method of training in which pace and training conditions are varied

FITT principles: Frequency, Intensity, Time, Type – the basis for planning a fitness programme

Peaking: producing your best performance at the right time

Periodisation: dividing a training programme into different parts, for example pre-season, peak season and off-season

Plyometrics: a training method using explosive movements to develop muscular power, for example, bounding and hopping

Progression: gradually increasing the amount of training or exercise you do

Overload: making the body work harder than normal to improve fitness

Recovery rates: length of time required for the cardiorespiratory system to return to normal after activity

Reversibility: loss of improvement when training is decreased or stopped

Specificity: the principle that training must closely resemble the sporting activity and be tailored to individual needs in order for improvement to take place

SPORT-P principles: Specificity, Periodisation, Overload, Reversibility, Tedium, Peaking – principles on which to base a training programme

Tedium: the principle that training methods must be varied to prevent boredom and overuse injuries

Training threshold: minimum rate at which heart must work to bring about fitness improvements

Training zone: range of heart rate within which a specific training effect will take place.

Key to Exam Success

For your GCSE you will need to:

■ know how training can be planned to improve the components of fitness (health-related fitness) and skill-related fitness

■ understand and apply the SPORT-P and FITT principles to a training programme.

❝ KEY THOUGHT ❞

'Thoughtful training delivers the goods.'

Training for success

In order to make steady progress while training and to avoid injury, we should follow the **SPORT–P** principles:

- Specificity
- Progression
- Overload
- Reversibility
- Tedium
- Peaking.

Specificity

Our training must be **specific** to our sport and our individual needs. Every type of exercise has a particular effect on the body. The type of training we choose must be right for the type of improvement we want to see.

If we want to improve the strength of our arms, running will not help: we must use strength-training exercises that work our arms. We must always use a training programme that puts regular stress on the muscle groups or body system that we want to develop.

Our training programme must also be designed to suit the needs of our sport. For example:

- Sprinters need to include a lot of speed work in their training. This helps their fast-twitch muscle fibres to develop.

- Endurance athletes need to develop their slow-twitch muscle fibres. They need to train over longer distances or for a longer time.

- Games players need to include both speed and endurance training in their programmes to develop both types of muscle fibres.

Progression

Our body takes time to adapt to more or harder exercise. We must build up the stress on our bodies in a gradual, or **progressive**, way – by lifting heavier weights or running further. If we build up the stress too quickly, we may injure ourselves or find the challenge too great and give up. If we build up the stress too slowly, we may become bored and give up.

The body needs time to recover and adapt to training. Our bones, ligaments and tendons may take longer to change than our muscles or other body systems. Our training thresholds tell us if we are training at the right level.

If we are unfit we can improve our fitness level quickly. The fitter we are, the harder it is to improve.

Overload

To improve the fitness of our body systems we need to work them harder than normal. The body will then adapt to the extra stress and we will become fitter.

We can **overload** our bodies by training more often, by working harder or by spending more time on an exercise. For example, to improve aerobic fitness by running, we could:

- run more times a week
- complete the run in a shorter time
- increase the distance we run.

Each of these methods will overload the aerobic system. The aerobic system will gradually adapt to cope with the overload and we will become fitter.

Reversibility

Just as our bodies adapt to the stress of exercise by becoming fitter, they also quickly adapt to less exercise by losing fitness. If our muscles are not used, they atrophy or waste away. We cannot store fitness for future use. It will disappear if we stop training. It takes only 3–4 weeks for our bodies to get out of condition.

We lose our aerobic fitness more easily than our anaerobic fitness. This is because our muscles quickly lose much of their ability to use oxygen. Our anaerobic fitness is less affected by not training. If we follow a strength-training programme for four weeks, we will lose the extra strength we have gained after about 12 weeks of inactivity.

Tedium

Our training programme must be varied to avoid **tedium**, or boredom. By using a variety of different training methods we will keep our enthusiasm and motivation. For example:

- We can follow a long workout with a short one, a hard session with a relaxed one or a high-speed session with a long, slow one.

- We can change where we train and when we train.

- We can avoid overuse injuries by varying the way we train. For example, shin splints can be avoided by running on grass rather than on hard roads.

Peaking

Peaking means producing your best performance at the right time. This will vary for different sports, but for most of us it will mean aiming for a major championship or cup final. Professional sportspeople need to maintain a high level of performance throughout their season. However, they will still wish to peak for their most important occasion.

In order to peak at the right time we must arrange our training programme and competition to ensure that we are in the best possible physical and mental condition to achieve our goal for the season.

activity ☺☺☺

Evaluating a training programme
Examine the following training programmes. Decide how far you think each programme has been based on the principles outlined above. Summarise your findings and be prepared to discuss them with the whole class.

activity

Programme 1: Six-week programme for Sharon, a cross-country runner

	Monday	Tuesday	Wednesday	Thursday	Friday	Saturday	Sunday
Week 1 programme	10-mile run	Gym work, concentrating on upper body strength	Fartlek	Track work, 400-metre repetitions ×10	Rest day	Race	30-minute swim, continuous lengths
Following 5 weeks	No change	Increase weights gradually	Increase total distance run	Reduce rest time between repetitions	Rest day	Race	No change

Programme 2: Six-week programme for Errol, a badminton player

	Monday	Tuesday	Wednesday	Thursday	Friday	Saturday	Sunday
Week 1 programme	Skill practice for 1 hour	Endurance training on court – 1 hour	Light weights (high reps.) in gym	Gym work: 30-min. run, 20-min. bike, 20-min. rowing	Match practice	Stretching and plyometrics	League game
Following 5 weeks	No change	No change	Increase speed and reps.	Increase work rate	No change	No change	League game

Programme 3: Six-week programme for Mandy, a football player

	Monday	Tuesday	Wednesday	Thursday	Friday	Saturday	Sunday
Week 1 programme	5-aside matches	Power lifting in the gym	Match	Rest day	10-mile run	Match	Rest day
Following 5 weeks	No change	Heavier weights	No change	No change	No change	No change	No change

Programme 4: Six-week programme for Ahmed, a swimmer

	Monday	Tuesday	Wednesday	Thursday	Friday	Saturday	Sunday
Week 1 programme	100-metre repetitions – various strokes ×20	200-metre repetitions – various strokes ×10	1 hour technique improvement, including turns	2 miles continuous – fast	1 hour technique improvement, including turns	Competition	5 miles continuous lengths
Following 5 weeks	Reduce time for both reps. and recovery	Reduce time for both reps. and recovery	No change	No change	No change	No change	No change

Sharon **Errol** **Mandy** **Ahmed**

activity 😊😊😊

Summary sheet

	Specificity	Progression	Overload	Reversibility	Tedium	Peaking	Overall suitability
Prog 1							
Prog 2							
Prog 3							
Prog 4							

Thresholds of training

In order to improve our sporting performance, we need to know exactly how hard and for how long we should train. If we train at too low a level we will make little improvement in our fitness. If we try to train too hard, we will quickly become exhausted or be likely to suffer injury and as a result, will be unable to complete our training programme. We need to calculate our own individual **thresholds of training** so that we can work to best effect.

To train effectively we need to know:

- the amount of **anaerobic training** we need for our sport

- the amount of **aerobic training** we need for our sport

- our present level of fitness.

To calculate our individual threshold of training we can use our **Maximum Heart Rate (MHR)**. This can be estimated using the following formula:

- MHR (males) = 220 – age

- MHR (females) = 226 – age

Our **aerobic threshold** can then be calculated by working out 60% of our MHR. If we work above this level we will be improving our aerobic fitness.

Our anaerobic threshold can be calculated by working out 80% of our MHR. If we work above this level, we will be improving our anaerobic fitness.

	Males		Females	
	15 years	16 years	15 years	16 years
60% MHR Aerobic threshold	123	122	127	126
80% MHR Anaerobic threshold	164	163	169	168

Different sports require different amounts of aerobic and anaerobic fitness. For example, a marathon runner will rely almost entirely on aerobic fitness, whilst a 100-metre sprinter will not use aerobic fitness at all during the race. Sprinters need instant energy which is provided in the absence of oxygen. They will therefore need to develop their anaerobic fitness. Games players need both aerobic and anaerobic fitness and their training programmes will need to develop both types. The aerobic and anaerobic energy systems are dealt with in more detail on pages 246–248.

- **Aerobic training**: training our cardiorespiratory system to provide the working muscles with enough oxygen to work for a long period of time

- **Anaerobic training**: training our cardiorespiratory and muscular systems to work for a limited amount of time without enough oxygen

- **Aerobic threshold**: the minimum rate at which our heart must work in order to improve our aerobic fitness

- **Anaerobic threshold**: the minimum rate at which our heart must work in order to improve our anaerobic fitness.

 activity 😊😊 😊

Calculating training zones

*To achieve results, we must train in the appropriate **training zone**. Consider the following training sessions for Floella, Jim, Janice and Lee. Calculate their individual **aerobic** and **anaerobic thresholds** and decide in which training zone they are working.*

- **Floella** is a 26-year-old racing cyclist. During a sprint training session she tries to maintain her heart rate at 155 beats per minute.

- 30-year-old **Jim** is doing a cross-country run and has maintained a heart rate of 158 for the last 15 minutes.

- **Janice** is 18-years-old and is doing interval training. Today's training session involves her completing ten 60-metre sprints with her heart rate raised to 170 beats per minute.

- **Lee**, who is 47 years old, swims regularly and keeps his heart rate above 105 throughout his swim.

Planning a training programme

We need to train to improve our fitness and therefore our performance. When planning a fitness programme we should follow the **FITT principles**:

- Frequency
- Intensity
- Time
- Type.

Frequency – how often we train
- We should train at least three times a week to improve our fitness.
- Our body needs time to recover from each training session.
- We should spread these sessions out over the week.

Intensity – how hard we train
- We will only get fitter if we work our body systems hard enough to make them adapt.
- We must start at the right intensity, depending on our current fitness.
- We must understand and use our training thresholds.

Time – how long we train
- To improve aerobic fitness, our training sessions should last longer and our working heart rate should rise.
- Each session must last at least 20 minutes to achieve real benefit.

Type – what kind of training we do
- We should analyse our particular sport to know the fitness and skills we need.

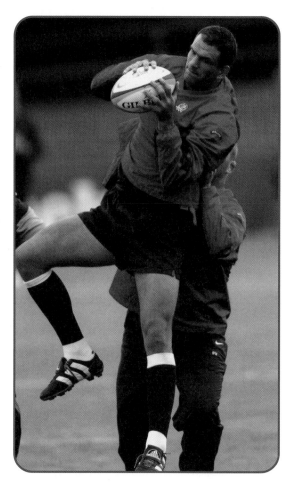

- Our training programme should include different types of activity to develop these skills and fitness.

Designing an individual training programme

The training programme for an elderly recreational tennis player would be very different from one for a young, competitive pole vaulter. We must design our training programme for:

- a particular sport
- a specific level of ability
- an individual sportsperson or group of sportspeople at a similar level of ability.

Before planning the programme we must find out about:

- the sport (skill requirements)

- the type of fitness needed (muscular strength, cardiovascular endurance, flexibility, muscular endurance, speed, agility, co-ordination, balance, speed of reaction and timing)

- the sportsperson's individual needs (age, health, fitness level, experience, sporting ability, motivation)

- the principles of training (SPORT-P: Specificity, Progression, Overload, Reversibility, Tedium, Peaking and FITT: Frequency, Intensity, Time, Type)

- the types of training available (continuous, Fartlek, interval, circuit, weight, flexibility, plyometric)

- the training year for the sport (pre-season, peak season, off-season).

Planning individual training sessions

To avoid injury and to get the most out of training, we should divide each session into three phases: warm-up, main activity and warm-down.

Warm-up

Our warm-up should include:

- gentle exercise for the whole body, such as light jogging. This gradually increases heart rate, breathing and blood supply to the muscles. It warms up our muscles and prepares us mentally for the session.

- gentle stretching, to prepare, muscles, ligaments and joints and to prevent injury

- practising techniques and skills to be used in the session.

Main activity

Our main activity could be fitness training, skill development or a combination of both, depending on our needs.

- **Fitness training**: our fitness activities will depend on the demands of our sport, but we can design fitness activities to develop skills as well. If training is too intense at the start of the session we may be too tired to practise our skills well later. However, games players need to practise their games skills when they are tired.

- **Skills development**: the skills and techniques practised will depend on the particular sport. We may need to work in pairs, in small groups, or in teams as well as on our own. We may play small-sided and modified games.

Warm-down

Every training session should end with a period of lighter exercise. Always avoid going from hard exercise immediately to rest. Light exercise during the warm-down decreases recovery time by helping to remove carbon dioxide, lactic acid and other waste products from the body. It also ensures that the blood continues to circulate well and prevents it pooling in the skeletal muscles, which may reduce blood pressure and cause dizziness.

While the muscles are thoroughly warm, flexibility exercises can be carried out with less chance of injury through over-stretching. Light exercise will also prevent muscle soreness and stiffness later.

How do we plan our training programme for a year?

If we take part in competitive sport we will naturally want to be at our best at the time of our most important competition. This is called **peaking**. Our training programmes will vary with the type of sport and the level of competition. We therefore need to plan well ahead. Dividing a training programme into different parts is called **periodisation**. For example, for many sports we could talk about three main periods: pre-season, peak season and off-season.

Pre-season
During the pre-season period you should:

- focus on fitness for your particular sport
- concentrate on muscular endurance, power and speed work
- develop techniques, skills and strategies.

Peak season
During the peak season you should:

- emphasise speed
- practise your skills at high speed and in competitive situations

- add extra fitness sessions if you do not compete enough.

Off-season
Following the competitive season, you need a period of active rest at first. You then need to:

- maintain a high level of general fitness through moderate activity
- develop muscular strength, flexibility and aerobic fitness
- develop your sports skills.

 activity

Planning an individual training session

Prepare a training session specific to your chosen sport. Be sure to consider periodisation. You must match what you include in the training session with the training period (pre-, peak or off-season) in which it is to fit. Include enough detail to allow someone else to lead the session.

QUESTIONS

11 Fitness training principles

1 **Specificity, progression, overload and reversibility are all principles of training. Link each one to these statements:**

a gradually increasing the work done

b working harder than normal

c closely resembling the sporting activity

d returning to original condition.

(4 marks)

2 **A games training session should always start with a warm-up. Name the other parts of a training session.**

(4 marks)

3 **Darren is a 16-year-old basketball player in training.**

a He wants to apply the SPORT-P principles of specificity, progression, overload, reversibility, tedium and peaking to his training programme. Select three of these principles. Explain what each means and give an example of the way in which Darren can apply each one in his training.

(6 marks)

b Darren has decided that he needs to develop both his aerobic and anaerobic capacity for basketball. Work out his aerobic and anaerobic thresholds.

(2 marks)

c Explain what is meant by periodisation when producing a year-long training programme.

(2 marks)

4 **Nisha is an enthusiastic 16-year-old footballer but finds it hard to get a regular place in the school team. She is advised to plan and follow a fitness programme based on the FITT principles of frequency, intensity, time and type.**

a Give two ways in which each of the FITT principles could be applied to her training programme.

(8 marks)

Nisha has been asked to take a football training session for some younger players. She plans to include five sections in this training session.

b Name each of the five sections she should use in this training session and give an example of an activity which she could include in each section.

(10 marks)

c Suggest two differences in the training carried out during pre-season and during peak season.

(2 marks)

(Total 38 marks)

12 Training methods

Success in sport only comes with dedicated training – and the key to success is to select the right methods of training. There are many different training methods available and it is important to understand their individual benefits and disadvantages. Together with the practical application of the principles of training, this will help you to achieve your potential in your chosen sport.

Understanding and applying the information in this chapter will enable you to create an effective **Personal Exercise Programme (PEP)**. This in turn will improve your sporting performance.

activity

Training for success
Look at these photographs of sportspeople in action. What methods of training do you think they used to reach this level of performance?

Discuss your ideas.

KEYWORDS

Aerobic activity: 'with oxygen'. If exercise is steady and not too fast, the heart can supply all the oxygen the muscles need

Anaerobic activity: 'without oxygen'. If exercise is done in short fast bursts, the heart cannot supply blood and oxygen to the muscles as fast as the cells can use them

Fartlek: 'speed play' – a method of training in which pace and conditions are varied

Interval training: any training using alternating periods of very hard exercise and rest

Isometric contraction: muscular contraction which results in increased tension but does not cause the length of the muscle to alter

Isotonic contraction: muscular contraction that results in limb movement

Personal Exercise Programme (PEP): a programme of training drawn up for a particular sport and sportsperson

Plyometrics: training method using explosive movements to develop muscular power, for example, bounding and hopping.

Key to Exam Success

For your GCSE you will need to:

- understand the different types of muscular contraction – isotonic and isometric
- know what is meant by circuit, weight, interval, continuous, plyometric, flexibility and Fartlek training
- be able to describe the effects of exercise and training on the skeletal, muscular, cardiovascular and respiratory systems.

66 KEY THOUGHT 99

'Train well, play well.'

How do our muscles work?

Before looking at methods of training, it is important to understand how our muscles work.

Our muscles can work in different ways according to the actions we are performing. Although they can only contract to cause movement, the way they are positioned in our body means that this movement can vary enormously. For example, the very large muscles in our thighs not only drive us forward at a sprint start, they can also be used to help us hold a delicate balance in gymnastics.

There are two main types of muscular contraction: **isometric** and **isotonic**.

Isometric muscular contraction

In isometric contraction, the muscle tension is increased but the muscle length does not alter and there is no movement around the joint. Throughout sport we can see isometric muscle contraction at work, for example, when we hold a handstand, hold the bow bent in archery or push in the scrum in rugby. Many of our muscles help to stabilise our body as our limbs move. They do this by working isometrically.

Isotonic muscular contraction

Isotonic contraction is muscular contraction that results in limb movement. It takes place when our muscle fibres shorten or lengthen causing movement around our joints. Most sporting action involves isotonic muscular contraction.

Isotonic contraction can be either **concentric** or **eccentric**.

- **Concentric muscular action** takes place when the contracting muscle fibres

shorten. This is the action we see most often in sporting movement. For example, when we do pull-ups on a bar, the muscle fibres in the biceps shorten as they contract, to bring the shoulder up, level with the wrist.

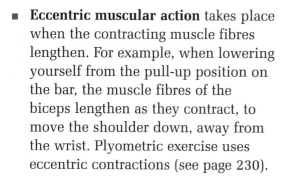

- **Eccentric muscular action** takes place when the contracting muscle fibres lengthen. For example, when lowering yourself from the pull-up position on the bar, the muscle fibres of the biceps lengthen as they contract, to move the shoulder down, away from the wrist. Plyometric exercise uses eccentric contractions (see page 230).

Isotonic contraction with muscles working concentrically

- The muscles shorten as they contract.

- The ends of the muscle move closer together.

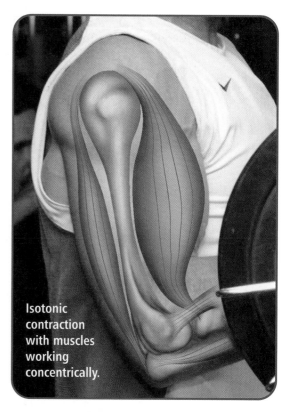

Isotonic contraction with muscles working concentrically.

Isotonic contraction with muscles working eccentrically

- The muscles lengthen as they contract under tension.

- The ends of the muscle move further apart.

Isotonic contraction with muscles working eccentrically.

Isometric contraction

- The muscles stay at the same length as they contract.

- There is no movement, so the ends of the muscles stay the same distance apart.

Isometric contraction.

  activity 😊😊

Feel the difference

This activity will helps you to understand the three different ways in which muscles work.

1 Hold a textbook in your preferred hand with your arm extended by your side.

2 Bend your arm to raise the book to your shoulder. Place the fingers of your other hand on your biceps and feel the contraction. This is an isotonic, concentric contraction.

3 Slowly lower the book to the starting position and feel your biceps contracting as it lengthens. This is an isotonic, eccentric contraction.

4 Raise the book again, but pause before your forearm is parallel to the floor. Hold the book steady and feel your biceps contracting. This is an isometric contraction as there is no movement taking place.

Training options

There are many different training methods. They are all based on the different ways our body adapts to regular exercise. They include:

- continuous training
- Fartlek training
- interval training
- circuit training
- weight training
- plyometric training
- flexibility training.

Continuous (aerobic) training

Continuous training consists of working for sustained periods of time, using all major muscle groups of the body. Activity can include running, swimming, cycling, rowing, taking part in aerobics or any other whole-body activity.

Continuous training requires working at the same pace for between 30 minutes and two hours and being moderately active, that is, working in the aerobic training zone at 60–80% of MHR (Maximum Heart Rate).

Why use continuous training?

- to improve cardiovascular endurance
- to help improve health-related fitness
- to reduce amounts of body fat
- to maintain fitness in the off-season.

Who uses continuous training?

Everyone, because it forms the basis of all health-related fitness. In sport it is essential for all activities which continue over a period of time. Examples include all major team games, racket sports, swimming and running.

Fartlek training

The name Fartlek comes from a Swedish word meaning 'speed play'. Fartlek involves deliberately varying the speed and intensity at which you walk, run, cycle or ski and the type of terrain over which you travel. A Fartlek session normally lasts a minimum of 30 minutes.

Why use Fartlek training?

■ to improve aerobic and anaerobic fitness, depending on how you train

■ to help games players who need both aerobic and anaerobic fitness

■ to enable you to enjoy moving quickly but within your own ability

■ to reduce tedium in training.

Who uses Fartlek training?

Everyone can benefit from this type of training, as it can improve both aerobic and anaerobic fitness. In sport, it is regularly used in the training programmes of runners and skiers and can also be used simply to avoid tedium.

Interval training

Interval training consists of using alternating periods of very hard exercise and rest. Rest periods are essential for recovery and enable you to train for longer.

During interval training you can vary:

- the time or distance of each exercise

- the amount of effort (intensity) you put into each period of exercise

- the type of activity you take part in during each period of rest

- the number of exercise and recovery periods in the training session. For example, an interval training session on the track could involve six 200-metre runs in 30 seconds with 90 seconds rest between each.

Why use interval training?
The aim of interval training is to improve anaerobic and aerobic fitness. Your aerobic fitness will improve if you train for a long period at 60–80% of MHR. Your anaerobic fitness will improve if you train over a short period at 80–95% MHR.

Using this high-quality speed training you will need rests of 2–3 minutes, but it will develop your ability to work when tired.

Who uses interval training?
Interval training is a specialist training method for serious sportspeople and is not normally used for health-related fitness. It can be used to meet the needs of a variety of sports. Sprinters, for example, will allow sufficient time between sprints in order to recover fully. Games players will use

programmes which alternate between hard and light working – which is what happens in a game.

Circuit training

Circuit training involves performing a series of exercises or activities in a special order, called a circuit. A circuit usually consists of 6 to 10 exercises or activities, which take place at stations. At each station, a set number of repetitions is completed as quickly as possible, or as many repetitions as possible are completed in a fixed time, for example, one minute.

Circuits should be designed to avoid working the same muscle group at more than one station in succession. They should also include exercises that work opposing muscles around a joint.

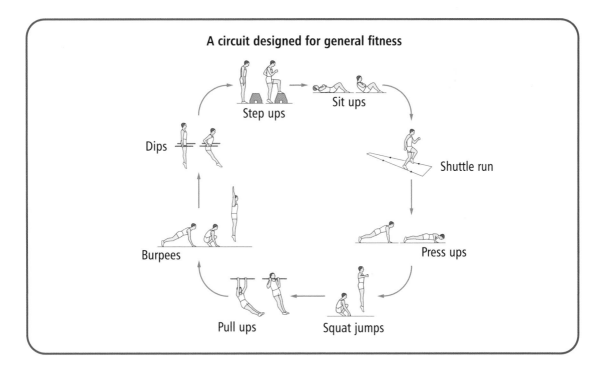

A circuit designed for general fitness

Step ups · Sit ups · Dips · Shuttle run · Burpees · Press ups · Pull ups · Squat jumps

As fitness improves, the circuit can be made more difficult by increasing:

- the number of stations
- the time spent at each station
- the number of repetitions at each station
- the number of complete circuits.

Why use circuit training?
Circuit training enables you to improve either aerobic or anaerobic fitness, or both at the same time. A great variety of exercises can be included, making it extremely adaptable for the needs of different sports.

Who uses circuit training?
Circuit training is a valuable training activity for almost all sports. For example, high jumpers can use programmes which concentrate on developing leg power, while basketball players can use programmes which

develop leg power together with upper body strength and aerobic fitness. It is also possible to construct circuits for games players in which exercises are replaced by short skills practices – for example, passing a ball against a wall. At the same time, anyone who wants to achieve a basic level of health-related fitness can benefit from a suitably designed circuit.

Weight training

In **weight training**, free weights or weights in machines are used to provide resistance to muscle power. Training consists of sequences or sets of exercises, and the weights used are gradually increased, allowing you to overload your muscles safely over a sensible period of time.

Any weight training programme should take account of your current state of fitness. Over the page are some guidelines for weight training:

- Decide which muscle groups are important for your sport and choose exercises to develop them.

- Aim for at least three training sessions a week.

- Make sure you are thoroughly warmed up before starting.

- Breathe in when you lift the weight and breathe out as you lower it.

- Never hold your breath, as this could make you faint.

- Work the different muscle groups in turn, to give time for recovery.

- Increase the weights as your muscles grow stronger.

Why use weight training?

The aim of weight training is to improve your strength – that is, muscular strength, muscular power and muscular endurance.

- Muscular strength is improved by using at least three sets of six repetitions at near-maximum weight.

- Muscular endurance is improved by using at least three sets of 20–30 repetitions. The weight should be 40–60% of the weight which you can lift just once (your one repetition maximum, or 1 RM).

- Muscular power is improved by at least three sets of 10–15 repetitions. These should be done at speed, using 60–80% of your 1 RM.

Who uses weight training?

Anyone who wants a basic health-related fitness level can benefit from a suitable weight training programme.

Sportspeople looking to improve their sporting performance can design their own weight training programme by comparing the physical demands of their sport with their own current level of fitness.

Weight training programmes are included in the training programmes of most sportspeople. They are of particular importance to power athletes such as jumpers, sprinters and throwers.

Plyometric training

Plyometric training involves a series of explosive movements including bounds, hops, jumps (on to and off boxes) leaps, skips, press-ups with claps, throwing and catching a medicine ball, all of which are designed to improve muscular power (explosive strength). The muscles can be stretched before they contract. This stores up elastic energy. When they next contract, they will produce extra power.

For example, in a vertical jump, you:

■ bend at the knees, which stretches the thigh muscles

■ immediately contract these muscles as you jump upwards.

This movement converts the stretch into an elastic recoil, and the extra power enables you to jump higher.

Plyometric training puts great stress on the muscles and joints, so it is vital to warm up thoroughly first. Beginners should take special care and should start by training on grass (if outdoors) or on mats if indoors.

Why use plyometric training?

The aim of plyometric training is to improve power by training the muscles to contract more strongly, and to improve sports performance by using your own body weight in movements similar to those found in your sport.

Who uses plyometric training?

This is a specialist training method for serious sportspeople who need to develop power and is not normally used for health-related fitness. It can be used to meet the needs of a variety of sportspeople, particularly jumpers, basketball and volleyball players. It is of benefit to all games and racket players.

Flexibility training

Flexibility training involves using a series of exercises to improve and extend the range of movement at a joint by stretching and moving the tendons and ligaments just beyond the point of resistance. A variety of exercises can used, involving static, passive, active and PNF stretching (see below).

Static stretching

In static stretching the limbs are extended beyond their normal range and the position is held for at least 10 seconds. After a few seconds the stretch is repeated. This is continued for at least five repetitions of 10 seconds, with the length of time the stretch is held being gradually increased.

Active stretching

In active stretching we extend a movement beyond our normal limit and repeat this rhythmically over a period of 20 seconds. It is very important that the muscles are warmed up before active stretching is started. Active stretches should be performed slowly at first, and bobs or bounces avoided.

Passive stretching

In passive stretching we increase the flexibility of our joints by using a partner to apply external force. He or she moves the limb being exercised to its end position and keeps it there for a few seconds. It is most important that this type of stretching is carried out carefully to avoid injury.

PNF stretching

PNF (proprioceptive neuromuscular facilitation) stretching is based on the principle that muscles are most relaxed (and therefore can most easily be stretched) immediately after contraction. The muscle is first contracted as hard as possible. It is then stretched fully and the stretch held for a few seconds. The muscle is then relaxed briefly before repeating.

Why use flexibility training?

The aim of all flexibility training is to improve flexibility and therefore

performance. Good flexibility is important for most sports and can reduce the risk of joint injury as well as allowing us to use our strength more effectively through a full range of movement.

Who uses flexibility training?

Everyone who wants a basic health-related fitness level can benefit from a suitably designed flexibility programme. It is a valuable training activity for almost all sports and is particularly important for gymnasts, dancers, skaters and hurdlers.

activity

Methods match

1 Match each of the different types of training listed on the next page with the type of fitness they are designed to improve.

2 Use this information to complete the first two columns of the table.

3 In the third column give an example of a suitable training activity to match the training type.

4 In the fourth column give an example of a sport for which the training activity might be used.

The first example is completed for you.

activity 😊😊😊

Type of training	Type of fitness	Activity	Sport
Continuous	Stamina	45-minute run	Athletics – 5,000 metres

Training type	Fitness type
Flexibility	Muscular endurance
Fartlek	Muscular power
Interval	Muscular strength
Plyometrics	Agility
Weight training	Aerobic fitness
Circuit training	Anaerobic fitness
	Flexibility

Your Personal Exercise Plan (PEP)

You are required to produce a six-week PEP as part of your GCSE course. This gives you an opportunity to show how much you know about fitness and training. The programme may be designed for health and well-being or a specific activity. It is helpful if you select the same sport for the Fitness Match exercise, your Analysing Performance task and your PEP. In this way everything that you do combines into one project.

What is a Personal Exercise Plan?

A **Personal Exercise Plan (PEP)** is a training programme that is designed for an individual sportsperson. It is prepared using knowledge about the individual's own needs, the needs of the sport for which he or she is training, and an understanding of fitness and training principles.

Your six-week plan should be designed to improve your levels of:

- flexibility
- cardiovascular endurance
- muscular strength
- muscular power
- speed
- muscular endurance.

Above all, it needs to be specific to you and to your sport/event.

What do I need to include in my PEP?

Introduction
You need to begin with an introduction, which explains what a PEP is and which sport you are designing it for.

Types of fitness
In this section you should define each of the types of fitness so that the reader can see that you understand each one.

Effects of exercise on the body
You should show that you understand the effects of exercise on the body. Your explanation should include details about:

- the difference between aerobic and anaerobic exercise

- oxygen debt

- the effect of lactic acid in the muscles

- the difference between inhaled air and exhaled air

- the effects on breathing and heart rates.

Effects of training
You should include a description of the effects that you expect to see from completing the PEP. You will need to list the long-term effects of exercise on the circulatory system, the respiratory system and the muscular system. You should include details about:

- how muscles change in size, strength and endurance

- changes to vital capacity and tidal volume

- changes to stroke volume, cardiac output, resting heart rate, recovery rate and blood composition.

SPORT-P principles of training
In the next section you should explain each of the SPORT-P principles of training (see pages 210–212) and show how they apply to your PEP.

For example:

> 'I am planning to use cycling, running and swimming to increase my level of stamina. This will help to avoid tedium.'

When writing about specificity, you should describe your individual needs, using evidence from the Fitness Match exercise, and compare your levels of fitness with those required for your sport. This will produce a list of priorities. For example:

> 'I need to work very hard on improving my stamina, but my flexibility levels are already high, so I just need to maintain them.'

FITT principles of training

You then need to explain the FITT principles and show how you will use them to design your PEP. You need to consider the types of fitness that you wish to improve and relate them to the types of training that will lead to improvement. Make clear statements. For example:

> 'Plyometric training will improve my muscular power.'

You will also need to be scientific when explaining the intensity of your training. For example:

> 'To improve my stamina I will train at 70% MHR for the first two weeks. By the sixth week I will be training at 75–80% MHR. This shows progression.'

You need to show your understanding of the phases of a training session. You can do this by describing the three phases (see page 216), but you need to mention that skill is not included in your PEP. However, you can use activities that are specific to your sport and you should provide examples:

> 'I will complete three sets of 15 blocking movements in volleyball to improve my muscular endurance.'

Example of 1-week PEP

Week 1 Session 1	Venue: school field and gymnasium
Warm-up	See description
Cardiovascular endurance	20-minute run at 70% MHR
Flexibility	15 minutes active stretching of major muscle groups
Muscular strength	–
Power	Five sets of 10 reps plyometrics using two gymnastic box tops
Muscular endurance	Circuit of biceps, triceps, abdominals, shuttle exercises (2 x 30 seconds on each)
Warm-down	See description
Date/notes	

Week 1 Session 2	Venue: local leisure centre
Warm-up	See description
Cardiovascular endurance	25-minute swim at 70% MHR
Flexibility	15 minutes active stretching of major muscle groups
Muscular strength	Weight training in fitness centre. Heavy weights, low reps
Power	–
Muscular endurance	–
Warm-down	See description
Date/notes	

Week 1 Session 3	Venue: school field and gymnasium
Warm-up	See description
Cardiovascular endurance	25-minute run at 70% MHR
Flexibility	15 minutes active stretching of major muscle groups
Muscular strength	–
Power	Five sets of 10 reps plyometrics using two gymnastic box tops
Muscular endurance	Circuit of biceps, triceps, abdominals, shuttle exercises (2 x 40 seconds on each)
Warm-down	See description
Date/notes	

This athlete is avoiding tedium by training in two different environments. Muscular strength training is only taking place in the fitness centre, where swimming is the chosen exercise to improve cardiovascular endurance.

In this section you should describe your warm-up and warm-down exercises in detail. There is no need to repeat the description for every session, as they will be similar each time.

If you are planning a flexibility programme you should describe it in some detail in this section.

Training sessions

You need to outline training sessions for six weeks, taking into account all of the above. It is likely that you will train three times a week. This takes into account reversibility – you will have explained this in the FITT section when describing the frequency of training.

You must be sure that the exercises are set at your level of fitness. You can show progression by making the exercises a lot more demanding by the end of Week 6.

Your PEP must be designed for you. If you have access to a fitness centre, you might choose to do all of the training there. If not, you may have to plan to use the school gymnasium, fields or local park.

As each session is completed you should add the date and make notes about how it went, or any changes you made.

Monitoring and evaluation

Once you have prepared your PEP you have to actually do the work! As you complete each session you should note any changes or comments about it.

At the end of six weeks you will need to evaluate the PEP as a whole. A good way of doing this is to retake the fitness tests that you completed for your Fitness Match. It is important to use the actual scores that you achieved before and after completing your PEP. You may find that your cardiovascular endurance level has increased significantly from the low end to the high end of 'above average' in the

norm tables. If you only look at the tables, you might think that there has been no improvement.

Your evaluation should consider:

- if your fitness levels have improved – and by how much

- any changes to your heart rate at rest and when exercising

- changes to your recovery rate

- noticeable effects on your muscles

- good and bad points about your exercise programme and how you might improve it.

QUESTIONS

12 Training methods

1 Muscle contraction is usually either isometric or isotonic. Name the major muscle contraction for the following:

a netball shot
b tug-of-war pull
c rugby scrum
d tennis serve. *(4 marks)*

2 Katy wants to improve her performance in the school netball team. She is following a fitness programme including interval training and plyometric training.

a Explain what is meant by:

  i interval training *(1 mark)*
  ii plyometric training. *(1 mark)*

  Give an example of each type of training.
  (2 marks)

b **i** Explain why Katy needs to improve her muscular power for netball.
    (1 mark)

  ii Which type of weight training will improve her muscular power?
    (1 mark)

c Two of the FITT principles are time and type.

  i Name the other two. *(2 marks)*
  ii Explain what is meant by type. *(2 marks)*

3 Hiren is a cross-country runner. His training includes continuous training and Fartlek running.

a Explain the difference between these two types of training.
  (2 marks)

b Which fitness component will they both develop?
  (1 mark)

c Describe what sort of circuit training would help Hiren's fitness.
  (2 marks)

Hiren's friend, Darren, goes to the gym and trains with weights.

d Explain the type of weight training needed to improve his:

  i muscular strength *(2 marks)*
  ii muscular endurance *(2 marks)*
  iii muscular power. *(2 marks)*

e Explain why flexibility training would help Darren's fitness.
  (2 marks)
  (Total 27 marks)

13 Training effects

When we train, our bodies have to do more physical work than they do normally. Our bodies respond by adapting to this increased workload. This means that they can cope better with the hard work when asked to do so again. The training effect is the way in which our body adapts. How it does so will depend on the type of training we do.

activity

Training effect

This activity is an experiment to see whether or not different types of training bring about an improvement in performance.

1 To begin with, form three groups with approximately equal numbers of boys and girls in each group.

2 Each member of the group attempts to juggle two tennis balls in one hand as many times as possible. Count the number of successful catches and record the best of three attempts.

3 Calculate:
- the average score for each group
- separate averages for boys and girls
  and enter the scores on the table.

4 Practise juggling as follows:

- **Group A**: juggling with two tennis balls using one hand for 20 minutes
- **Group B**: bouncing a tennis ball continuously on the ground for 20 minutes
- **Group C**: juggling with three tissues or scarves in two hands for 20 minutes.

5 After your practice session, re-test your juggling ability with three tennis balls and enter the results in the table.

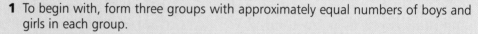

	Group average	Boys' average	Girls' average	Juggling Test 1	Juggling Test 2
Group A					
Group B					
Group C					

Use the information from your results to answer the following questions:

1 What sort of practice is most likely to improve your juggling skills?

2 Is this true for both boys and girls?

3 Is practising bouncing a tennis ball more likely to improve your juggling skills than practising with tissues or scarves?

4 Do you think your answers would apply to other sporting skills?

5 Does slowing down the skill, e.g. using the tissues or scarves, improve learning?

KEYWORDS

Aerobic activity: 'with oxygen'. If exercise is steady and not too fast, the heart can supply all the oxygen the muscles need

Anaerobic activity: 'without oxygen'. If exercise is done in short fast bursts, the heart cannot supply blood and oxygen to the muscles as fast as the cells can use them

Lactic acid: waste product produced in the working muscles

Oxygen debt: the amount of oxygen consumed during recovery above that which would ordinarily have been consumed in the same time at rest, resulting in a shortfall in the oxygen available

Recovery rate: length of time needed for cardiorespiratory system to return to normal after activity

Training target zone: the range of heart rates which need to be achieved in order to bring about a specific training result.

Key to Exam Success

For your GCSE you will need to:

- describe the effects of exercise and training on the skeletal, muscular, cardiovascular and respiratory systems
- understand the meaning and use of recovery rates and target training zones.

66 KEY THOUGHT 99

'The right training will get the right results'

The effects of exercise and training on our body systems

If we follow a well planned, long-term training programme, changes will occur in our bones, muscles, cardiovascular and respiratory systems. We must remember, however, that training is specific. This means that the actual changes that take place will depend on the type of training we have carried out. The long-term effects of aerobic, anaerobic and weight training will be different. On the pages which follow you will find a description of all the major changes which can be brought about by exercise and training.

The effects of exercise on bones, joints and muscles

What are the immediate effects of exercise on bones, joints and muscles?

- little effect on bones and joints

- increased flow of blood to working muscles

- muscles take up more oxygen from the blood

- muscles contract more often and more quickly

- more of the muscle fibres contract

- rise in temperature in the muscles.

What are the effects of regular training and exercise on bones, joints and muscles?

- bone width and bone density increases

- strengthens muscles, tendons and ligaments surrounding joints

- joint cartilage thickens, improving shock absorption at joints

- increased range of movement at joints (flexibility)

- muscles adjust to greater workload

- muscles increase in size (hypertrophy)

- depending on the type of training, the number of fast- or slow-twitch fibres will increase

- muscles can work harder and for longer.

What are the long-term benefits of exercise on bones, joints and muscles?

- increase in bone strength and thickness

- increase in stability of joints

- fuller range of movement at joints

- increased muscular strength, muscular endurance and muscular power

- improved capacity of muscles to tolerate fatigue by coping with lactic acid and oxygen debt.

The effects of exercise on the cardiovascular system

Immediate effects of exercise on the cardiovascular system

- The hormone adrenaline enters the blood system.

- Adrenaline causes the heart to beat more quickly – increased heart rate.

- The heart contracts more powerfully – increased stroke volume.

- Blood circulation speeds up, with more oxygen carried to the working muscles.

- Blood is diverted to areas of greatest need.

- Blood temperature increases, causing sweating response.

- Blood vessels to skin areas enlarge, allowing heat to be lost more easily.

The effects of regular training and exercise on the cardiovascular system

- Increased amount of blood pumped around the body

- Cardiovascular system copes more easily with increased demands.

- Body able to carry and use more oxygen per minute

- Body able to remove waste products (especially carbon dioxide) more efficiently

- Increased recovery rate after exercise.

Long-term benefits of exercise on the cardiovascular system

- Healthier heart and blood vessels

- Reduced risk of heart disease

- Increased cardiovascular endurance

- Reduced blood pressure

- Lower resting heart rate and quicker recovery after exercise

- Heart muscle increases in size, thickness and strength.

- Increased number of capillaries

- Volume of blood increases.

The effects of exercise on the respiratory system

What are the immediate effects of exercise on the respiratory system?

- Increased rate of breathing

- Increased depth of breathing

- Increased blood flow through lungs

- Increased oxygen take-up and use by the body.

What are the effects of regular training and exercise on the respiratory system?

- Increased strength of intercostal muscles and diaphragm allows deeper and faster breaths

- Greater number of alveoli

- Increased amount of oxygen delivered to the body

- Increased amount of carbon dioxide removed from the body.

What are the long-term benefits of exercise on the respiratory system?

- Healthier lungs

- Increased vital and tidal volume

- Increased capacity of lungs to extract oxygen from the air

- Increased capacity of the lungs to remove carbon dioxide and other waste products from the bloodstream

- Increased tolerance of oxygen debt as lungs can work harder for longer.

The immediate effects of exercise on our body systems

Action by our lungs
Our lungs breathe faster and deeper (increased tidal volume).
Increased exchange of gases:
■ more oxygen taken into our blood
■ more carbon dioxide removed from our blood.

We start to exercise
Our muscles work harder and use up more oxygen.
The amount of carbon dioxide in our blood increases. Our brain detects this increase and releases adrenaline.

Action by our heart
Our heart beats faster and stronger (increased heart rate and stroke volume).
More blood pumped to our lungs (increased cardiac output)
■ to collect oxygen
■ to remove carbon dioxide.
More blood pumped to our muscles (increased cardiac output)
■ to deliver oxygen
■ to remove carbon dioxide.

As a result:
■ Blood pressure rises but blood vessels then expand to reduce the pressure.
■ Body temperature rises, but surface blood vessels expand to reduce heat quickly through the skin, and sweating increases, producing water on the skin which evaporates and cools us.
■ Blood flow is redirected away from parts of the body not involved in exercise such as the digestive system, towards our working muscles.

Anaerobic and aerobic activity in training

Our bodies need energy so that our muscles can contract and make our body work. Our muscles can use energy only when it is in the form of a chemical compound called adenosine triphosphate, or ATP. Our muscles have only very small stores of this high-energy compound. As soon as it is used up we have to remake it. We can do this by using either of our two energy systems: the **anaerobic** or the **aerobic** system.

- **Anaerobic system**: our body works without oxygen as we cannot get enough to the muscles for them to work at the high rate demanded.

- **Aerobic system**: there is a constant supply of oxygen to the muscles enabling them to work hard, but not flat out.

The anaerobic system

The anaerobic system gives us both immediate energy and energy for the short term.

However, if there is not enough oxygen available at the same time, then **lactic acid** will be formed as well as ATP. If lactic acid builds up in the muscle, it makes muscular contractions painful and we become

tired. Therefore we cannot use the anaerobic system for very long. The energy from the anaerobic system will be enough for a maximum of about one minute of hard work.

Oxygen debt and lactic acid

When we use the anaerobic system we produce an oxygen deficit – that is, our muscles need more oxygen than they can get at the time. As we saw above, we can continue the activity by using glycogen, but the disadvantage is that we also produce lactic acid.

A build-up of lactic acid causes muscle fatigue. This makes us feel tired and our working muscles start to stiffen and ache.

This will force us to stop and rest eventually if no more oxygen is supplied.

If we are able to carry on, at the end of the exercise we have to rest and take in the extra oxygen we need to remove the lactic acid. This makes up our oxygen deficit.

The extra oxygen we have to take in at the end of the activity is called the **oxygen debt**.

Feel the burn!

Feel the effects of lactic acid by straightening and curling your index finger as quickly as possible and for as long as possible. Discuss the effects as muscle fatigue begins to occur.

The aerobic system

The function of the aerobic system is to give us long-term energy. It can be used only when enough oxygen reaches the working muscles. The aerobic system is used for all light exercise, including most of our daily activities. It gives us energy much more slowly than the anaerobic system.

The energy provided by the aerobic system comes from using glucose, formed by the breakdown of carbohydrates and fats, combined with a plentiful supply of oxygen. Although this gives us energy much too slowly for intensive activity, it can supply energy for a very long time.

Energy systems and sport

This aerobic system is important for nearly all sportspeople. It is very important for those who need energy over a long period of time – such as runners, cyclists, swimmers and games players. But the energy we need for different sports varies a great deal.

- A shot-putter uses one huge burst of energy lasting just a few seconds. This comes from the anaerobic system; energy from the aerobic system would take too long to arrive.

- A 100-metre sprint swimmer needs a longer, but still quite short burst of energy. The creatine phosphate supplies would soon be exhausted. The aerobic system will not be able to supply oxygen fast enough. The swimmer will therefore rely on the anaerobic system to supply the energy needed. At the end of the swim there will be an oxygen debt.

- A marathon runner needs a continuous supply of energy over a long period and has no need of the anaerobic energy system. He or she must rely on a well developed aerobic system to send a steady stream of oxygen to the muscles over a long period of time.

In many sports the two energy systems work together at different times to supply the particular type of energy needed. For example, a hockey player will need the anaerobic system when shooting for goal and when repeatedly sprinting short distances, and the aerobic system when jogging into position when the ball is out of play.

The anaerobic system works without oxygen and supplies our muscles with energy quickly. In contrast, the aerobic system must have oxygen to work and only supplies energy slowly to our muscles.

To train your energy systems for your particular sport you need to know to what extent you use each energy system. You can then decide, with your coach, what type of training is likely to improve your performance. You will also need to think about training thresholds and **target training zones**.

Training thresholds and target training zones

To train effectively you must know:

- your present level of fitness
- the amount of anaerobic training you need for your sport
- the amount of aerobic training you need for your sport.

Maximum heart rate

To work out our fitness level, we need to know our maximum aerobic capacity (VO_2 Max), which involves scientific calculation. Fortunately there is a very close link between our VO_2 Max and our maximum heart rate (MHR), and we can use MHR instead.

As we saw earlier, maximum heart rate can be estimated as follows:

- MHR males = 220 minus age

- MHR females = 226 minus age.

For example, a 16-year-old male has an MHR of 220 − 16 = 204 beats per minute. For a female of the same age, the MHR would be 210 beats per minute.

(Remember that the percentages of MHR which we give here are only approximate. Personal levels of activity and fitness will cause differences. The less fit we are, the lower our training thresholds will be.)

Aerobic target zone

When we train in this zone we improve aerobic fitness. To achieve this, we need to exercise above our aerobic threshold, which means keeping our heart rate between 60–80% of our MHR.

For a typical 16-year-old athlete, the aerobic target zone would therefore be:

- Male: 60–80% of 204 = 120–160 beats per minute
- Female: 60–80% of 210 = 125–170 beats per minute.

Anaerobic target zone

When we train in this zone we improve our anaerobic fitness. To achieve this we need to exercise above our anaerobic threshold, which means keeping our heart rate above 80% of MHR. For a typical 16-year-old athlete, the anaerobic target zone would therefore be:

- Male: 80%+ of 204 = over 160 beats per minute

- Female: 80%+ of 210 = over 170 beats per minute.

Recovery rates

Whenever we exercise, our heart rate increases to supply more oxygen to our working muscles. As a result our pulse rate increases from its resting level to a higher level depending on how hard we work. (Our pulse rate is simply our heart rate measured at the wrist or throat.)

A sportsperson's fitness can be estimated by checking their resting pulse rate. The fitter they are, the lower their resting pulse rate. A fit person will have a larger and stronger heart than an unfit person. This means that a fit heart can supply the same amount of blood to the muscles but uses fewer beats than an unfit heart. Therefore the resting pulse for the fit heart is lower.

However, a better way of measuring fitness is to work out how long a person's pulse rate takes to return to normal after exercise. This is called the **recovery rate**.

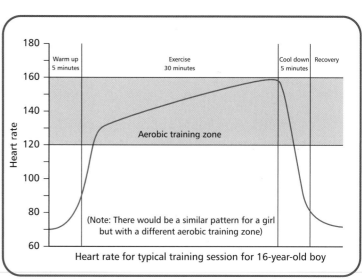

Heart rate for typical training session for 16-year-old boy

(Note: There would be a similar pattern for a girl but with a different aerobic training zone)

Resting pulse rates: comparative scores

85 and above	Poor
70–84	Average
56–69	Good
55 and under	Excellent

During the recovery period the body deals with the oxygen debt. This is achieved by breathing deeply, transporting more oxygen from the lungs and removing the lactic acid. The recovery process is helped by gentle aerobic exercise immediately after the vigorous activity. This aids the removal of lactic acid, reduces the possible effect of muscle soreness and improves recovery time.

activity ☺☺ ☺

Measuring recovery rate

You can estimate your recovery rate by comparing your heart rate before and after exercise.

In pairs, the resting pulse rate of each participant is taken over 15 seconds and recorded.

One member of each pair runs 400 metres as fast as possible.

Immediately after their run their partner records their pulse over 15 seconds at 30 second intervals for 5 minutes.

The process is then repeated for the second person in each pair.

A table is completed for each runner based on the format below, and a graph plotted.

Name of runner:	Pulse for 15 seconds	Pulse per minute
Immediately after exercise		
30 seconds after exercise		
1 minute after exercise		
1.5 minutes after exercise		
2.0 minutes after exercise		
3.0 minutes after exercise		

QUESTIONS

13 Training effects

1 **Explain what is meant by:**

a aerobic training *(1 mark)*

b anaerobic training. *(1 mark)*

Give one example of each.
(2 marks)

2 **As we start a 400-metre race, explain what are the immediate effects on our:**

a heart *(2 marks)*

b blood supply to our working muscles *(1 mark)*

c lungs *(2 marks)*

d tidal volume *(1 mark)*

e blood pressure *(1 mark)*

f body temperature *(1 mark)*

g blood flow. *(2 marks)*

3 **Complete this table by giving one possible effect of each training activity on the heart and muscular system.**

4 **During training, Ricky's heart rate is recorded. The results show that in the first five minutes of activity his heart rate climbed from 65 to 150 and remained there for the rest of the hour. Over the next half hour it gradually came down to 65.**

a Why did his heart rate increase in the first five minutes? *(2 marks)*

b For a long period his heart rate is constant. Suggest the type of activity he was doing at this time. *(2 marks)*

c In which training zone was he working? *(1 mark)*

d What is the relationship between his training activity and his oxygen supplies? *(1 mark)*

e What happened during the last half hour? *(1 mark)*

f What is this period called? *(1 mark)*
(Total 26 marks)

Possible effects of training activity	Long runs	Weight training with heavy weights and few repetitions
Heart		
Muscular system		

(4 marks)

Risk assessment in physical activity

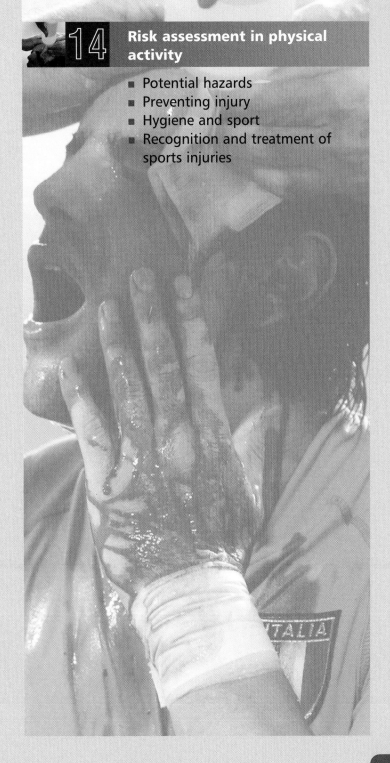

14 **Risk assessment in physical activity**

- Potential hazards
- Preventing injury
- Hygiene and sport
- Recognition and treatment of sports injuries

14 Risk assessment in physical activity

Many of us take part in sport because it is exciting and unpredictable, but this unpredictability can put great strain on our bodies and brings with it the risk of injury. Good preparation is important in trying to reduce the risk of injury. We should know the rules of our sport and the ways of working safely. We should wear the correct protective clothing and use safe equipment. Competition should be fair in terms of level of skill, weight, age and sex. Warming up and cooling down should be essential parts of any sporting activity.

If we are to perform to the best of our ability, we must avoid injury when training and competing. To do this we must assess the risks, plan to be safe and take every precaution to stay safe. If we do get injured, we must know how to recognise and treat the injury so that we recover quickly. Knowing when to return to training is also important: returning too soon can cause problems.

activity

Safety issues

Look at the following cartoons of sporting activities and copy and complete the grid listing all the potential safety hazards.

Sport	Facility	Clothing and equipment	Safety in general
Trampolining			
Climbing			
Gymnastics			
Rugby			
Cricket			
Basketball			

KEYWORDS

Dehydration: loss of body fluids, usually when working extremely hard in hot conditions, leading to heat exhaustion

Etiquette: special ways we are expected to behave in our sport

Heat exhaustion: state of fatigue in hot conditions caused by dehydration

Heatstroke: when the body becomes dangerously overheated through exercise in extremely hot conditions

Hygiene: good personal habits which keep us clean and healthy

Hypothermia: when the internal body temperature becomes dangerously low through exposure to extremely cold conditions

Overuse injuries: damage caused by using a part of the body incorrectly over a long period of time

RICE: Rest, Ice ,Compression, Elevation – a checklist to follow in the case of soft tissue injuries

Shock: an acute state of weakness caused by pain or emotional upset

Sprain: when we overstretch or tear a ligament at a joint

Stitch: a sudden sharp pain, usually caused by exercise, in the muscles in the side of the body

Strain: when we overstretch or tear a muscle or tendon.

Key to Exam Success

For your GCSE you will need to:

- be able to assess the hazards and risks involved in sporting activities, both to yourself and others
- identify how preventative measures can minimise the risk of injury to yourself and others
- understand the common causes of sports injuries
- recognise the signs and symptoms of a range of sporting injuries
- understand how to treat a range of common sports injuries.

66 KEY THOUGHT 99

'Most sporting injury is both painful and avoidable.'

Potential hazards

A hazard is a source of danger or risk. Taking part in sport always carries some risk of injury. We know that if we are playing rugby or climbing, there is a greater risk of injury than if we are playing table tennis or swimming. We are all willing to accept the risks of our sport.

However, if we are organising a sporting activity for other people, we have a responsibility for their safety. For this reason organisers of sporting activities must carry out an assessment of all potential hazards and ensure that risks are minimised before the activity takes place. All those taking part must also be made aware of any specific risks and ensure that they are properly prepared.

We can carry out a risk assessment by asking a number of important questions in different areas. We must then deal with any problems.

Assessing the risk to ourselves
The first step is to check that we are well prepared for our activity.

- **Health and fitness**: are we healthy and fit enough to take part in the activity?

- **Techniques and skills**: do we have the ability to compete at this level?

- **Training**: have we completed sufficient training to cope with the demands of the activity?

- **Warm-up**: have we warmed up our body to avoid injury?

- **Clothing, equipment and footwear**: do we have what is needed for the activity and conditions?

- **Jewellery**: have we removed rings and any other item of jewellery that might cause injury to opponents?

- **Rules**: do we have a good understanding of the rules?

- **Etiquette**: do we know the expected behaviour for the activity?

- **Respect**: do we have respect for our opponents?

Assessing the risk to others

We must be sure we have the right qualifications, knowledge and experience to teach, coach, train or instruct young people in an activity. If we are responsible for young people, we have a 'duty of care'. This means that we must take all reasonable precautions to see that they are safe. We must ask the following questions:

- Have we prepared the group members properly?

- Have we planned the activity carefully?

- Have we the right group size?

- Have we ensured fair competition in terms of age, size, weight, sex and skill?

- Are the facilities and equipment safe?

- Will we supervise the activity well?

- Have we taken safety precautions?

- Is First Aid equipment ready?

- Have we explained any emergency procedures?

Assessing the sporting environment

We must be satisfied that the sports facilities, both indoors and outdoors, are in a safe condition.

Indoor areas

- Is the floor surface suitable for the activity?

- Is the floor surface clean, dry and free from dirt?

- Is the area clear of unnecessary portable apparatus?

- Is all fixed apparatus, such as beams, secure?

- Are there any dangerous projections or wall fittings?

Playing fields

- Is the grass clear of litter, especially glass and cans?

- Is the playing surface suitable?

- Are the weather conditions suitable?

- Is the equipment, such as goal posts, in good condition?

Swimming pool

- Are the wet surfaces around the pool clearly indicated?

- Are rules of behaviour prominently displayed?

- Are depth signs clearly visible?

- Are lifeguards on duty?

Outdoor activities

- Are competent instructors present?

- Are the weather conditions suitable?

- Is appropriate specialist clothing and equipment available?

- Are First Aid facilities available?

- Are emergency procedures known and understood?

Organising a tournament

Imagine that you are organising a tournament for your chosen sport.

Describe the basic organisation of the event including the age of teams, the number of teams and the number of pitches, courts or other facilities involved.

Complete a risk assessment and describe the safety precautions you will take. Set it out in the form of a table as shown below:

Hazards	Risk factor (1–5) (1 = low risk; 5 = high risk)	Precautions (actions/instructions)

Preventing injury

We can look at prevention of injury in sport under a number of headings:

- rules of the game
- footwear, clothing and equipment
- balanced competition
- warm-up and warm-down.

Rules of the game

To avoid injury we need to know and understand the rules of our chosen activity. Rules encourage good sporting behaviour, help games to flow and also protect players from harm. Rules must be followed and players punished if they break them. Injury causes pain and stops us from playing. In high-risk collision sports such as rugby, injuries will inevitably happen, but players who break rules and harm opponents must be dealt with severely. In recent years some players have been taken to court when their deliberate foul play has led to serious injury.

Some sporting activities such as mountaineering, pot holing and sky diving have no formal rules as such. However, it is vital to follow the safety guidelines: failure to do so can be disastrous.

Etiquette means the special ways we are expected to behave in our sport. Etiquette is not a set of written rules as such, but a code of behaviour that has become part of each sport over a long period. Golf has many examples of etiquette; for example, when players complete a hole, they should immediately leave the green and record their scores elsewhere. Tennis players will always shake hands at the net after a match, and rugby players will clap their opponents off the pitch. Etiquette allows us to demonstrate fair play, sportsmanship, sporting spirit and respect for our opponents and helps to reduce violence and injury.

activity

Safety rules

All sports have rules designed to minimise the possibility of injury to those taking part. For example, in football girls are not allowed to play against boys after the age of 11, players who raise their feet too high close to an opponent are penalised and all players must wear shin guards.

Choose three sports and for each of them write down three rules designed to prevent accident or injury.

Footwear, clothing and equipment

All sports shoes must support and protect our feet as well as be comfortable. Shoes must grip the playing surface and absorb impact when we are running or landing. Cross-trainers are useful for moderate performers who play a number of sports, but top players will always choose shoes that are specially designed for their sport. They will also make sure that their shoes can provide maximum support and response to movement by tying the laces tightly.

Always wear the correct clothing for the activity. Check your clothing and equipment regularly to see that everything is in good order. For example, a damaged fencer's outfit could be dangerous if used in competition or practice.

In extreme weather conditions it is especially important to wear the appropriate clothing. Sports manufacturers now produce a wide variety of clothing suitable for very hot, very cold and very wet weather.

Some sports have rules to make sure that protective equipment is worn. For example, hockey goalkeepers and school-age batters in cricket must wear helmets and other padding. Footballers must wear shin guards. Sports often lay down few rules about clothing, but players still need to take sensible precautions.

Protective equipment must:

- properly protect the player
- allow freedom of movement
- permit air to flow around the body
- be comfortable
- be safe and reliable.

In very sunny conditions, players should wear protection against harmful ultraviolet rays, such as sunglasses, hats, long-sleeved shirts and skin creams.

Jewellery

As far as possible, players should remove all jewellery before playing sport. The risk of accidents due to jewellery will vary from sport to sport. For example, rings on fingers will be a much greater problem in judo than in running. People taking part in contact or combat sports should wear no jewellery at all.

Balanced competition

Many sports try to make their competition balanced for fairness and the greater enjoyment of the competitors. For combat and contact sports, balanced competition is important for safety reasons.

- **Age**: most competition in school sport is based on age. However, competition between players of the same age but with different physical development can be both unfair and unsafe.

- **Size and weight**: rugby and football can be very dangerous if there are large differences between the body size and skill levels of the players. For weight lifting and rowing there are weight categories to make competition fairer, whilst weight categories in boxing and wrestling make contests both fairer and safer.

- **Gender**: mixed-sex teams are acceptable in tennis, volleyball, hockey and badminton, but not in netball. Rugby union has non-contact forms of the game which are suitable for mixed teams, whilst mixed teams are allowed in soccer up to the age of 11.

- **Skill**: in karate and judo belts are awarded for different skill levels and competition takes place within these skill levels for reasons of safety and fairness. Golf has a handicap system to allow competition between players of different abilities.

These children are all the same age.

Warm-up and warm-down

These are essential parts of any training session or competitive situation. They are important in preventing injury and should be closely tailored to the individual sport.

If we start strenuous activity when our muscles and joints are cold, they are likely to suffer damage because they will be unable to cope with the sudden stresses. Gentle exercise for the whole body warms up the muscles and joints and prepares them for more vigorous activity. A combination of gentle jogging and stretching exercises will help to prevent injury.

If we simply rest immediately after strenuous activity, our recovery will take much longer and there is the possibility of dizziness. Light exercise will maintain the blood circulation, prevent pooling in the skeletal muscles, lower blood pressure and reduce the risk of dizziness. It will also help the speedy removal of waste products which will prevent muscle soreness and stiffness.

Hygiene and sport

Hygiene means the different ways we look after our body to keep it healthy and clean. We should keep our bodies healthy as part of our preparation for sport. We should also develop hygienic habits after taking part in sport and ensure we get enough sleep and rest.

Skin care

Our skin protects and maintains our body. If the skin is healthy, it can resist most forms of infection. Soap and warm water removes dirt and sweat, which encourage bacteria and cause body odour. We should wash our hands after going to the toilet, before meals and whenever they are dirty.

We can also keep our whole body clean by showering daily. It is essential to wash or shower thoroughly after taking part in any physical activity. Most of us use deodorants and anti-perspirants, but they are only really effective if the body is already clean.

Nails

Nails should be kept clean and cut regularly. This will help to reduce injury in sport from scratches. Ingrowing toenails can be avoided by keeping nails short and having footwear of the right size.

Hair

Hair is found on nearly every part of our skin. We must wash our hair regularly to keep it clean and healthy. In some sports long hair can be a hazard and should be tied back.

Feet

Shoes and sports footwear must fit well. This will help to prevent corns and other infections. We must wash our feet regularly and dry them carefully. If we also change our socks daily this will also help to prevent foot odour.

- **Athlete's foot** is a fungal infection which affects our feet, especially between the toes, causing the skin to crack open and become itchy. It can be treated by drying the feet carefully and using antifungal creams, sprays and powder.

- **Verrucas** are warts which can be found on the feet. They are caused by a virus and can be quite painful. They can be treated by applying a prescribed liquid.

Foot conditions are easy to treat if recognised at an early stage. We should check our feet for problems regularly and treat them immediately.

Causes of sports injuries

In order to avoid sports injuries, we need to know what they are and why they happen. A sports injury can be any damage caused to a sportsperson whilst in action. This can include hypothermia brought on by cold weather conditions as well as broken bones and pulled muscles.

Some sports have a greater risk of injury than others – for instance, we are more likely to be injured when playing rugby than when taking part in archery. Being aware of the risk can help to reduce it.

Sports injuries can be caused in many different ways. They can be classed as:

- accidental injuries (due to violence or the environment)

- overuse injuries

- chronic injuries.

The force that causes accidental and overuse injuries can be:

- **internal**: from inside our bodies

- **external**: from outside our bodies.

Accidental injuries

Accidental injuries are caused unintentionally and usually happen when we least expect them. They can be caused by internal and external forces.

- **Internal forces** are those created when our body works during exercise. When we perform at our highest level, the extra strain on some body parts can cause damage. A sudden stretch or twist can strain or tear muscles, tendons or ligaments. These injuries may be caused by forgetting to warm up, by very sudden powerful movements or by lack of skill. For example, sprinters can tear hamstrings in a race. Footballers often suffer groin strain through stretching for the ball or knee ligament damage through twisting.

activity

Injuries

Working in groups, look at the following photos of injured sportspeople. See if you can agree on the following:

- What type of injury have they sustained?
- What was the likely cause of their injury?
- How could the injury have been avoided?

■ **External forces** come from outside our bodies. Direct contact, or violence, from another player is one external force. Another external force is the environment.

Violence

Injuries caused by violence are due to direct contact between players or equipment. Many sports involve violent contact between opponents. Collisions may result in fractures, dislocations, sprains and bruises. They may also be caused by being hit by equipment such as balls, sticks or rackets. Breaking the rules can lead to violent injury.

The environment

The environment can lead to injury in two different ways:

■ An injury may involve equipment or facilities – for example, you might trip and land heavily on the playing surface or collide with the goalposts.

■ Alternatively, an injury may be due to weather conditions. Extreme heat can cause dehydration, heat exhaustion and then heatstroke. Extreme cold may lead to hypothermia.

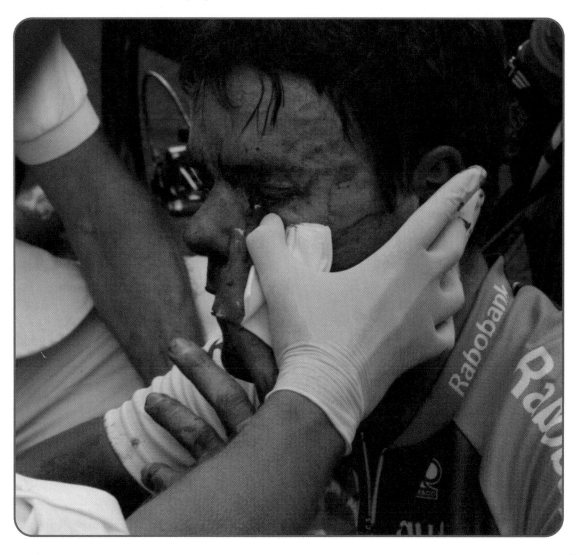

Overuse injuries

Overuse injuries are caused by using a part of the body again and again over a long period of time. These injuries produce pain and inflammation.

Common overuse injuries include:

- 'tennis elbow' or 'golf elbow' – an inflamed elbow joint

- 'shin splints' – pain on the front of the shins

- 'cricketers' shoulder' – damage and inflammation to the front of the shoulder

- blisters and calluses – caused by gripping equipment very tightly during the activity, for example, in rowing.

The only cure for overuse injuries is rest. However, where injuries are caused by incorrect technique, the action must be corrected to prevent the injury recurring.

Chronic injuries

All injuries must be treated immediately and given time to heal. If we put an injury under stress before it is healed, it

will get worse. If this continues, we will develop a chronic injury, which is difficult to heal. Chronic injuries can lead to permanent damage such as arthritis in the joints.

Recognition and treatment of sports injuries

Whenever we have to deal with an injury the first step is to look for signs and symptoms. These help us to assess the injury and decide on any action.

- **Signs**: what we can see, feel, hear and smell – for example, swelling, bruising, bleeding, skin colour

- **Symptoms**: what the sufferer feels and describes – for example, pain, discomfort, nausea.

Fractures

A fracture is a break or crack in a bone. There are two types:

- In a simple (closed) fracture the bone stays under the skin.

- In a compound (open) fracture the bone breaks through the skin.

More complicated fractures also involve damage to nerves and muscles. Whenever the skin is broken there is a danger of infection. All fractures are serious and need urgent medical treatment.

Stress fractures

These are small cracks in a bone, often the result of an overuse injury, such as too much running on hard surfaces. The signs of a stress fracture are steadily increasing pain in a particular part of a limb, swelling and tenderness. In such cases the sufferer needs to:

- use ice to reduce inflammation

- get immediate rest

- keep fit by doing other activities

- check running action and footwear for problems

- run on softer surfaces after recovery.

Joint injuries

The joints of our body are often extremely complex and vulnerable to injury. Simple joint injuries may be treated using the **RICE** procedure – that is, Rest, Ice, Compression, Elevation. However, if serious damage or dislocation are suspected, the injury should be treated as a break and medical help sought.

Dislocations

A dislocation means that a bone is forced out of its normal position at a joint. The ligaments around the joint may also be damaged. The cause may be a strong wrench to the bone, perhaps in a rugby tackle. Treat all dislocations as fractures (see above). Do not attempt to replace the bone into its socket.

Tennis and golf elbow

These two injuries to the tendons at the joints are both caused by overuse. The tendons become inflamed and should be treated using RICE in the first instance. If the symptoms persist after a lengthy period of rest, then further medical advice should be sought to prevent chronic injury and the development of arthritis.

Cartilage injury

We have two cartilages between the bones of our knee joint which act as shock absorbers. They can be torn when the joint is twisted or pulled in an unusual way, for example, during a tackle in football. Sometimes cartilage injury causes the knee to lock. If this happens, medical advice should be sought.

Twisted ankle

This refers to damage to the ankle when the joint is forced beyond its normal range of movement. This is a relatively common injury in games such as hockey, football and rugby. The ligaments supporting the joint are torn, causing pain, swelling and loss of movement. Immediate treatment should be RICE.

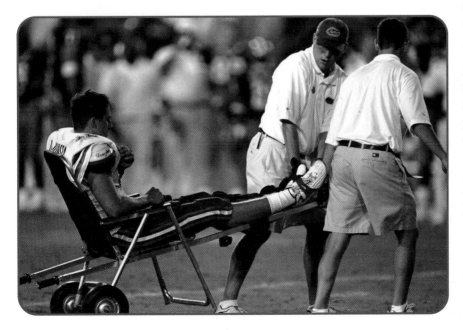

How do we treat bone and serious joint injuries?

The first step is to identify the problem. The following are all possible indicators of serious bone or joint injury:

- a recent blow or fall

- snapping sound of breaking bone or torn ligament

- difficulty in moving the limb normally

- pain made worse by movement

- tenderness at the site (fracture)

- severe 'sickening' pain (dislocation)

- deformity – that is, the limb has an unusual shape

- swelling, bruising

- signs of shock.

Some injuries are hard to diagnose. A sprained ankle and a broken ankle are very similar. An early sign of a break is that the casualty becomes pale and the skin is clammy. This is a sign of shock that does not often occur when the ankle is only sprained. If in doubt, treat the injury as a fracture:

- Keep the casualty still, steady and comfortable.

- Support the injured part.

- Reassure the casualty.

- Send for medical help.

Soft tissue injuries

Soft tissue injuries include damage to:

- muscles

- ligaments

- tendons

- cartilage.

When soft tissues are injured they become inflamed. Treatment aims to reduce the swelling, prevent further damage and ease the pain. Soft tissue injuries are usually dealt with by using the RICE treatment.

- A **sprain** happens when we over-stretch or tear a ligament around a joint. A sprain can be caused by a twist or sudden wrench, for example, a sprained ankle. In this case we must use the RICE treatment. If the injury is severe, we would treat it as a fracture.

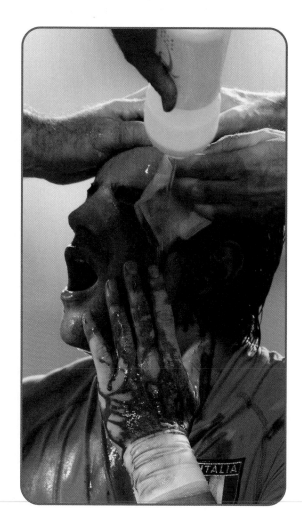

- A **strain** happens when we overstretch or tear a muscle or tendon. This can be caused by a sudden stretch or extra muscular effort (for example, a pulled muscle). In this case we must use the RICE treatment.

Even minor problems should be attended to quickly and carefully. If ignored, they may become more serious.

Skin damage

- **Cuts**: clean the cut with running water. Dab dry and cover with a dressing. Clean and dry the skin around the cut. Use an adhesive plaster over the dressing. Some lint-free dressings stick directly to the wound. These are designed to remain in place until they fall off naturally.

- **Grazes (abrasions)**: the top layer of skin has been scraped off through friction with a rough surface. Treat it as a cut, but use a specialist non-stick dressing. Be careful to check that the wound is clean.

- **Blisters**: damage to the skin by heat or friction can cause a bubble to form to protect the skin. Do not break the blister. Cover it with a special plaster that stays in place until it falls off naturally. This will ease pain and protect the area from further damage.

- **Bruises**: these are formed by damaged capillaries bleeding under the skin and are the result of an impact. The skin changes colour, the area is painful and can swell. Treat by raising and supporting the bruised part. Put a cold compress (ice pack) on the affected area.

Other injuries:

- **Winding**: this is a temporary paralysis of the diaphragm. It is usually caused by a blow to the upper abdominal area, just below the ribs (sometimes called the solar plexus). The symptoms are pain, 'doubling over' and an inability to breathe. Treat by sitting down and resting until recovery takes place.

- **Cramp**: this is a sudden and painful muscle contraction caused by strenuous exercise or loss of fluid and salt through sweating. Treat by drinking fluid, stretching and massaging the muscle.

- **Stitch**: a sharp pain in the abdominal area caused by a cramp in the diaphragm. Treat by sitting down and resting. Light massage can also help.

The RICE procedure

The treatment known as **RICE** (Rest, Ice, Compression, Elevation) is a checklist to follow in the case of most soft tissue injuries, including sprains, strains and impact injuries. We should treat such injuries as soon as possible after they occur to prevent them from becoming worse.

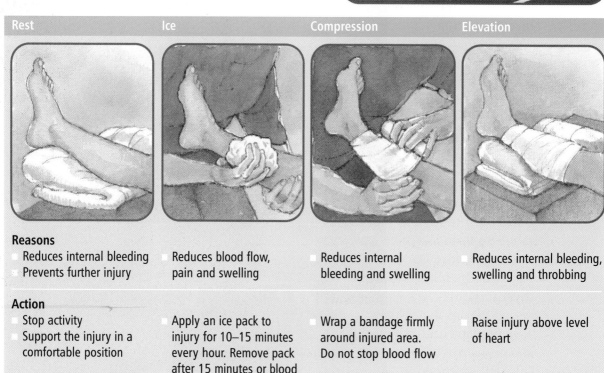

Rest	Ice	Compression	Elevation

Reasons

Reduces internal bleeding	Reduces blood flow, pain and swelling	Reduces internal bleeding and swelling	Reduces internal bleeding, swelling and throbbing
Prevents further injury			

Action

Stop activity	Apply an ice pack to injury for 10–15 minutes every hour. Remove pack after 15 minutes or blood flow will increase to try to heat up the area	Wrap a bandage firmly around injured area. Do not stop blood flow	Raise injury above level of heart
Support the injury in a comfortable position			

Returning to sport

All injuries need time to heal. We can reduce the time before we return to sport by acting quickly when we are first injured. We also need to continue to treat the injury properly throughout our recovery period. If we try to return to play too soon, we can make the injury worse.

There are three stages of treatment for sprains and strains.

Stage 1: The first 48 hours
Ice should be applied for 10–15 minutes every hour during this period.

Remember **HARM** – things to be avoided in the first 48 hours after an injury:

- Do not use **Heat** because it increases internal bleeding.

- Do not drink **Alcohol** because it increases the swelling.

- Do not **Run** because the weight and impact will cause further injury.

- Do not **Massage** the injured area because it increases internal bleeding.

Stage 2: 48–72 hours
Apply ice and heat alternately for five-minute periods to increase blood flow to and from the injured area. This will encourage healing.

Stage 3: 72 hours onwards
Use heat from baths, hot water bottles, etc., to increase blood flow and encourage healing. Most injuries will now be at the stage where some movement will help to speed up recovery, but do not try to move or play at full strength until you are sure you can do so safely.

This phase is called rehabilitation. It can last for between 10 days and 6 weeks. It has four stages:

1 **Active movement**: gentle movements that do not cause any pain. If movement is painful it should not be continued.

2 **Passive stretching and active exercise**: stretching and light endurance work that does not cause any pain.

3 **Active strengthening**: the muscles will have lost some strength during the period of injury. You should first train to improve endurance and only then develop power and speed.

4 **Re-education**: if you have no pain or swelling, your muscles and joints will need to be worked through their full range of movement. You can return to full training and then return to play.

Dealing with serious injuries

We expect help whenever we are injured whilst playing sport and we also expect organisers and helpers to have a knowledge of First Aid. Every sports club should have a qualified First Aider at every match and training session. We can all become qualified quite easily and should take the opportunity to do so. The St John Ambulance Brigade and the Red Cross organise First Aid courses. With a little training we may be able to provide life-saving help in an emergency. There are a number of serious injuries and conditions that need prompt action. We should all know what to do if we have to deal with someone who is seriously injured.

The recovery position

Always use the recovery position for an unconscious person who is breathing. You may need to alter the position slightly if the person is injured, but you can roll the body towards you and into the basic recovery position as follows:

- Tilt the head well back. This prevents the tongue blocking the throat.

- Keep the neck and back in a straight line.

- Keep the hip and knee both bent at 90°. This keeps the body safe, stable and comfortable.

- Use the casualty's hand to support their head, which should be slightly lower than the rest of the body. This allows fluids to drain from the mouth.

Remember to:

- check pulse and breathing regularly

- send for medical help.

Unconsciousness and concussion

All blows to the head are potentially dangerous. A person may lose consciousness after a violent blow to the head and may suffer from concussion on recovery. Sometimes there is a delay between the injury and losing consciousness. This is a sure sign of concussion.

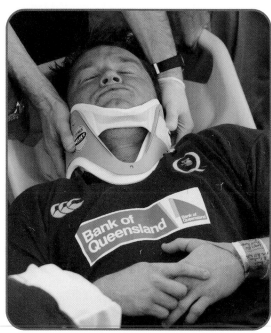

If you suspect concussion, you should check for dizziness, sickness and headache. People suffering from concussion often cannot remember what has happened to them. Always put someone with concussion in the recovery position and check their breathing and pulse regularly. Never allow anyone who has been knocked unconscious to continue with activity until medical advice has been obtained. In many sports, players who have suffered concussion are barred from playing again for a period of time in order to prevent further injury to the brain.

Shock
Serious injuries of many types may cause **shock**. If you suspect that a person is suffering from shock you should check for:

- a rapid pulse

- paleness

- cold, clammy skin

- light-headedness

- nausea (feeling sick)

- thirst.

Eventually the person may become restless, anxious and aggressive, may yawn and gasp for air or even become unconscious.

Treat shock by removing or treating the cause, if possible, then:

- lie the person down, with head low and feet high to assist blood flow to the brain

- give room and air, loosen tight clothing to assist breathing and increase oxygen intake

- keep the person warm

- send for medical help

- give reassurance

- keep checking for pulse and breathing.

Extreme conditions

Extreme sports are becoming very popular. These, and many mainstream sports, take place in very cold or very hot conditions. Such conditions can create very serious problems for sportspeople. Three common but dangerous conditions that we should be able to recognise and treat are **hypothermia**, **heat exhaustion** and **heatstroke**.

Hypothermia
Hypothermia is a condition in which the internal body temperature becomes dangerously low. It can be caused by being outdoors in the cold and wind, or being in very cold water. Signs of hypothermia include:

- shivering

- cold, pale, dry skin

- slow, shallow breathing and slow, weakening pulse

- feeling confused and lacking energy.

If someone is suffering from hypothermia, send for help, then:

- insulate the person with extra clothing and cover their head to keep in heat

- move to a sheltered place and protect them from the ground and weather

- use a survival bag, if you have one

- give hot drinks if the person is conscious

- check pulse and breathing regularly.

Heat exhaustion

When the temperature around you is the same as your body temperature, your body cannot lose heat by evaporation. If the air is also humid, then sweat will not evaporate from the body and heat exhaustion or heatstroke can occur.

Heat exhaustion develops during activity in hot conditions. It is caused by dehydration – that is, loss of fluid and salt from the body due to excessive sweating.

Signs of heat exhaustion include:

- headaches and light-headedness
- feeling sick
- sweating
- pale, clammy skin
- muscle cramps
- rapid, weakening pulse and breathing.

If someone is suffering from heat exhaustion, send for help and then:

- lie them down in a cool place
- raise and support the legs
- give plenty of water and sips of weak, salty water
- if they are unconscious, place them in the recovery position.

Heatstroke

Heatstroke is the result of the body becoming dangerously overheated after being in the heat for a long time. Signs of heatstroke include:

- headaches
- dizziness, restlessness and confusion
- hot, flushed, dry skin
- very high body temperature
- a full, bounding pulse.

If someone is suffering from heatstroke, send for help and then:

- move them to a cool place
- remove outer clothing
- cool the body with wet towels or a cold, wet sheet
- if they are unconscious, place them in the recovery position.

Careful planning and proper training, together with the right clothing and equipment, can help to prevent all the dangerous conditions described above.

QUESTIONS

14 Risk assessment in physical activity

1 **All sports can be dangerous. For each of the following sports, list one possible risk and one way to reduce the risk:**

a football *(2 marks)*

b javelin throwing *(2 marks)*

c white water canoeing *(2 marks)*

d cycling *(2 marks)*

e gymnastics. *(2 marks)*

2 **Explain how the following can help reduce the risk of injury in sport. Give two reasons for each.**

a rules of the game *(2 marks)*

b footwear, clothing and equipment *(2 marks)*

c balanced competition *(2 marks)*

d warm-up and cool-down. *(2 marks)*

3 **Give three rules of personal hygiene related to sporting activities.**
(3 marks)

4 **a** Describe two signs and symptoms of a sprain. Suggest one method of treatment.
(3 marks)

b Describe two signs and symptoms of heat exhaustion. Suggest one method of treatment.
(3 marks)

5 **John is a hockey player.**

a Name two items of protective clothing which he wears every time he plays.
(2 marks)

b Suggest two potential risks that John faces when playing hockey.
(2 marks)

c Soft tissue injuries often occur in hockey. Explain the RICE procedure used to treat them.
(4 marks)

d During a recent game a player was knocked unconscious. Name the type of injury that this causes.
(1 mark)

e Name the position in which John placed the injured player whilst waiting for the ambulance to arrive.
(1 mark)

f Why did he use this position?
(2 marks)
(Total 39 marks)

INDEX